The Heavens Might Crack

THE
HEAVENS
MIGHT
CRACK

The Death *and* Legacy *of*
Martin Luther King Jr.

JASON SOKOL

BASIC BOOKS
New York

Basic Books
Hachette Book Group
1290 Avenue of the Americas, New York, NY 10104
www.basicbooks.com

Printed in the United States of America

First Edition: March 2018

Published by Basic Books, an imprint of Perseus Books, LLC, a subsidiary of Hachette Book Group, Inc. The Basic Books name and logo is a trademark of the Hachette Book Group.

The Hachette Speakers Bureau provides a wide range of authors for speaking events. To find out more, go to www.hachettespeakersbureau.com or call (866) 376-6591.

The publisher is not responsible for websites (or their content) that are not owned by the publisher.

Print book interior design by Timm Bryson, em em design, LLC

Library of Congress Cataloging-in-Publication Data
Names: Sokol, Jason, author.
Title: The heavens might crack : the death and legacy of Martin Luther King Jr. / Jason Sokol.
Description: New York : Basic Books, 2018. | Includes bibliographical references and index.
Identifiers: LCCN 2017042658| ISBN 9780465055913 (hardback) | ISBN 9781541697393 (ebook)
Subjects: LCSH: King, Martin Luther, Jr., 1929–1968—Assassination—Public opinion. | King, Martin Luther, Jr., 1929–1968—Influence. | United States—Race relations—History. | African Americans—Social conditions. | Public opinion—United States. | BISAC: HISTORY / Social History. | HISTORY / United States / 20th Century. | SOCIAL SCIENCE / Discrimination & Race Relations. | POLITICAL SCIENCE / Political Freedom & Security / Civil Rights.
Classification: LCC E185.97.K5 S63 2018 | DDC 323.092—dc23
LC record available at https://lccn.loc.gov/2017042658

ISBNs: 978-0-465-05591-3 (hardcover), 978-1-5416-9739-3 (ebook)

LSC-C

10 9 8 7 6 5 4 3 2 1

For Nina and Arlo, with love

CONTENTS

Introduction
SHOT RINGS OUT

B EFORE THE EVENING performance of April 4, 1968, conductor Robert Shaw put down his baton and stood to address the Atlanta Symphony audience. He announced that Martin Luther King Jr. had been killed. The concertgoers gasped and moaned. A Roman Catholic priest prayed for King and exclaimed, "The king is dead! Long live the king!"[1]

On the opposite side of the country, author James Baldwin sat by a Palm Springs swimming pool with the actor Billy Dee Williams. The phone rang, and a friend told Baldwin of the tragedy in Memphis. "It took awhile before the sound of his voice—I don't mean the *sound* of his voice, something *in* his voice—got through to me." At first, Baldwin felt numb. Then an "unbelieving wonder" overtook him. He wept briefly, and finally succumbed to a "shocked and helpless rage." For years, that evening would remain a blur in Baldwin's memory. "It's retired into some deep cavern in my mind."[2]

In Blacksburg, Virginia, hundreds of college students had packed an auditorium to watch Senator Strom Thurmond, the longtime segregationist from South Carolina, debate the liberal satirist Harry Golden. A Virginia Tech dean interrupted the debate to inform the audience that King had been assassinated. Though the student body was almost all white, "no Negro audience could have been more shocked by the news," Golden recounted. "I heard groans of despair." The dean asked

1

Golden to say a few words about King. Golden offered an affectionate tribute, calling it "a sad day for the world and a sad day for Americans." The students sat in silence, shifting in their seats, too stunned to applaud. Then Thurmond spoke: "I disagree with Mr. Golden's estimate of Dr. King. He was an agitator, an outside agitator, bent on stirring people up, making everyone dissatisfied." Mere minutes after hearing of King's death, Strom Thurmond denounced him. Thurmond was no outlier—he spoke for the millions of white Americans who thought King had received his just deserts.[3]

The fatal shot rang out in Memphis, and it quickly rippled across the nation and the world. News of King's murder stopped people in their tracks and rendered them speechless, moved many to tears and others to celebration, drove some to violence and still others to political activism.

African Americans were overcome with grief and gripped by rage. Despair seized Dorothy Newby, an eighteen-year-old who attended Hamilton High School in Memphis. "I wanted the world to end completely . . . I felt there was no reason to continue living, and above all I wanted to kill myself." If such a foul deed could occur in this world, she wanted to opt out of it. Her classmate, seventeen-year-old Frankie Gross, broke down in tears. Gross "knew that people all over the world mourned his death, and I felt better knowing it." At the same time, he realized that a violent anger was surging through the black neighborhoods of Memphis. "You could see and feel the hate in the Negro community after the assassination. People took guns to work the next day just waiting for any white person to do anything wrong." The actions of law enforcement officials only intensified their fury. The National Guard rolled through the city in tanks and attempted to seal off African American neighborhoods. Black Memphians felt doubly victimized. Their leader was slaughtered by a white assailant and then *they* were treated as criminals.[4]

Clarence Coe, an African American who worked at Memphis's Firestone factory, believed the race war had finally arrived. On Thursday evening, April 4, Coe's foreman advised him that the plant was closing early and that a citywide curfew would be imposed. Coe asked why, and the foreman told him of King's assassination. He left the factory with a coworker, climbed into his new Buick, and headed toward home. Coe drove carefully through a city under siege. National Guardsmen shined their lights on Coe's car at Chelsea Avenue in North Memphis, and again at the intersection of Manassas Street and Union Avenue. He encountered more probing lights all along Mississippi Boulevard. Coe arrived at home and appraised his arsenal of firearms. He resolved to walk to the cemetery across the street, burn down a wooden bridge there, and take control of a small hill. "That's what I thought everybody else was going to do," he explained. But Coe was in for a surprise. "When I found out they [blacks] weren't going to do nothin'... it took a lot out of me ... I just expected to go to war... and I thought that would happen all over the world." While Dorothy Newby had the impulse to take her own life in the aftermath of King's assassination, Clarence Coe prepared for armed conflict.[5]

Martin Luther King was in Memphis to stand with striking sanitation workers, 1,300 black men whose struggle for dignity dovetailed with King's own Poor People's Campaign. King spent the final months of his life waging that fight against economic inequality. He envisioned masses of the nation's poor, black and white and Latino, converging on the Washington Mall in a show of nonviolent civil disobedience. After King's death, many African Americans in Memphis felt an unspeakable sense of loss. They were ashamed by the thought that their own community had failed to shelter him. They were also enraged—angry with Mayor Henry Loeb for bitterly opposing the sanitation strike, and infuriated at Memphis's white citizens for denigrating King and denouncing the strikers. They were incensed that FBI officials could seemingly spy on King at all hours, yet fail to protect him from an assassin's bullet and then allow the shooter to flee the city. Like African Americans across the country, they were outraged at the many whites who had given encouragement—tacit as well as explicit—to all of the King-haters and created a favorable climate for the assassin.

In the days after King's assassination, hundreds of cities burned. African Americans rose up in violent rebellions, the largest of which occurred in Washington, Chicago, Baltimore, and Pittsburgh.

With King gone and with riots shaking America's cities, it appeared impossible to reclaim the hopes of an earlier time. It felt like a gear in the machinery of the universe had shifted. Just a few years prior, upon the enactment of landmark civil rights laws, interracial harmony appeared conceivable; continued progress toward civil rights seemed probable. Such optimism quickly vanished.

King's death acted as a tipping point in the nation's racial history. It seemed as though the final flicker of hope for a multiracial America had finally gone out. And King's death helped to steer the country toward a new course. King's own vision of interracial fellowship appeared to have died with him. In its place reigned outrage and indifference, anger and apathy. King's death and its aftereffects contributed to a rising militancy among African Americans and exposed an enduring white racism, all of which turned his ideal of the beloved community into a fanciful dream.

MARTIN LUTHER KING Jr. was a preacher and an activist, an orator and an organizer, a patriot and a dissident. By the age of thirty-nine, he had achieved so much.

King was born in 1929 to a middle-class family in Atlanta's Sweet Auburn neighborhood. Throughout his childhood, he navigated the Jim Crow South. King graduated from Morehouse College at the age of nineteen, continued his education at the Crozer Theological Seminary in Pennsylvania, and earned his PhD from Boston University. He married Coretta Scott in 1953. The following year, young King became pastor of the Dexter Avenue Baptist Church in Montgomery, Alabama. Blacks in Montgomery began a boycott of the city's buses in December 1955, and elevated King to a leadership position in that struggle. The yearlong bus boycott would help to galvanize the southern civil rights movement. The larger freedom struggle evolved in tandem with King, the man and the movement each lifting one another to greater heights. Soon, he was the country's most well-known civil rights leader.

The events of 1963 further cemented his standing. King led demonstrations in Birmingham, Alabama, that provoked gruesome white violence, gained national and international attention, and ultimately pushed President John F. Kennedy to propose major civil rights legislation. In August 1963, King stood before the Lincoln Memorial and delivered his "I Have a Dream" speech. He not only told the audience about his dream of a colorblind America, but also addressed the "unspeakable horrors of police brutality" and warned that the "whirlwinds of revolt" would shake the nation for as long as injustice prevailed. Through the years, King employed the language of the Bible as well as the Constitution. He spoke to whites and to blacks, urging African Americans to join in the nonviolent struggle for freedom and counseling whites that if they could overcome their racism, attack the inequality in their cities, and help to build a just nation, they too could join the beloved community. King often imagined the "beloved community" as his end goal—where racial harmony, economic equality, love, and peace prevailed.[6]

King began to exert more influence on the White House, working for the passage of civil rights laws, just as he continued to march along the dusty roads of the Deep South. President Lyndon Johnson signed the Civil Rights Act in July 1964, outlawing segregation in public life. At the end of that year, King received the Nobel Peace Prize. In 1965, he joined a campaign for voting rights in Selma, Alabama, eventually leading marchers across Selma's Edmund Pettus Bridge and all the way to Montgomery. The Voting Rights Act, which Johnson signed in the summer of 1965, enfranchised African Americans and buried the last legal vestige of the South's Jim Crow system. King then committed himself more fully to battling segregation in the North. He had led marches in northern cities before, notably in Detroit in 1963 and Boston in 1965. In 1966, he took up residence in a Chicago slum and waged a struggle for open housing. During King's final two years, he spoke out more forcefully on issues of economic inequality as well as foreign policy. He became a fierce critic of the Vietnam War and began to organize the Poor People's Campaign. Throughout, he remained committed to nonviolent resistance.

King shaped how many people thought about America and its ideals, both within the country and around the world. For so long he held out hope. He asked the nation to live up to its promises of freedom and democracy, goaded it into enacting civil rights and voting rights laws, jabbed it for its barbarism overseas, implored it to see its poor people—to clothe them and house them and feed them. He kept faith in the principles expressed in the Constitution and the Declaration of Independence, thinking of those documents as "promissory notes" on which America had yet to make good. By the force of his will and with the eloquence of his voice, he convinced many others to believe in their nation even when that seemed to be asking the impossible. Despite the fire hoses and attack dogs, the lynchings and bombings, and the untold demonstrations of white supremacy's savagery, many African Americans still clung to the hope that one day the country might deliver on its rhetoric of freedom and equality. The gap between American ideals and reality had yawned so wide, even since the founding. In the early and mid-1960s, because of the struggles and demands of African Americans, the nation seemed to be narrowing that gap.[7]

But the coming years would witness vicious racial strife, generational division, and pitched controversies over the Vietnam War. The latter half of the 1960s brought shattering episodes of violence: riots in the streets, the assassination of Malcolm X in 1965 and eventually of King and Senator Robert Kennedy. During his life, King encouraged Americans to commit themselves to collective sacrifice—and to remain hopeful about the nation's potential. His death helped to destroy that sense of possibility and of shared purpose.

By King's last years, the black freedom struggle had split into at least two divergent movements. Moderates like Roy Wilkins of the National Association for the Advancement of Colored People (NAACP) and Whitney Young of the Urban League occupied one end of the spectrum. They believed African Americans could still advance their causes through legislation, lawsuits, and electoral politics; they continued to support President Lyndon Johnson even as he escalated the Vietnam War. They had gained a foothold in the Washington establishment, and remained committed to working within the system. At the other end of the spectrum stood the adherents of Black Power, who increasingly viewed America as irredeemable.

Only one leader retained credibility with both camps: Martin Luther King. Wilkins and Young had criticized King for his antiwar activity, but they nonetheless admired his devotion to nonviolence and his efforts for civil rights legislation. Black Power proponents thought King's persistent belief in nonviolence was absurd, as was his willingness to work within America's political system. But with King's scathing critique of the Vietnam War, and with his campaign for the poor, he was regaining the "cautious respect" of radical activists. In his final months, he was attempting to broaden the civil rights insurgency.[8]

King knew that two worlds existed within black America. He realized that the chasm between them might already be too wide to traverse. But he felt that if anyone was going to try for unity, he had to be that person. In the fall of 1967, he urged African Americans to follow "the militant middle between riots on the one hand and weak and timid supplication for justice on the other hand." King tried doggedly to heal the rift. "There must be somebody to communicate to the two worlds," he said early in 1968. He wanted to build a "coalition of conscience," as he called it, which would draw together Black Power radicals and mainstream civil rights advocates as well as white activists. King was not parting the waters; he was bridging them. Yet because of his death, the prospects for cooperation became even bleaker. The "militant middle" would be no longer viable.[9]

THE HEAVENS MIGHT *Crack* explores a wide range of responses to King's assassination in the hours, days, weeks, and months afterward.

Some whites celebrated King's death, revealing the depths of a hatred that persisted late into the 1960s and well beyond. King's assassination also propelled African Americans toward militancy and led directly to the nationwide rise of the Black Panthers. Yet many African Americans, as well as liberal whites, continued to revere King even in his last years. After his death, such citizens gathered to express their enduring commitment to an interracial America. They mourned and prayed and marched in cities large and small. King's death also sparked massive protests on many college campuses. From Duke to Columbia, King's assassination awakened privileged white students to the ongoing travails of African Americans. In addition, King's death spurred legislation on Capitol Hill. It surely expedited the passage of the Fair Housing Act. Less well known, it helped to break a multiyear deadlock in the Senate Judiciary Committee on the issue of gun control. The assassination of King, coupled with Robert Kennedy's two months later, led to the most expansive gun control legislation in American history.

This book offers a new perspective not only on King's death, but also on several aspects of his life. While Americans tend to think of King in a purely national context, he stood—throughout his career— as an inspiration for freedom struggles across the world. In Africa and Asia, and on both sides of the Cold War, global citizens fashioned King into a hero for their causes. His death only amplified that dynamic. Once he was gone, they continued to shape King to fit their particular circumstances and enlisted his legacy in their own struggles.

After King's death, mourners took to the streets in cities across the world. King's murder also inspired a copycat assassination attempt in West Berlin, which intensified student rebellions throughout Germany. In Britain, King's assassination worked to accelerate the passage of civil rights legislation. But the urban riots in America reverberated across the Atlantic; they helped to strengthen racial prejudices and to spur a wave of anti-immigrant activity in the United Kingdom. Before 1968, King often found a sanctuary overseas where he could escape the growing hatred at home. But King's death ultimately helped to create a more hostile world, unleashing forces that turned some of those havens into places of enmity.[10]

This book also highlights King's connection to his most loyal followers: ordinary African Americans. Mainstream American leaders denounced King's antiwar speeches and his Poor People's Campaign. Critics claimed that King—because of his international fame, his interest in foreign policy, his espousal of democratic socialism, or his unyielding commitment to nonviolence—had lost touch with the common folk. In reality, black workers wrapped King in a loving embrace. And in the wake of King's death, many African Americans emphasized that link with their fallen leader.

The Heavens Might Crack concludes with the story of how the American public ultimately shaped King into a saint. By the end of the twentieth century, King had become a hero for all seasons. In the popular mind today, he remains an unthreatening figure who supposedly transcended race. King stands beyond reproach. White children are taught to identify with him. He is lionized and sanctified. We forget the deep hatred he attracted, right up to the end of his life. Many white Americans loathed King, not only in the South but across the country. They perceived him as a rabble-rouser and an agitator; some rejoiced in his death. Even among African Americans, King inspired skepticism and frustration as much as awe and adulation. Many African Americans viewed his messages of nonviolence and interracialism as no longer relevant. In the spring of 1968, King was by turns idolized and despised. And there were millions of Americans in between the two poles: their disposition toward King was far more complex, and more ambivalent, than we now realize.

King's funeral, and the accompanying tributes to him, started a longer process of canonization. How so many Americans got from loathing to loving is less a tale of diminishing racism, and more about the ways King's legacy has been sculpted and scrubbed.

In the end, *The Heavens Might Crack* shows how King's death impacted America's broader racial history. It made the struggle toward a multiracial America that much more difficult, dashing dreams for harmony both within the black freedom struggle and between whites and blacks.

This book is less about King than his impact on others. The moment of King's death is so revealing because it crystallized his influence on Americans as well as others throughout the world. Citizens' differing perceptions of him, and their understandings of what his life and career meant, burst into public view.

KING'S DEATH HELPED to make 1968 a traumatic year for America and the world—a year of barricades and bullets. His assassination occurred not just within the American context of the 1968 presidential election, the Poor People's Campaign, the sanitation strike, and the growing antiwar movement, but also in a context of global revolution. Upon hearing the news of King's death, many struggled to make sense of the event and feared the world that it augured. They could not yet fully see, though many could already anticipate, the tumult that awaited.

At the end of January, North Vietnamese forces waged a bold attack on American strongholds. The Tet Offensive shocked the American public and swelled the ranks of the antiwar movement. In Orangeburg, South Carolina, in February, police officers fired on a crowd of unarmed black students who were protesting segregation at a bowling alley. The "Orangeburg Massacre" stole the lives of three students from South Carolina State University. On April 23, two weeks after King's funeral, students at Columbia University seized campus buildings for several days and were then bloodied by police officers. In June, at the Ambassador Hotel in Los Angeles, an assassin's bullet struck down Robert Kennedy. Then in August, chaos engulfed the Democratic National Convention in Chicago. Antiwar protesters gathered in Grant Park as delegates assembled inside the Hilton. Chicago police officers brutalized the protesters while the victims chanted, "The Whole World Is Watching!" The following month, feminists staged a dramatic demonstration outside the Miss America pageant in Atlantic City. Throughout the summer and fall, Black Panther chapters formed in cities across the country. Amid the unrest and protests, the blood and the tear gas, many believed that a new social order stood within reach.

Young people took to the streets throughout the world. Early in 1968, Czechs reveled in the Prague Spring. They celebrated their political and cultural freedom for several months before the Soviet military invaded and reasserted control. In May, millions of French workers and students organized a wave of protests that paralyzed the nation and captured the world's imagination. Students staged rebellions at Tokyo University and the London School of Economics, the University of Madrid and the Free University of Berlin. They protested world events like the Vietnam War as well as campus issues and government policies in their own countries. In Mexico City, some 300,000 people marched to the Zocalo in August. Two months later, in Tlatelolco Plaza, riot police massacred student demonstrators. On every continent, the spirit of revolution filled the air.[11]

It was a year of so many world-historical crises, one after the other, that it can be difficult to isolate any single event and assign to it a causal power. King's assassination was a powerful ingredient in the overall mix. It is hard to overstate what he meant, not only to African Americans but also to young activists around the world. King's death seemed to show what fate would befall those who dared to commit themselves to social change. And if one who worked nonviolently had met a gruesome death, what would become of peaceful avenues for change? Once King had taken his leave from the world, revolution looked ever more attractive to those who remained.

FROM THE VANTAGE point of April 1968, one sees more clearly how death dogged King, hovered over him, marked and marred his waking moments. He sensed that somewhere along the journey for racial equality, he would sacrifice his own life. Hours before King's death, the British Broadcasting Corporation (BBC) aired an interview in which King told the BBC's Gerald Priestland, "I live every day under the threat of death, and I have no illusions about it." During the interview, which was recorded in December 1967, Priestland asked King whether he had "moments of apprehension that you may meet a violent death?" King replied:

> I don't have any apprehension about it, I'm very realistic about it and, I guess, philosophical. . . . And if something happens to me, physically or if I come to a violent end, I will go on with the faith that unmerited suffering is redemptive. And I don't think the important thing really is how long you live, but how well you live. And I'm not concerned about my longevity or the quantity of my life, but the quality of my life . . . I want to remain busy, trying to do a good job for humanity and for my race and for the human race and for my children and for God.

That sensibility was crucial to King's leadership, fortifying him through sacrifice and struggle.[12]

From the early days of the Montgomery bus boycott to the eve of his assassination, King regularly confronted the prospect of his own death. In January 1956, his Montgomery home was bombed with his wife and child inside. Two years later, a deranged black woman stabbed him in a Harlem department store. The letter opener she wielded was lodged just centimeters from King's heart, his life preserved by a team of surgeons at Harlem Hospital. King spent many nights in the jails of the Deep South, and endured countless death threats. In response to a threat he received in St. Augustine, Florida, in 1964, King said, "If physical death is the price that I must pay to free my white brothers and sisters from a permanent death of the spirit, then nothing can be more redemptive." Over the years, he had been violently attacked by many of those "white brothers and sisters," from a white supremacist who punched him in an Alabama hotel to rock-throwing hordes in a Chicago park. The FBI urged King to take his own life. King ultimately learned to make peace with the possibility of his death. He was not unafraid, but undeterred. From those encounters with his own mortality, he derived a unique strength.[13]

In a sermon on February 4, 1968, exactly two months before his death, King confided in his Atlanta congregation: "Every now and then I think about my own death and I think about my own funeral." He issued specific instructions to the worshippers at Ebenezer Baptist Church. He hoped the eulogist would highlight his service. "I'd like somebody to mention that Martin Luther King, Jr., tried to give his life serving others. . . . I want you to be able to say that day that I did try to feed the hungry. And I want you to be able to say that I did try in my life to clothe those who were naked." Above all, "I tried to love and serve humanity." If the world would allow him that much, then "all of the other shallow things will not matter. . . . I just want to leave a committed life behind." This speech was eventually replayed during King's funeral.[14]

King's repeated brushes with violence forced him to anticipate and even accept his own death; it was a price he had agreed to pay. He lived with that truth each day, as did his family. For those closest to him, one part of loving King was knowing they would lose him. That anticipation of loss, and the feeling of danger, was ever present.

For every badge of mainstream success King collected—the hundreds of honorary degrees and magazine covers, the meetings in the White House, the Nobel Peace Prize—he received an equal measure of scorn and revulsion. Yet he did not identify as an outcast. More precisely, he stood at odds with the way of things. King was unable to rest while suffering existed anywhere, a trait that lay at the heart of his genius. "Some people thought he was crazy," reflected Vincent Harding, a former associate of King's and a civil rights scholar. "King did not accept conventional wisdom, conventional patriotism. But maybe the 'mad' men and women have something to tell us." This was why King terrified so many segregationists and racial conservatives. He refused to accept things as they were. Fully realizing the perils of this pursuit, he pressed on.[15]

1

LOSING KING

I N THE LAST year of his life, King faced persistent questions about his effectiveness, his relevance, and his stature as a national leader. Because King had stridently denounced the Vietnam War early in 1967, many political leaders and journalists turned against him—including President Lyndon Johnson and even some of King's allies in the civil rights movement. And as he continued to trumpet nonviolence and interracialism amid the rise of Black Power, his star faded among younger African Americans. David Levering Lewis, one of King's first biographers, explains, "The verdict was that Martin was finished." The conventional wisdom portrayed King as a leader without a constituency. Yet that analysis underestimated the power and endurance of King's connection with ordinary African Americans. Only after his death did it become clear just how much he had meant to them. For so many black people, the feeling of loss was both personal and profound.[1]

The Poor People's Campaign was King's last gambit, and his most explicit attempt to take up the cause of impoverished Americans. As he planned it, participants from all corners of the nation would march on Washington in the spring of 1968, exposing the depths of poverty in America. They would disrupt everyday life in the capital, jar the nation's conscience, and push the federal government into action. Elected officials bristled at King's ideas for this final crusade, and criticized him further. He became even more alienated from the powerful in

Washington and from many mainstream white Americans. King understood that to attack poverty in this way was to challenge capitalism
itself. "For years, I labored with the idea of reforming the existing institutions of the society," he told journalist David Halberstam in 1967.
"Now I feel quite differently. I think you've got to have a reconstruction
of the entire society, a revolution of values." The Poor People's Campaign represented one struggle in this larger revolution.[2]

King's assault on economic inequality led him to Memphis in March
1968. The striking sanitation workers had asked the city of Memphis to
recognize their union, and to allow them to implement a dues-checkoff
system. Mayor Henry Loeb refused to negotiate, and maintained that
the strike was illegal. The white community rallied behind Loeb. The
strikers were weathered old black men who for their adult lives had
hauled garbage cans through heat and humidity and rain. They worked
for low wages with virtually no benefits. They were peaceful, church-
going folk. Few of them advocated Black Power. And the issue they
were highlighting—poverty—had become King's foremost priority.
These were King's people. The strikers seemed to galvanize King with
a kind of energy he had not felt since Selma. On March 18, King spoke
at Mason Temple before a crowd of 25,000, a larger indoor audience
than any he had previously encountered in the South. He returned to
Memphis on March 28 and led a march through downtown. Some of
the demonstrators behind King turned violent. They broke store windows and scuffled with the police. Chaos took hold of the streets. King
was whisked to the Holiday Inn Rivermont, a new white-owned hotel.[3]

King endured caustic criticism—for the violence at the march, for
his larger Poor People's Campaign, and even for his choice of hotel.
King's critics claimed he was finished as a nonviolent leader. In response, he reassessed everything. He returned to Memphis on April 3,
and this time he chose the Lorraine Motel instead. It was shabbier than
the Rivermont and patronized exclusively by African Americans. As
King committed himself more fully to the workers' cause in Memphis,
he was "relearning, what had made him great," wrote the scholar and

Martin Luther King Jr. arrived in Memphis on April 3 with other members of the SCLC: Andrew Young, Ralph Abernathy, and Bernard Lee.

Preservation and Special Collections Department,
University Libraries, University of Memphis

journalist Garry Wills, "learning what motels to stay at; what style to use; what were his roots." Through the Poor People's Campaign, King had been identifying with America's dispossessed. And in Memphis, he could get back in touch with his own identity as a black southerner. "He did not so much climb to the mountaintop there as go back down into the valley of his birth." When King lowered himself into that world of trash and toil, he rediscovered the deep connection he shared with his people. Through the strike and after King's death, black workers would emphasize that relationship with their slain hero.[4]

ANDREW YOUNG, THE executive director of the Southern Christian Leadership Conference (SCLC)—a civil rights organization led by King—spent the day of April 4 in federal court in Memphis. Young was trying to persuade the court to legalize a march planned for April 8; the city of Memphis had obtained a restraining order against the march. After spending the day on the witness stand, Young returned to the Lorraine Motel and walked into room 201, where the other preachers convened a "general bull session" that devolved into a pillow fight. Martin Luther King wrestled Young onto the bed and started beating him with a pillow. "He was like a big kid," Young remembered. King was perturbed that Young had not kept him updated on the events at the courthouse. "He was just standing on the bed swinging the pillow at me," Young recalled. "I'm trying to duck with him saying, 'You have to let me know what's going on.' . . . Finally I snatched the pillow and . . . people just started throwing pillows and piling on top of everybody, and laughing." As the preachers indulged in a grand pillow fight, the tension of the past months seemed to lift.[5]

The night before, King had delivered an extraordinary speech at Mason Temple. A storm produced claps of thunder that rattled the church's windows and bolts of lightning that illuminated the Memphis sky. Despite tornado warnings, 3,000 people turned out at the church. James Lawson, a Memphis minister and a leader of the sanitation strike, remembered this as "a rare moment, with the rain on the outside and the feeling of intense humanity on the inside." Lawson recalled "a great feeling of oneness . . . a great enthusiastic spirit, a great warmth. And I remember sort of basking in that feeling." Rev. Billy Kyles recollected, "The magnetism that was in that temple that night is really indescribable." From King's first words, the crowd was with him, urging him on with rollicking applause and a spirited call-and-response. Amid the howling wind and the thunderclaps, King reflected on the urgency of the struggle in Memphis and on his own mortality. He recounted his experience in Harlem in 1958, when he was stabbed at a book-signing. The doctors later told him that if he had so much as sneezed, the blade would have severed his aorta. King received mail from well-wishers, among them a ninth-grader at White Plains High School who wrote, "I'm so happy that you didn't sneeze." King told the Memphis crowd that he would have missed so much: the student sit-ins, the Albany Movement, the mass demonstrations in Birmingham, and the Selma-to-Montgomery march. And he "wouldn't have been in Memphis to see a community rally around those brothers and sisters who are suffering. I'm so happy that I didn't sneeze."[6]

During the last year of his life, King thought even more about his death. Coretta Scott King recalled, "Throughout 1967, and during the planning of the Poor People's Campaign early in 1968, we had, beyond everything, a sense of fate closing in." King had been living with the taste of death in his mouth for more than a decade, but the early months of 1968 felt different. As King continued to passionately oppose the Vietnam War, the criticism he attracted seemed ever more vicious, the death threats more numerous. A depression was enveloping him. "Around this period there was an even greater kind of anxiety," remembered Bernard Lafayette, the national field coordinator for the SCLC. "This was abnormal, the heavy climate and volume of threats." King knew there would be more attempts on his life, as scholar and journalist Lerone Bennett Jr. wrote in *Ebony,* and "he knew that someday somebody would succeed." In February, he had spoken of this to his own congregation at Ebenezer Baptist. Now, in Memphis's Mason Temple, he took the audience into his confidence.[7]

The "Amens" and "Yesses" willed King toward his peroration. "Like anybody, I would like to live a long life," King admitted. His voice soared as his eyes teared. "Longevity has its place. But I'm not concerned about that now. I just want to do God's will. And he's allowed me to go up to the mountain. And I've looked over. And I have *seen* the promised land. I may not get there with you. But I want you to know tonight that we as a people will *get* to the promised land." The audience stood on the verge of eruption. One man shouted, "Go ahead, go ahead!" And King went ahead. "So I'm happy tonight. I'm not worried about anything. I'm not fearing any man. Mine eyes have seen the glory of the coming of the Lord!" King turned and collapsed into his seat, almost in a controlled fall, having pushed his way through the open arms and outstretched hands of his associates. He was exhilarated and exhausted. The crowd had lifted him to one of the great oratorical peaks in a career filled with such crescendos. "It was an ecstatic moment," recalled Andrew Young. "The crowd had brought him back to life."[8]

On the morning of April 4, while Young toiled in court, King had a long and rejuvenating sleep. He and his confidant Ralph Abernathy shared a late lunch in room 306 at the motel. Then they sauntered downstairs to join their brethren. Young arrived at five o'clock and was pressed into the pillow fight. King finally extricated himself and announced, "Let's go." It was time for the men—Young, Abernathy, Bernard Lee, and Martin's brother A. D. King among them—to decamp to the home of Rev. Billy Kyles before that night's mass meeting. Gwen Kyles was preparing the mother of all soul-food feasts. It was to be a meal of excess. For the peripatetic SCLC preachers, a home-cooked meal was a special treat, Gwen Kyles noted. "The staff and Dr. King, they were ready to relax a little bit, and wanted some soul food." She had called in the best cooks from her church, and they cut no corners. "We just had everything that we thought they might want." The menu held copious delights: roast beef and ham, chitlins and sweet potatoes, corn muffins, cornbread and hot rolls, macaroni and cheese, spaghetti, greens, several types of salads, cakes and pies and ice cream. "It was an honor," said Kyles, "and it was perfect." The cooks were excited. The preachers were giddy.[9]

King returned to his room to get dressed for the evening. Andrew Young and James Orange shadowboxed in the parking lot below. Minutes before six o'clock, King walked out to the balcony and leaned over the railing to speak with the musician Ben Branch. He asked Branch to play "Precious Lord" at the mass meeting later that evening. King said, "I want you to play it real pretty." And King asked his friends, "You think I need a coat?" They answered that he ought to go back inside and put on an overcoat, as it was chilly and he was getting over a cold. King said, "Okay, I will." Then an awful sound pierced the Memphis night. "It sounded like a firecracker," Young recalled. "And I looked up and didn't see him."[10]

An ambulance took King to St. Joseph's Hospital. Police officers swarmed the area, with King's aides close behind. "The waiting room was like walking into Grand Central Station," Dr. Frederick Gioia remembered. Gioia rushed to the emergency room. The surgeons could not save King, and pronounced him dead at seven o'clock central time. Ralph Abernathy and Bernard Lee accompanied King's body to the morgue, and then to the funeral home: R.S. Lewis and Sons. The morticians worked until morning to reset King's jawbone, build it up with plaster, and embalm the body. They listened to replays of King's speeches on the radio. As King's voice boomed from the speakers of the funeral home, his body lay lifeless.[11]

Coretta Scott King, at the family's home in Atlanta, had spent the afternoon shopping for Easter clothes with her daughter Yolanda. Shortly after she returned home, the phone rang. Jesse Jackson, a young SCLC leader, told her Martin had been shot, but was still alive and at the hospital. It was "the call I seemed subconsciously to have been waiting for all our lives," Coretta explained. She contacted Dora McDonald, Martin's executive secretary, and asked her to come over. That was at 7:20 eastern time, and Coretta planned to take the 8:25 flight to Memphis. She flipped on the television, but turned down the volume when her children realized what had occurred. She told the children that their father had been shot, and that she was heading to Memphis. Then Ivan Allen Jr., the mayor of Atlanta, called Coretta to offer his help. Allen told Coretta he would send over a police officer, and he would head to the King home himself.[12]

Mayor Allen first learned King had been shot the same way many Americans found out: he was at home watching television with his wife. "I suppose millions of others all over the world had the same feeling of shock and anger at that same second," he recalled. After Allen hung up the phone, he and his wife Louise hurried into their car and raced toward the King home. A police car was already waiting with Coretta in the front seat. Coretta had spoken with Martin's mother and kissed her own children goodbye. Ivan Allen jumped into another police car, and Louise Allen followed in their Chevrolet. The caravan set off for the airport as Allen radioed to Eastern Air Lines with orders to hold the plane. Allen and King dashed through the terminal, and as they approached the gate, Dora McDonald came walking quickly toward them. She pulled Coretta into the entrance of the ladies' lounge for some privacy. Meanwhile, Allen was directed to a telephone where an Eastern Air Lines official in Memphis informed him that Martin Luther King had died. Allen walked toward the ladies' lounge. When the women emerged from the lounge, he said to Coretta, "Mrs. King, I have to inform you that Dr. King is dead." Coretta recalled the moment: "Of course I already knew. But it had not yet been *said*. I had been trying to prepare myself to hear that final word, to think and accept it." They all stood there and wept. Coretta wanted to get back home to her children. The plane to Memphis took off without her.[13]

Allen sat in the Kings' living room with some friends of the family, watching Lyndon Johnson's televised address to the nation. Coretta retired to her bedroom and turned on the television. She watched newscasts that were spliced with her husband's speeches. Her daughter Yolanda sat on the floor, her hair in curlers. Coretta's friend Xernona Clayton stayed with her for much of the night. Coretta "was glued to

King's wake was held at R.S. Lewis and Sons Funeral Home in Memphis.

Preservation and Special Collections Department,
University Libraries, University of Memphis

the television set," Clayton remembered, "eager for every detail. She got annoyed if people obstructed her view. She seemed to gain new strength from knowledge. It helped her to understand. After the doctor called and described the wound to her, she related it to me, enthusiastic about being knowledgeable." She grasped for any piece of information that might make the catastrophe more comprehensible.[14]

Back in Memphis, R.S. Lewis and Sons opened its doors for the wake at eight o'clock in the morning on Friday, April 5. Several hundred people circulated through the tiny, lavender-encased chapel. Day laborers, maids, and secretaries came dressed for work; teenagers arrived in blue jeans; families brought their children. Only a "pitiful handful of whites" showed up, wrote journalist Joan Turner Beifuss. Young men removed their hats. Several women approached King's body and snapped photos with their Polaroids, stooping to touch the body or to

King's coffin was loaded into an airplane at the Memphis airport, headed for Atlanta. Coretta Scott King waited inside the plane.

kiss King on the cheek. Others remained silent and composed, holding their sobs until they stepped out of the chapel. Groups of people milled about outside, mostly sad and stunned and cordial. But there were whiffs of anger in the air. One woman walked out the front door and said to everyone within earshot, "I wish it was [Mayor] Henry Loeb lying there." Like many blacks in Memphis, she blamed Mayor Loeb for King's death. Ralph Abernathy led an impromptu service, then the bronze casket was closed.[15]

A twenty-car procession set off for the Memphis airport, where Coretta Scott King had just landed. She stayed in the airplane as SCLC staff members boarded and King's body was loaded in. National Guardsmen wielded bayonets and menaced a small crowd of onlookers. The group of African Americans huddled on the tarmac and sang

"We Shall Overcome." Shortly before eleven in the morning, the plane revved its engines and took off, bound for Atlanta.[16]

THE SANITATION WORKERS held a meeting at the United Rubber Workers Union Hall on the afternoon of April 5. Through songs and sobs, they vowed to press on with their struggle. Fourteen different speakers regaled them—union leaders, ministers, and civil rights activists. The SCLC's James Bevel was the final speaker. Bevel experimented with a phrase he had been using for the past year: "on the case." He had previously employed it to describe musicians who were perfectly in sync, and the SCLC came to apply it to the black struggle. "Dr. King died on the case," Bevel told the crowd. "Anyone who does not help forward the sanitation workers' strike is not on the case. You getting me?" His audience was indeed getting him, as Garry Wills reported from his seat in the union hall. They realized that King had known their oppression and had sympathized with their plight; they recognized King as their champion and their hero. Then Bevel pivoted, invoking a higher leader. "There's a false rumor around that our leader is dead," Bevel continued. But "*our* leader is not dead." The crowd had heard variations on this theme from the thirteen prior orators. They well knew that King's spirit lived on. Yet Bevel had in mind a figure even more venerated. "Martin Luther King is not our *leader*!" The crowd wanted to stay with him, but they didn't know quite what he meant. Did he mean Ralph Abernathy was their leader? Not exactly. "*Our* leader is the *man* who led *Moses* out of *Israel*." The crowd rose as one. They yelled, "*That's* the man!" Bevel elaborated. "Our leader is the man who walked out of the grave on Easter morning. Our leader never sleeps nor slumbers. He cannot be put in jail. . . . *Our* leader is *still on the case*." The crowd hollered, "That's it! On the case!" Bevel mixed the holy with the profane, the heavenly with the hardened. By his lights, the garbage workers' cause was not only right and just; it was blessed and divine.[17]

On that morning of April 5, a federal judge in Memphis legalized the march that was planned for Monday, April 8. Originally, King was to stand at the helm. Now the march would become a memorial to him.[18]

King's body remained in motion. After Coretta Scott King's aircraft touched down in Atlanta, a black Cadillac carried the casket to Hanley's Funeral Home. Fifty cars followed behind. African Americans congregated along the sidewalks throughout the city. On Auburn Avenue, some flew flags upside down—a sign of distress. King's body was then ferried from the funeral home to Ebenezer Baptist Church. A memorial service began at seven thirty on the evening of April 5. The church stayed open all night as a steady stream of mourners offered silent tribute. On Saturday, April 6, King's body was transported to Sisters Chapel at Spelman College, where it would lie in state until Monday. Coretta Scott King held a press conference shortly before she appeared at Spelman. "He knew that at any moment his physical life could be cut short," she remarked, "and we faced this possibility squarely and honestly. He knew that this was a sick society, totally infested with racism and violence that questioned his integrity, maligned his motives, and distorted his views, which would ultimately lead to his death." She highlighted one part of her late husband's legacy: his devotion to the impoverished and the dispossessed. "He gave his life for the poor of the world, the garbage workers of Memphis and the peasants of Vietnam." By the middle of the afternoon, 1,000 people had converged upon the Spelman campus. The hearse arrived at 5:40, when Harry Belafonte—the famous calypso singer, civil rights activist, and friend of the King family—escorted Coretta Scott King into the chapel for a private prayer service. An hour later, a shaken Coretta emerged from the chapel as the restless crowd pushed toward the door. Coretta later recalled, "For so long, Martin had been in the heart and soul of the masses. Now they wanted their time with him." They entered, quietly and humbly, to view King's body, outfitted in a black suit with a gold tie.

By the time darkness engulfed Spelman, the line stretched far across its blooming campus.[19]

Even in the heyday of Black Power, many African Americans still held King in high esteem. Early in 1968, a poll was conducted among blacks in fifteen cities. Fully 72 percent approved of King; only 5 percent disapproved. By contrast, just 14 percent approved of Stokely Carmichael while 35 percent disapproved. According to an additional poll, some 90 percent of African Americans judged that King had the "best approach" to racial change and said they trusted him more than any other black leader. Even at King's lowest point, he remained their prince.[20]

Polling data seemed an antiseptic way of measuring a relationship— between King and the people—that was emotional and even spiritual at heart. In the heat of the black church, in the rhythm of call-and-response, through the endless marches and the long nights in jail, they were with him. They had propelled him to lofty heights. In turn, he spoke for them eloquently; he fought for them valiantly; and finally he sacrificed his life for them.

Few felt this attachment more deeply than the sanitation workers. Clinton Burrows remembered the moment in March 1968 when he heard that King would be coming to Memphis. "It was just like Jesus was coming into my life . . . I was full of joy and determination. Wherever Dr. King was, I wanted to be there." Black youths testified to similar feelings. After the assassination, a teacher at Memphis's Porter Junior High School directed her students to write essays about King. Of the fifty-two students in Ann Benson's Home Economics classes, virtually every one of them wrote in worshipful tones. Many referred to King as a member of their family. Mary Mayhue called him "The Black Prince of Peace." Older students agreed. Sherry Echols, an eighteen-year-old at Hamilton High School, regarded King as "a right hand of God." She recounted the scene in her church on Palm Sunday, April 7, when the congregation was overcome with grief. A sanitation worker named George Houston "prayed like he never prayed in his life. . . . Everyone in church began to cry and shout." The service had the solemnity of a funeral with the emotion of a revival meeting. As James Lawson explained, "There was a great realization . . . that Martin had died on behalf of all of us." This was neither a fanciful theory nor an overstatement. It was a hard truth: King had given his life for their cause.[21]

THE NATION'S EYES turned back to Memphis on Monday, April 8, the day of the memorial march. The city was awhirl with buses and airplanes and people. James Lawson instructed the marchers to walk in complete silence. He also conveyed a warning: "Each of you is on trial today." Millions of Americans would watch them on television, and they would attract the gaze of the world. Lawson counseled the marchers: "March with your head high—with pride." And they did. They marched "proudly and reverently," as Myra Dreifus remembered. They walked eight abreast, arms locked, without so much as a chant or a song—let alone a cigarette or a stick of chewing gum. They marched in suits or work shirts, sunglasses or mourning veils, high heels or mud-caked work boots. Tens of thousands of feet pounded out a silent tribute to the man whose own words had echoed so loud.[22]

People started gathering at Clayborn Temple before eight o'clock in the morning, though the march was not scheduled to begin until eleven. Coretta Scott King's plane from Atlanta was delayed because of fog, so the procession began without her at eleven fifteen. Two huge trailers were placed on either side of Hernando Street to form a funnel, allowing only eight people to pass through at a time. The marchers walked from Hernando Street to Linden Avenue, down Beale Street and onto Main Street, finally striding into City Hall Plaza. When the first line of marchers reached the intersection of Beale and Main, word arrived that Coretta was en route from the airport. The marchers paused for twenty minutes. Coretta made her way to the head of the march just before noon, flanked by her three older children. Joining

Tens of thousands marched in Memphis on April 8. They walked silently, and peacefully, in honor of King and in support of the striking sanitation workers.

Preservation and Special Collections Department,
University Libraries, University of Memphis

them on the front line were Ralph Abernathy, Andrew Young, and Harry Belafonte. Memphis's police chief walked alongside Coretta, watching anxiously for snipers. National Guardsmen lined the route, clutching rifles and bayonets. White spectators flung racist comments and issued death threats, reserving their most hateful vitriol for the white marchers. Overall, the march was a tremendous show of unity, and of nonviolence. While other cities exploded in violence, tens of thousands gathered in Memphis—tense and reeling Memphis—to honor King's memory in a public display of peace. Leaders distributed three different signs. One was the slogan of the sanitation workers, in its brusque elegance: "I AM A MAN." Another said, "UNION JUSTICE

NOW!" A third sign read, "HONOR KING: END RACISM!" This message was aspirational and even fantastical. But to judge by the sincere determination on the faces of the marchers, they seemed to believe that this utopian goal stood within reach.[23]

Speeches began in City Hall Plaza before even half of the marchers had arrived. An hour later, they were still streaming in, eight at a time. The police claimed 19,000 people had marched, but that seemed a low estimate. Bayard Rustin, the march's logistical organizer, counted 42,000; an NBC News broadcast estimated 35,000. If these many thousands marched with pride and reverence, some of them also marched in fear. To recall King's assassination is to recall a moment of collective fright. Memphis simmered with enmity while other cities were already burning. Ted Hoover, an Episcopal chaplain, left his will in his secretary's hands before he headed to Clayborn Temple for the march. The city of Memphis initially secured an injunction on the grounds that the marchers themselves would resort to violence. But for the African Americans who marched—and they constituted a vast majority—the National Guardsmen were a source of fear. The National Guard had been patrolling Memphis's black neighborhoods for more than a week, acting with open hostility. Most generally, a great unknown loomed over the event: how many more white supremacists were out there, armed with rifles and lying in wait?[24]

Actor Ossie Davis opened the proceedings in City Hall Plaza. Three years prior, Davis had delivered the eulogy for Malcolm X. On this day, he declared that the "seed" of Martin Luther King's love "has already taken root in our hearts." He promised to continue King's nonviolent struggle. For the next three hours, a bevy of speakers would make the same pledge. The speeches were a mixture of rousing religious sermons, somber eulogies, and defiant calls for labor justice.[25]

Harry Belafonte spoke about the long legacy of white violence and the endurance of racism. He spoke with anger. Yet he tried his best to channel King, and to hold out hope for white Americans. Perhaps "the white man will be able to come to his senses. . . . Perhaps, after this, we might be able to appeal to his soul because that's all that's left." After Belafonte's scathing message, a local minister led the throng in a rendition of the African American spiritual "Guide My Feet." The thousands raised their voices: "Lord guide my feet, while I run this race / Lord hold my hand, while I run this race." They moved Coretta Scott King to tears.[26]

She was the person whom so many marchers had come to hear. "I came today because I was impelled to come," King allowed. SCLC leaders had wanted to write her speech, but she refused. While on the plane, she jotted down some notes, just in case she felt overwhelmed by the moment. But once on the speakers' platform, which rose high up above the doors of city hall, she barely glanced at her notes. She emphasized the global fight against poverty. "We're concerned not only about the Negro poor, but about the poor all over America and all over the world." The audience responded with deafening applause. Television cameras captured some of the faces in the crowd—youthful faces with earnest and focused expressions. Coretta reflected on her husband's life and death. "He often said that unearned suffering is redemptive. And if you give your life to a cause in which you believe, and which is right and just . . . then your life could not have been lived in a more redemptive way." She pleaded with the crowd and with the nation: "How many men must die before we can really have a free and true and peaceful society? How long will it take?" Finally, she reaffirmed her belief that the nation could be transformed "into a society of love, of justice, peace and brotherhood, where all men can really be brothers." The marchers erupted in another thundering ovation. The peaceful, multiracial crowd itself symbolized that commitment to nonviolent change and brotherhood.[27]

Shortly after Coretta's speech, Ralph Jackson delivered a defiant address that brought the crowd to the edge of elation. Jackson, a conservative black minister, had not participated in civil rights activities before the sanitation strike. But on February 23, during a march for the strikers on Main Street, Jackson was maced. In that instant, he morphed into a political crusader. And he embraced his activism with the zeal of a convert. Now, on April 8, Jackson spoke of Memphis as a "racist community" where "the mayor has no interest in black people." He urged the city's elected officials to settle the strike, and he advised African Americans to boycott white-owned stores as well as the city's two daily newspapers. "No new clothes for Easter! No new hats for Easter!" Jackson bellowed the instructions, and the crowd roared back its approval. Many speakers followed, including Rev. Ben Hooks of Memphis, who delivered a marvel of public oratory. Ralph Abernathy added a comparatively lackluster speech, and Walter Reuther, head of the United Auto Workers, contributed a passionate diatribe. Reuther aimed his arrows straight at Henry Loeb. "I say to Mayor Loeb: Even though it may be painful, before this fight of the sanitation workers is over, we're going to drag you into the twentieth century somehow!" The silent march had given way to a stirring protest rally.[28]

Bayard Rustin had also organized the March on Washington in August 1963. That march seemed of a different era altogether. King, both Kennedys, and Malcolm X were all still alive at that time. Vietnam seemed a distant and irrelevant land. The chaotic 1960s had not yet arrived. On this day in Memphis in 1968, some observers thought the silent marchers were turning back the clock to the peaceful, interracial struggles of the earlier 1960s. But Rustin hesitated to declare a victory for nonviolence. "I think Dr. King's death had a polarizing effect. Those who practice violence have in their own minds further justification for using it. Those who believe in nonviolence . . . have a deeper commitment to achieving democracy and integration." In this view, King's death compelled those on each side of the debate to dig in deeper.[29]

That dynamic certainly applied when it came to the strike itself. The marchers' cries for union justice, and the speeches that lacerated Mayor Henry Loeb, only incensed many white Memphians. The editors of the *Commercial Appeal* gave voice to their anger. The editors had no problem with the march's "peaceful prelude" or with its homage to King. But the more "fiery oratory," like that of Walter Reuther and Ralph Jackson, struck the editors as "racial agitation" and "demagoguery." The *Commercial Appeal* resorted to old-fashioned paternalism: "As we have said for years, our Negro community deserves more attention than it has received." But the strikers' demands were an example of "one group working to exert its will over the will of the American majority." In this twisted logic, the poor and dispossessed garbage workers had become the coercive ones. And the white leaders of Memphis, longtime segregationists and lifelong union-bashers, supposedly stood as the true democrats.[30]

For many white Memphians, King's death had done nothing to alter their views on the strike. After King's assassination, the Jackson Avenue Lions Club sent Henry Loeb a telegram: the club was "standing 100 percent behind you." Other whites in Memphis launched a letter-writing campaign, assuring Loeb that they continued to support his anti-union stance. Telegrams flooded the mayor's office and citizens walked the streets to collect signatures on a pro-Loeb petition. In the weeks prior to King's death, such endeavors seemed only obdurate and small-minded. Now that King had sacrificed his life while assisting the strikers, those actions looked odious and sickening.[31]

As whites fumed at the calls for labor justice, African Americans in Memphis basked in the glow of the memorial march. Eighteen-year-old Joseph Smith Jr., one of the marchers, walked in honor of the "God-sent prophet of the twentieth century." At the outset, Smith felt "incomplete, for I had lost something." But the spirit of the crowd worked on him. "The atmosphere was one. Hope was given to the world." A feeling of unity permeated the streets. "We all seem to be drawn together now." That same spirit leaped through the television screen, infecting those who stayed at home. Seventeen-year-old Frankie Gross found himself glued to the television in the days after King's death. Gross explained that he initially sided with militant black leaders. "I agreed with Stokely Carmichael's philosophy of burning at first, and wondered why Negroes hadn't burned down more than they had." As

This photo was taken at the beginning of the march, before Coretta Scott King arrived. The marchers included Bayard Rustin (foreground, left); Jerry Wurf, head of the American Federation of State, County, and Municipal Employees (center, in tie and trench coat); local union leader T. O. Jones (to the right of Wurf); and Ralph Jackson (far right).

Preservation and Special Collections Department, University Libraries, University of Memphis

Gross watched Coretta Scott King appeal for peace, he began to feel differently. "When I saw Mrs. King on television I respected what she had to say. I realized that Martin Luther King's dream wasn't of killing and looting, but a dream of life where all races could live together in a world of brotherly love." The display of nonviolence in downtown Memphis had won over Frankie Gross.[32]

Barbara Chandler, also seventeen years old, sat transfixed by the scenes from the "sacred" march. "As I looked at the television I could picture him leading that march." In her mind's eye, she saw Martin Luther King next to his wife and children, alongside Ralph Abernathy and Andrew Young, with the tens of thousands trailing behind. In the picture Barbara Chandler conjured, King was leading the march and all was right with the world. "I've been told that the dead can look back and see what's happening. If this is true, Dr. Martin Luther King saw a great sight that Monday, and I know he is happy."[33]

WHEN THE SILENT march concluded, the herd of media and celebrities flew to Atlanta for King's funeral. The union chartered buses for those sanitation workers who wished to bear witness. The workers had only a few hours at home between the end of the silent march and the buses' departure—time to change, eat dinner, and pack. Each man was told to bring a toothbrush and a change of clothes. It remained unclear whether the buses could accommodate their wives as well.

Union leaders had alerted the Memphis police that workers would be traveling to Clayborn Temple late at night, notwithstanding the citywide curfew. The police stopped some of the workers nonetheless, ordering them out of their cars and forcing the men to explain themselves. Everyone gathered at Clayborn Temple, where three buses eventually arrived. After an hour of head counts and huddles, it became apparent that the buses could fit the workers and their wives—if folding chairs occupied the middle aisles. Author Garry Wills asked whether there was room for him. The workers put it to a vote, and welcomed Wills aboard. Wills later published an article in *Esquire*, a deeply textured account of how the workers experienced King's assassination.[34]

The four-hundred-mile trip would wind through the foreboding terrain of Mississippi and Alabama. After midnight, the buses began to trudge southward and out of Memphis. The workers could see that many whites drove their vehicles unmolested, despite the curfew. In the back of Garry Wills's bus, one worker started to preach. He had served as a marshal all day long in the silent march. His legs were weary, but his voice needed the exercise. "That Dr. King was for us. He didn't have to come here." His fellow passengers played their part. Their responses came "like sleepy respirations," as Wills put it, "as if the bus's sides were breathing regularly in and out." The man in the back announced, "King was *one* with us." His comrades agreed: "That he was. That he was." The other passengers were tired but still willing to engage; it was sufficient encouragement. "You know what Dr. King said? He said not to mention his Nobel Prize when he died." The others agreed: "That's what he *said*." The man explained, "What matters is that *he* helped *us*." The passengers focused on King's devotion to them, and the powerful bond between the workers and their leader.[35]

The buses crossed the state line. "We're in Mississippi now," noted a man seated behind Garry Wills. His wife blurted out what everyone else was thinking: "Oh no!" As T. O. Jones, the leader of the local union, told Wills, "This is risky country. And it gets more dangerous as you go down the road." Well into Mississippi, the caravan stopped for a bathroom break. The buses eased into a parking lot. Two of the three buses were equipped with restrooms, but the folding chairs rendered them useless. So the passengers folded up the chairs and exited. Women lined up in one bus, men in the other. Some of the men wandered toward trees to relieve themselves, but T. O. Jones called them back. He knew that the sight of two hundred black people, in the middle of the night, was more than enough to inflame white Mississippians. He offered, "Well, we're in Mississippi, and folk tend to get fluster[ed] at—"[36]

The buses rolled through Mississippi and Alabama, and the dawn light finally revealed Georgia's red clay. The funeral was scheduled to start at ten thirty. But the buses had not left Memphis until past midnight, and they reached Atlanta after the funeral service had begun. The buses pulled up near the capitol and emptied the tired passengers onto the sidewalk. The workers and their wives did not have time to change their clothes.[37]

ON THE MORNING of King's funeral, the rest of the country paused for a moment of silence. Many government offices and schools were closed. Stock exchanges took the day off as well, the first time the New York Stock Exchange closed to honor a private citizen. One hundred twenty million Americans tuned in to watch the service on television.[38]

People poured into Atlanta. The city "felt like the center of the universe," recalled Maria Saporta, an Atlantan who was twelve years old at the time. Newsstands at the airport stocked *Life*'s commemorative King issue, and raised the price from thirty-five cents per copy to one dollar. They quickly sold out of all 100,000 copies. The SCLC put out a frantic call for volunteers to assist with the influx of visitors. Atlanta residents opened up their homes. For many whites, it was the first time they had hosted African Americans. Local churches and schools prepared to receive the fatigued travelers. Krispy Kreme donated 150 dozen doughnuts and Coca-Cola contributed 16,000 bottles of soda. Central Presbyterian Church acted as the de facto headquarters. It provided food, blankets, and sheets, and bused visitors to churches and colleges throughout the city. Rows of army cots dotted classrooms and gymnasiums. It seemed every structure in the city held grieving visitors, a mourner in every bed.[39]

James Baldwin traveled to Atlanta by himself. He had last seen King when they both appeared at an event at Carnegie Hall earlier in 1968. Baldwin, the celebrated black writer, bought a new dark suit for that occasion. And he wore it again to King's funeral.

On the morning of Tuesday, April 9, Baldwin left his Atlanta hotel and walked toward Ebenezer Baptist Church. Throngs of people stretched in every direction. Baldwin squeezed his way closer to the church, inch by inch, until an impenetrable wall of humanity finally stopped him in his tracks. The people "were like rows of poppies," recalled June Dobbs, a lifelong friend of King's. Outside the church, Baldwin leaned up against a Cadillac carrying football star Jim Brown, but Brown did not see him. Baldwin gesticulated wildly until someone on the church steps recognized him, pushed toward the Cadillac, and "sort of lifted me over." He followed his escort into the church and found a seat among the 1,000 souls pressed into Ebenezer. The pew in front of him held a lineup of celebrity entertainers: Marlon Brando, Sammy Davis Jr., Eartha Kitt, and Sidney Poitier. Harry Belafonte sat up front, alongside Coretta Scott King. Ralph Abernathy occupied the pulpit. "The atmosphere was black," Baldwin wrote, "with a tension indescribable—as though something, perhaps the heavens, perhaps the earth, might crack."[40]

As the service began, Baldwin tried to keep himself together. "I did not want to weep for Martin, tears seemed futile." His death was too terrible, the void too deep. "I may also have been afraid, and I could not have been the only one, that if I began to weep I would not be able to stop."[41]

Abernathy offered a prayer and read from the Old and New Testaments. Harold DeWolf, King's professor from Boston University, delivered a short tribute. Then the Ebenezer choir sang one of Martin's favorite hymns, "Softly and Tenderly," as well as "Where He Leads Me I Will Follow." Choir member Mary Gurley delivered a breathtaking performance of "My Heavenly Father Watches Over Me." Jethro English, a church deacon, had sung in the choir for several decades. English noted, "I sang at his wedding to Coretta—and I sang at his *parents'* wedding." But English had trouble during the funeral. "It was hard to sing. There was so much emotion. But we had an obligation to share." After the choir finished, Martin's voice filled the church. Coretta played his speech of February 4, in which King had reflected on his funeral wishes. Finally, the pallbearers carried King's casket toward the door. Abernathy followed the casket, trancelike, chanting psalms. The crowd filed out behind him. When James Baldwin emerged in the sunlight, he noticed the enormity of the spectacle, which he had failed to appreciate on his way in. He saw that masses of people not only lined both sides of the road, but that they occupied every imaginable space. They stood on every rooftop, baking in the Georgia heat. "Every inch of ground, as far as the eye could see, was black with people, and they stood in silence." They offered a mute testament to King. "It was the silence that undid me," Baldwin explained. "I started to cry, and I stumbled." Sammy Davis Jr. grabbed his arm and steadied him for the march ahead.[42]

King's coffin was loaded into a wagon drawn by mules. King had envisioned for the Poor People's Campaign a similar scene: impoverished citizens would hitch their wagons and set out for Washington. As Bernard Lafayette put it, the wagon "symbolized what he lived for and what he died for." The mule-drawn wagon brought King down from the plane of Nobel laureates and the rarefied air of angels. It placed him squarely alongside ordinary black laborers. It highlighted his ties with those whose hands had picked cotton, those who still worked with mules across the rural South, those who cleaned the toilets or carried the trash. They were King's people.[43]

The idea of the mule-led wagon came from the SCLC's Hosea Williams. Coretta and the SCLC staff considered many options, but everyone agreed in the end that the wagon was most appropriate. It fit with the specific image of King that Coretta and the SCLC were projecting: of a man in touch with the poor, a leader who toiled for society's most alienated. Days after King's death, his closest confidants thus engaged in the shaping of his legacy. Once they decided on a wagon, SCLC members then started to look for the perfect one. "It had to look a certain way," explained Elizabeth Omilami, the daughter of Hosea Williams. She was seventeen years old at the time, home from boarding school to attend the funeral. "It couldn't be nice, it had to look rugged." SCLC staffers searched for a working wagon that fit the bill. They eventually found one at an antique shop in Atlanta's West End. Ed Peek, a farmer from Clayton County, Georgia, agreed to lend two mules.[44]

At noon, the great funeral march began with the clop of the hooves on the street. It would snake for four miles, from Ebenezer to Morehouse College. "When the procession would go by," mayoral intern Sam Williams remembered, "people would get quiet." Forty years later, the sound stayed with him—silence broken by the rapping of hooves upon pavement. Kennedys and Rockefellers marched together with tens of thousands of anonymous African Americans. As a *Newsweek* reporter wrote, the funeral procession featured "the powerful and mighty marching along with a gnarled sharecropper wearing his only oversized Sunday suit." Princes and paupers alike donned their Sunday best. On the front page of the *New York Times*, Homer Bigart described it as "one of the strangest corteges ever seen in the land."[45]

The streets of Atlanta were illuminated in red, white, and black. Blooming red azaleas lined the route as the dogwoods reached their spring peak, painting a bright ivory background behind the march. Of the 150,000 marchers, as many as 140,000 were black. While the funeral demonstrated the powerful link between King and ordinary black people, it also showed the depths of white apathy. The white neighborhoods on the city's outskirts seemed untouched by the day's events. In northeast Atlanta, the Lenox Square shopping center buzzed with affluent whites. Though Rich's department store closed its downtown location for the day, its Lenox Square store welcomed the hordes of Easter shoppers.[46]

While virtually every white American was touched by John F. Kennedy's assassination in 1963, these shoppers were among the millions of whites who merely noted King's death and hoped it would not disrupt their everyday lives. In the weeks after King's assassination, the Emory Center for Research in Social Change conducted a survey of Atlanta residents. Eighty-three percent of African Americans reported strongly emotional reactions to King's death. Only 42 percent of whites registered such responses. As the Emory social scientists concluded, "White Atlantans simply did not identify with Dr. King; his death to them was simply an event which would not affect the individual lives of white people." The researchers asked whether King's death had affected individuals' attitudes toward racial problems. Fully 84 percent of whites in Atlanta answered "No." The audience at the Atlanta Symphony may have gasped at the news of King's death, but for most white Americans,

King's assassination was not a tragedy to wrestle with—much less an event that would affect their lives or their outlook. It was just another inconvenience to navigate.[47]

Senator Robert Kennedy came to this conclusion during the march. Kennedy walked with black activist Charles Evers, whose older brother Medgar had also been assassinated in 1963. Few white people participated in the march, or even stood among the thousands of well-wishers who lined the route. Reporter Jimmy Breslin said to Kennedy, "You'd think even a few of them would come out and just look, even for curiosity." Kennedy replied, "You'd think so." Breslin inquired, "Then maybe this thing won't change anything at all?" "Oh," said Kennedy, "I don't think this will mean anything." Kennedy looked at Evers and asked, "Charles, do you think this will mean anything?" Evers said, "Nothing. Didn't mean nothing when my brother was killed." Kennedy answered, "I know." To so many white Americans, King's death registered as someone else's horror. It was a wound inflicted upon another people.[48]

For the African Americans who made the pilgrimage to Atlanta, however, that wound cut deep. One South Carolina man could not quite explain why he had traveled the two hundred miles. "It's just something I felt I had to do. I don't know exactly why, other than I had a great respect for King." He was pulled ineluctably to Atlanta. Laurence Smith Jr. viewed such people as the true heroes of the day. Smith, a graduate student in sociology at the University of Kentucky, was already in Atlanta to attend an academic conference. He both participated in the funeral march and analyzed it. He collected his thoughts and drafted a letter to Ralph McGill, publisher of the *Atlanta Constitution*. Smith focused not on the elected officials, the movie stars, the famous athletes, or the foreign ambassadors. He wrote about the "*real* dignitaries," by whom he meant "the people of little known public identity who stood in silent vigil, who march the 30-odd blocks to Morehouse College, who stood, pressed against one another in ... summer temperature, sharing their collective grief." He described some of these "*real* dignitaries" in more detail. They were "the high school girls from

Detroit who had sacrificed their money, saved to buy an Easter outfit, in order to ride a bus and to be in Atlanta to pay their respects; they were the plumbers from Stamford, Connecticut, the working girls from Chicago, the seminary student from Philadelphia, the unemployed laborer from Biloxi, the soldier home on leave from Vietnam, the off-duty Atlanta cab-driver, the hotel porter from Augusta." He included on his list a "weeping white policeman from Cleveland" as well as postal workers from Richmond and schoolteachers from Cleveland. "The sacrifices they made to be there was their mutual gift to Dr. King's memory." King had toiled for them. In return, they tolerated every mundane inconvenience in order to make sure the streets of Atlanta would be clogged with mourners.[49]

They sang as they walked. They sang "This Little Light of Mine" and "Swing Low, Sweet Chariot." Dizzy Gillespie sang "Freedom." Eartha Kitt led a portion of the crowd in "We Shall Overcome," and Aretha Franklin picked up where she left off. The mules trotted onto the Morehouse College campus shortly after two thirty in the afternoon. The classic portico of Harkness Hall served as the speakers' platform. Benjamin Mays, the former president of Morehouse, took his place at the lectern in a rich crimson robe. Next to Mays sat Andrew Young and then Rosa Parks, wearing a black dress with a black straw hat. She sobbed quietly into her handkerchief. Rows of green-cushioned folding chairs were positioned just beneath the platform. Martin Luther King Sr. sat in the front row, looking "alternately bewildered, perturbed, and proud," according to a *Newsweek* reporter. Behind the folding chairs, the vast throng of mourners overflowed the Morehouse quad. They climbed onto tree limbs or stood atop parked cars for a better view. Some fainted from the oppressive heat and the suffocating crowd. At one point, a disoriented older woman wandered into an open area in front of the main platform. Nelson Rockefeller rose and ceded his seat to the woman, a former domestic worker. She sat next to Happy Rockefeller and the two women shared a cup of crushed ice. Nelson Rockefeller retreated to the grass and sat down, legs crossed.

Mahalia Jackson took the podium and sang "Precious Lord," the song King had requested in his last moments. Finally, Benjamin Mays gave the eulogy. Mays and King had forged a pact: whichever man passed away first would have his eulogy delivered by the other. Mays stood thirty-five years older than King. Mays lamented, "I always wanted him to preach mine." Although King's family and confidants lived for so long with the prospect of his death, there was a painful awareness that he had died too soon. Cut down at age thirty-nine, he was survived by the president of his alma mater, by his father and mother, and by the gray-haired woman who stumbled into a front-row seat.[50]

Abernathy closed the service at four fifteen. Jesse Jackson dropped to his knees in front of the coffin, bobbed his head, and wept. Jackson seemed to have released something. Many of the other men remained calm and controlled through the service; now they dissolved in tears as well. The mule train left Morehouse and headed toward South-View Cemetery. African Americans had founded the cemetery in 1886, seeking an alternative to Atlanta's segregated graveyards. Several lynching victims were buried there, including those who perished in Atlanta's 1906 race riot. A brief ceremony capped the long day. King was the most recent, and the most famous, among the victims of white violence to be buried in that ground.[51]

Few of the celebrities or politicians made the trek to South-View Cemetery. Some lacked the stamina for the seemingly interminable day of mourning. More to the point, they lacked the commitment. Many political leaders had recently admonished King and denounced the Poor People's Campaign. After the assassination, they suddenly turned around and offered mealy-mouthed encomiums to King. As the liberal southerner Pat Watters wrote in *The Nation*, "the outpouring of grief and guilt and bathos after the assassination, coming from such an officialdom, a press, a society . . . had to be called obscene."[52]

Jesse Jackson felt a similar disgust. He was incensed by the sight of 150,000 mourners in Atlanta. He wondered where they had been in the past weeks, months, and years. "There was a total outpouring of people. My anger was, in part, because—how many people had been with us April 3, fighting for the garbage workers, the Poor People's Campaign?" To avoid the strike in Memphis, and then just to show up in Atlanta, was an easy salve. "It's cheap grace to admire a sacrificial person. There were many who admired him but few who followed him." The elected officials who attended the funeral had engaged in "politically inspired commiseration," wrote David Levering Lewis in his 1970 biography of King. They had lambasted King for his stance on Vietnam and whipped up revulsion toward him. Their denunciations had "fostered, condoned, or finessed the rising opposition to Martin's activities during the past three or more years." On this day, with their hypocrisy barely disguised, they sought photo opportunities under the boiling Georgia sun.[53]

Only one senator or congressman from the South attended the funeral: Georgia's Fletcher Thompson. The other southern politicians knew how deeply their constituents loathed King, and realized that their own presence at the funeral could become a political liability. (Indeed, Thompson's constituents assailed him.) A few of them expressed "polite statements of regret" about King's assassination, as Ralph McGill reported. But they were "privately relieved that Dr. King was no longer alive." King had long stuck as a thorn in their sides. He confronted, challenged, and discomfited those in power.[54]

Now his voice was stilled.

PRESIDENT LYNDON JOHNSON declined to attend the funeral.

Lady Bird Johnson described the moment when the Johnsons learned of King's assassination as "one of those frozen moments, as though the bomb had fallen on us." President Johnson immediately called Coretta Scott King to express his remorse. Then he appeared on television and told the nation, "I am sure that every American of goodwill joins me in mourning the death of this outstanding leader." In his statement, Johnson said more about the need for peace than about the loss of King. His chief aim was to deter Americans from rioting.

Although Johnson praised King as an "outstanding leader," the two men were no longer on speaking terms. They had worked together closely in the past—particularly on the 1964 Civil Rights Act and 1965 Voting Rights Act—but that seemed long ago. By 1968, Johnson disdained King's antiwar position and expressed anger at the prospect of the Poor People's Campaign. Some of Johnson's aides despised King, while J. Edgar Hoover continued to bombard the president with anti-King slander. Johnson was not mourning the passing of an ally.[55]

Johnson attended a memorial service for King at the National Cathedral on April 6. He designated April 7, Palm Sunday, as a national day of mourning. As the funeral approached, Ralph Abernathy claimed to have received word that Johnson was planning to attend. On April 8, during the televised broadcast of the Memphis silent march, CBS's Douglas Kiker reported, "There is some talk that President Johnson might go to Atlanta for the services. We understand from the White House that the Secret Service has been urging him not to go, and a decision has yet to be made." In his 1971 memoir, Johnson explained that he had wished to attend the funeral so he could express his condolences to the King family, but he "had to heed the unanimous judgment of the Secret Service and the FBI. The situation in Atlanta was tense and dangerous; they recommended in the strongest terms that I not attend the funeral."[56]

Many in Washington assumed Johnson would attend the funeral; the question was which individuals would fly with him to Atlanta. Donald Kendall, the president of Pepsi, called an FBI secretary on April 5 to suggest that Johnson should bring on his plane the leading presidential candidates: Eugene McCarthy, Robert Kennedy, and Richard Nixon. That way, Kendall thought, none of the candidates would be tempted to play politics with King's funeral—they would have to present a united front. Other administration officials called and wrote to the White House staff, jockeying for a seat on Air Force One.[57]

Johnson received plenty of advice. Several white southerners fretted about the prospect of Johnson's traveling to Atlanta. On the morning of April 8, a New Orleans oilman named Bill Helis called the White House and urged the president to stay in Washington. Johnson "ought not expose himself to any of the extremists who undoubtedly will be in the area." Georgia congressman Phil Landrum, alarmed by local newspaper reports stating that Johnson would attend the funeral, spoke with Johnson's chief of staff. "I frankly don't think it is safe in any respect," Landrum said to Marvin Watson. He worried that African Americans would harm the president. "It looks like they are looking for a martyr. I think the possibility of physical harm is there. Just like the possibility was in Memphis." Landrum, a longtime opponent of racial integration, added, "I don't think it will do anybody, including him, any good . . . what he has done is already enough." He meant that Johnson had accomplished quite enough for African Americans and for King. Tennessee governor Buford Ellington offered a similar opinion: "The country knows the President has done enough for this man. . . . His going very likely would cause serious white backlash." John Davis, another Georgia congressman, called the White House to warn that Klansmen had vowed to attack Johnson if he appeared in Atlanta. And Joseph Califano, Johnson's chief adviser, added one more consideration to the mix: "I still believe that you should not go to the funeral, especially now that Bunker is coming in." He referred to Ellsworth Bunker, the ambassador to South Vietnam, who was scheduled to meet with Johnson about the prospects for peace. Califano counseled Johnson to focus on those talks rather than pay his respects to Martin Luther King. Johnson needed to sort through an array of concerns. Would he be safe in Atlanta? Had he indeed "done enough" for civil rights already? Should he just focus on Vietnam instead?[58]

The Secret Service, FBI, and Johnson's staffers agreed: the president ought not travel to Atlanta. On April 8, Secret Service director James Rowley sent Johnson a blunt recommendation: "Both the U.S. Secret Service and the Federal Bureau of Investigation strongly recommend that the President should not attend the funeral services." The Secret Service also forwarded to Johnson a long FBI report. Alarmist in tone and thinly researched, it anticipated violence on every Atlanta corner. The report was not so much a levelheaded evaluation of whether it might be feasible for Johnson to attend the funeral. Instead, it was an ominous portrait of every group that might possibly cause disorder. It noted that Stokely Carmichael would be attending the funeral, and that Carmichael had previously encouraged "mob violence" and advocated "use of firearms by Negroes." It also expressed general panic about activists from the Student Nonviolent Coordinating Committee (SNCC). According to one FBI source, "Violence will break out immediately following funeral services for King . . . all contacts feel SNCC activists will seize the moment of highest emotional tension to start rioting." This informant "could not imagine circumstances more likely to result in violence than those that will exist in Atlanta on day of King's funeral." The FBI also detailed the plans of assorted black nationalist groups. Members of the Revolutionary Action Movement were supposedly gathering in Philadelphia, then traveling to Memphis for the silent march and on to Atlanta for the funeral. The FBI report warned, "All persons recruited will be armed with pistols in shoulder holsters." The Ku Klux Klan also posed a threat. "Sources state there are numerous Klansmen in Atlanta area who are capable of making an attempt to do bodily harm to the president and vice president." To read the FBI report with a believing eye was to view King's funeral as a certain bloodbath.[59]

Yet there is no evidence that Johnson actually wished to travel to Atlanta. "The truth was, Johnson didn't *want* to go to Martin Luther King's funeral," as author Hampton Sides puts it. "The president could not quite bring himself to honor the man who'd so brazenly undermined him on Vietnam." Clay Risen agrees, noting that Johnson "had more or less checked out of the King ceremonies." Assistant Attorney General Roger Wilkins was angered by Johnson's actions. According to Wilkins, Coretta Scott King wanted to keep the number of other politicians to a minimum. "I had relayed the family's request that only the President come and if he couldn't then only Vice-President

Humphrey." Wilkins was furious that the administration sent "a whole planeload of Washington dignitaries, who took seats that could have gone to the people who risked their lives on lonely roads with Martin." Not even Robert Kennedy escaped Wilkins's wrath. Kennedy marched through the Atlanta streets, waving to well-wishers along the funeral route. "I hated those smiles," Wilkins recalled. "A man was dead." Wilkins found the number of white leaders who took part in the funeral procession offensive. "The white politicians started to come. And they came. And they came. And they came. And a lot of people—both black and white came to see the show—like to a carnival. And that made me resent the politicians—and the President, who didn't come—even more." Johnson's response felt like one final insult.[60]

Events did not bear out the FBI's shrill predictions. Although 150,000 mourners packed the Atlanta streets, there was no violence. They came to grieve, and they came in peace. This outcome showed that the FBI continued to misunderstand the various forces that composed the black freedom struggle. For years, Hoover's FBI had treated black leaders like King and Malcolm X as subversive enemies. And when it came to King's funeral, they misread the civil rights movement once again. Where the FBI predicted all manner of violence, peace prevailed. Peace reigned in Memphis for the silent march, and many thousands traveled to Atlanta for a similar display of nonviolence.

In the end, the critical issue is not whether the FBI correctly predicted the likelihood of violence. The question is how that prediction factored into Johnson's absence. Was it the overriding consideration? If the FBI had presented a less alarming assessment, would Johnson have attended? If Johnson could have peered ahead by several decades, and could have seen the saint King became, would he have found his way to Ebenezer?

Johnson's anger toward King likely colored his decision. Vice President Hubert Humphrey did appear at the funeral, despite protestations from the FBI and Secret Service. Yet the two living former presidents,

Dwight Eisenhower and Harry Truman, declined to travel to Atlanta. Both Truman and Eisenhower were elderly and unlikely to travel in any case. They were also following Johnson's lead.

Perhaps Johnson knew that April 9 was not his day, and realized—in some deeper sense—that King's funeral was not his place. It was a day for King's family, for the SCLC staff, and for the anonymous thousands: the Atlanta residents who perched on their rooftops for a glimpse of the mule train, the schoolteachers who trekked from Cleveland, the plumbers from Stamford, and the group of garbage workers who sat in folding chairs on the bus, who hurtled through the Deep South in the middle of the night, who arrived in Atlanta without enough time to change their clothes.

After King's funeral, James Baldwin flew back to Hollywood to continue working on the screen version of *The Autobiography of Malcolm X*. Baldwin then returned briefly to his native New York, where he ran into the journalist Leonard Lyons. He told Lyons about his suit—the suit he bought for his event with King at Carnegie Hall, and that he had also worn to King's funeral. Baldwin confessed that he would never be able to wear the suit again. Lyons relayed this anecdote in his *New York Post* column. Soon, Baldwin began to receive repeated phone messages from an old junior high school friend. Guessing that his friend needed money, Baldwin took his time to respond. When they finally spoke, Baldwin discovered that his friend had read Leonard Lyons's column and had deduced that Baldwin possessed an extra suit. The two men were the same size.[61]

Baldwin agreed to dine at his friend's Harlem home that evening, and he brought the suit with him. In the decades since the men last saw each other, Baldwin had gained international fame; his friend worked for the postal service. Before the meal, Baldwin and his friend argued over the Vietnam War. His friend's mother recoiled at Baldwin's coarse language. The fried chicken dinner quickly became an uncomfortable affair. Baldwin smoked and drank and ate, and felt the distance between them. Then Baldwin gave his friend the suit. "For that bloody suit was *their* suit, after all, it had been bought *for* them, it had even been bought *by* them: *they* had created Martin, he had not created them, and the blood in which the fabric of that suit was stiffening was theirs." His friend tried on the suit: it was a perfect fit.[62]

2

THE LAST PRINCE OF NONVIOLENCE

MILLIONS OF ORDINARY African Americans continued to revere King into his last months and after his death. But the nation and the world focused on a different segment of the African American population: those who turned to violence.

One photograph in particular came to symbolize the nation's ordeal. It showed thick plumes of smoke hovering over the Capitol dome. Fires blazed in Washington, DC, while thousands of people were arrested and stolen merchandise littered city streets. Army troops moved into Washington on April 6. "It was like how I always imagined Berlin must have looked after World War II," said Richard Zimmerman, a twenty-one-year-old private stationed on Seventh Street. "Everything was burned, gutted, and crumbling." Troops would soon occupy Chicago and Baltimore as well. The National Guard appeared in twenty other cities. Overall, more than 120 cities experienced sustained episodes of violence. Thirty-nine Americans died in the wave of riots. Yet to fixate on the smoke in Washington, and the riot statistics, is to risk distorting the story in one crucial respect. Among those individuals who rioted, very few cited King's death as their underlying motivation. His assassination was the catalyst rather than the root cause.[1]

Still, King's death did set in motion a deeper conceptual shift. It intensified a debate among African Americans about the virtues of nonviolence versus armed resistance. Many began to embrace the latter. The vast majority of African Americans remained peaceful. But more than ever before, nonviolence lost its allure. King's death represented a turning point in the growth of black militancy.

Few were radicalized more fully than Aaron Dixon. "Since the death of Martin Luther King," Dixon explained, "my life and the life of many other Black youth throughout America had taken on an overwhelming sense of urgency." Dixon soon helped to open a chapter of the Black Panther Party in Seattle, one of the first chapters outside California.[2]

Dixon had been a leader of the Black Student Union at the University of Washington. In March 1968, a black high school student told Dixon he had been unfairly suspended from Seattle's Franklin High. Moreover, the principal at Franklin refused to recognize the Black Student Union there. On March 29, Dixon and other activists, including his brother Elmer, helped to organize a protest at Franklin High. Several days later, on April 4, the protest leaders were arrested for unlawful assembly. Dixon spent that night in the King County Jail, an "archaic-looking dungeon, like something out of medieval times." He sat in a dark and cold cell, watching a tiny black-and-white television perched high on a metal shelf. Walter Cronkite delivered the news that King had been assassinated. As the night went on, images danced across the screen—scenes of violence and mayhem in city after city. "It was looking like the revolution had come—and here we were, sitting in jail. . . . My emotions were going wild. I kicked and banged the steel table, throwing whatever I could throw, wishing I were out there on the streets." He resolved to strike back. "I vowed to myself that Martin's death would not go unavenged. If a man of peace could be killed through violence, then violence it would be." Aaron Dixon was already headed toward aggressive activism; King's death turned him to the Black Panthers. That moment was decisive. As Dixon's story unfolded through the spring of 1968, it showed how King's assassination propelled the national expansion of the Black Panther Party.[3]

AMID THE VIOLENCE of the late 1960s, King struggled to adjust his message in a way that would resonate. The summer of 1967 witnessed violent uprisings in hundreds of American cities. The Black Power movement gained momentum, as did the "white backlash." In this context, King's admonitions to love one's enemy struck many younger African Americans as not only fanciful but absurd. In June 1967, King published *Where Do We Go from Here: Chaos or Community?* Two months later, journalist Andrew Kopkind issued a scathing appraisal of the book—and of King: "He has been outstripped by his times. . . . He is not likely to regain command. Both his philosophy and his techniques of leadership were products of a different world." During that "long hot summer" of 1967, "the black people of America are at the losing ends of shotguns, out weighed by thumb-heavy scales, on the outermost margins of power." Nonviolence was finished. "Martin Luther King and the 'leaders' who appealed for non-violence . . . *are all* beside the point." King was "not ready for the world," Kopkind asserted. "What is hardest now to comprehend," he concluded, "is King's irrelevancy." For many African Americans, the last years of the 1960s were no time to stand before fire hoses or to extend their hands across the racial divide. The man who led America toward a new day of racial equality seemed a relic of an earlier era.[4]

As the critics of nonviolence saw it, King's assassination clinched their argument. African Americans had tried nonviolence and failed. "Nonviolence is a dead philosophy," Floyd McKissick of the Congress of Racial Equality (CORE) said after King's death. "It was not the black people that killed it. It was the white people that killed nonviolence . . . Dr. Martin Luther King was the last prince of nonviolence." In that moment, Black Power leaders found themselves both distraught and emboldened. Many of them maintained that peaceful resistance was ill suited to a nation so barbaric. Julius Hobson, a longtime radical and a former CORE leader, declared, "The Martin Luther King concept of nonviolence died with him. . . . It was a foreign ideology anyway—as foreign to this violent country as speaking Russian." Another Black Power leader appealed for violence, explaining, "White America understands no other language." For these activists, King's murder demonstrated the ultimate futility of nonviolence.[5]

As American cities erupted in riots after King's assassination, elected officials asserted that King himself would have denounced such uprisings. Lyndon Johnson implored the nation, "I ask every citizen to reject the blind violence that has struck Dr. King, who lived by nonviolence." On a CBS News roundtable, the NAACP's Roy Wilkins declared that violence "would be an insult to Martin's memory." But other black leaders explained that the cities had exploded precisely *because* it was King who had been murdered. His reputation as a paragon of peace, and as one who worked for interracial harmony, made his slaughter that much more outrageous. Stokely Carmichael, the nation's leading proponent of Black Power, insisted, "It would have been better if" whites had "killed Rap Brown and/or Stokely Carmichael." King's death was an assault too hideous to abide.[6]

Charles Cabbage, a member of a Black Power group in Memphis called the Invaders, explained why King's death hit with such devastating force: "The majority of black people in this country saw Dr. King as possibly the greatest moral leader that this country had ever seen." They were "totally unprepared" for King's assassination because they "did not think that white America could stoop this low. Because here came a man talking love and nonviolence and walking hand in hand with white people, and they took his head off." The assassination was a profound insult. Cabbage predicted that King's absence would open the door for groups like his own. "I think that white America has put itself in one hell of a trick now." The actions of a twenty-one-year-old in Washington lent credence to Cabbage's view. This man, who had participated in looting after King's death, considered King "the best liaison between government and ghetto people and black people, a man who was preaching nonviolence but nevertheless . . . he was shot down." He ultimately concluded, "It seems as though I have no alternative but to take on some militant strives because nonviolence doesn't seem to be the answer."[7]

It was no exaggeration to call King the last prince of nonviolence. According to Cornelia Crenshaw, a civil rights activist and a longtime manager at the Memphis Housing Authority, that city's white citizens "did not know that really the greatest friend they had had been killed. He was the last of the people that I know whom the folk really respect, who had a non-violent attitude." King had indeed earned the respect of "the folk." This set him apart from others who preached nonviolence. Leaders like Roy Wilkins struck many African Americans as staid and out of touch. And although the philosophy of nonviolence may have seemed increasingly irrelevant in the time of Black Power, King himself still enjoyed the affections of so many black people—young and old. George Foster articulated African Americans' loss on the night of King's assassination. Foster, a young black anchor for CBS News, appeared on a roundtable forum with Roy Wilkins and Whitney Young. Foster was asked to summarize the views of the younger generation: "What has happened today underlined those points, those positions, that the militants of this country stress: that you cannot trust the white man, that the white man will indeed do away with you if you get in his way, that the . . . aware Negro or black man must arm himself and prepare to fight at all costs." King's leadership had been so meaningful because he "led the common people. He went into the beer halls and spoke with people about nonviolence . . . he tried to talk with people." King's common touch, as much as his soaring oratory, made him great. And this was what the black freedom struggle would be missing. "I am afraid that the common people will be persuaded to join a much more violent group now."[8]

THE RIOTS IN Washington quickly gripped the world's imagination. That was in no small part because they occurred within blocks of the White House. It was also due to the presence of Stokely Carmichael. Carmichael began his career as a SNCC organizer, dedicated to nonviolence and toiling on voter-registration drives in the Deep South. Carmichael was radicalized over the course of the 1960s, through his confrontation with the brutality of American racism. By 1968, he had drifted away from King in both theory and practice—yet he still harbored affection and admiration for the man. On the evening of Thursday, April 4, Carmichael appeared at the SCLC's Washington headquarters at Fourteenth and U Streets, and pressed for more details about King's shooting. Saddened and enraged, he took to the streets. He walked from store to store along Fourteenth Street, with a group of demonstrators in tow. He spread the word of King's assassination and asked shop owners to close down for the night out of respect. All the while, he urged his followers to refrain from violence. As the crowd of about 1,000 alternated between sorrow and anger, a teenager smashed the front window of the Republic Theater. Carmichael asked members of the growing crowd to go home. He was a peacemaker that night.[9]

Yet as darkness fell, businesses were ransacked and burned. The next day, April 5, looting and fires reached within two blocks of Pennsylvania Avenue. President Johnson mobilized army troops.[10]

Carmichael had previously scheduled a press conference for the morning of April 5. After King's assassination, it became a major event. At the New School for Afro-American Thought, Carmichael donned sunglasses and sat before posters of Malcolm X and H. Rap Brown. He delivered a lament, a tirade, and a warning all at once: "I think white America made its biggest mistake when she killed Dr. King last night because when she killed Dr. King last night she killed all reasonable hope." Carmichael called King "the one man of our race that this country's older generations, the militants, the revolutionaries, and the masses of black people would still listen to. He was the one man in our race who was trying to teach our people to have love and compassion and mercy for what white people have done." That was Carmichael's lament. Then he issued the warning. "When white America killed Dr. King last night, she declared war on us. . . . The rebellions that have been occurring around these cities and this country is just light stuff to what is about to happen. We have to retaliate for the deaths of our leaders." Carmichael noted that as long as King was living, African Americans debated the merits of violence versus nonviolence, separatism versus integration, Black Power versus the "beloved community." King, as if through the force of his own will, had kept alive the possibilities of interracial harmony and of nonviolent change. With his passing, the debate ended. King's death "made it a whole lot easier for a whole lot of black people today. There no longer needs to be intellectual discussion. Black people know that they have to get guns. White America will live to cry since she killed Dr. King last night." Those words landed with the force of an angry prophecy.[11]

The news media often mistakenly described Carmichael as the leader of the Washington riots. But the riots in Washington were not organized affairs. While King's killing angered and propelled many who joined in the riot, a deeper rage—one that had been gathering for months and years—ultimately drove their actions. "The assassination was deeply meaningful to some," noted Dr. Leonard Duhl, special assistant to Secretary Robert Weaver of the Department of Housing and Urban Development. "But to others, just a significant straw on a pretty weak camel's back." Though King's murder explained the timing of the riots, the living conditions for African Americans in cities like Washington were the riots' most basic cause.[12]

In the weeks after the riots, an interviewer from Howard University's Civil Rights Documentation Project sat down with three of the young men who had burned and looted. One was a part-time waiter; another was a Howard dropout from New York City; the third was an unemployed man, jailed for looting. These men all respected King and were wounded by his death, yet they also rejected his teachings of nonviolence. They attested to the riots' spontaneous nature, and gave voice to the long-simmering grievances that lay at the root of the uprisings.

The waiter, twenty-one years old and a lifelong Washington resident, considered himself "a rather moderate person." After learning of King's assassination, the waiter and some of his friends walked to the New School for Afro-American Thought "because we thought the brothers would probably have a discussion." They were looking for conversation and camaraderie. Many others had already gathered on the street. Upon seeing those crowds, "my attitude changed from an attitude of complacency to one of militancy." The rioting spirit quickly overtook him. From a corner delicatessen he swiped a loaf of bread, two packs of cigarettes, and a few cans of beer.[13]

The young waiter invested his actions with political meaning. "I felt that . . . this was the proper thing to do at that particular time—taking from the white merchants those things which I felt brothers had been denied because of oppression. . . . The black man is tired of [honkies] coming in and exploiting him, setting up businesses and then moving" to the suburbs. He advocated burning all of the white-owned stores on the Fourteenth Street corridor. "I think it was a form of fighting the system by all means. I had hoped to see as many of the establishments go down as did go down." He was surprised by how much of the community participated in the looting. "Many people who I would consider to be extremely moderate were out there taking practically anything they could get their hands on." One study of the riots substantiated his impression. An analysis by the *Washington Post* estimated that roughly 20,000 people participated, accounting for one in eight of the residents in the affected areas. The waiter looted more aggressively on Friday, April 5. But federal troops took control of Washington the following day. Their presence began to quell the uprising.[14]

The waiter insisted that the conditions in Washington's black neighborhoods motivated his actions. "I can't say that it was the death of Dr. King. You might say that that was what one would call a precipitating factor. It was something that triggered off the event here in Washington. But burning and mass-scale looting . . . was something that was inevitable here in the District as well as in a number of other ghettos across the nation." With or without King's death, riots would have come to Washington. "This is something which has been building up over the years. It's not something that was touched off because Martin Luther King was assassinated . . . but because the people had been oppressed and depressed, because the people were living in poverty." The second interviewee was a twenty-four-year-old native of New York City who had attended Howard for two years, dropped out, then worked an array of menial jobs. He explained, "King was—you might say, the catalyst or the trigger—but this thing has been brewing for a long time, a long time and it wasn't just because King was killed. . . . It was because of the fact that all the other things piled up and then this." Well before King's murder, African Americans were ready to rise up.[15]

The riots brought chaos and destruction, but also pride. Blacks in Washington "feel that they have done something which they should have done quite some time ago," noted the waiter. "I've sensed the development of a great deal of pride in the Negroes in the area." This seemed to startle James Mosby, the Howard University interviewer. Mosby asked, "Because of the riots?" The waiter confirmed, "Some pride has been elevated in Negroes. They feel that this is a way of letting the white man know they really don't want him in the area, that they want to develop a community of their own involving their own people." He linked the riots to a desire for empowerment. These were neither random spasms of violence nor planned affairs. They inhabited a middle ground. The incidents of looting and arson were spontaneous, but they carried a social meaning forged through years of oppression.[16]

After King's assassination, the second interviewee looted and burned. He took up arson "because if you hit the man in his pocketbook you really hurt him. . . . We feel that it's legitimate." He also derived pride from the destruction. "It's a peculiar type of pride or dignity that one gets from destroying property that belongs to the enemy, you know? And the white man is our enemy." To this participant, the Washington riots were expressions of vengeance as well as assertions of selfhood.[17]

When he first heard King had been shot, he sat in his apartment and discussed the news with his roommate. At nine thirty that night, he walked out of his home: "I thought I would get some air." He strolled

Riots decimated Washington, DC, in the hours and days after Martin Luther
King's assassination. Firefighters battled blazes throughout the city.

Warren K. Leffler, Library of Congress

to the corner of Fourteenth Street and Euclid Street, and saw people
running toward U Street. "A couple of minutes later a group of young
kids ran by and they said, 'They're going to riot tonight.' And I thought
to myself, 'Yes, they are.'" At about ten o'clock, he walked with a group
of eight up Fourteenth Street toward Columbia Road. They watched
the looting of Maxie's Clothing Store, where police officers dispersed
the looters but did not try to arrest them. He stayed up all night with
a friend, and eventually burned down a store. The police came out in
force on the morning of Friday, April 5, but even in the light of day
they could not stop the rampant theft. At about seven o'clock in the
morning, he looted a dry cleaner and a liquor store. Still, the burning
remained his primary focus. "We really wanted to put the man out of
business. . . . We wanted to gut his store and get rid of him."[18]

Given his tendencies toward violence and revenge, one might have
expected this arsonist to disparage King. But he did not. "I dug King
from the standpoint that I knew that he was working for us, black

people, and I dug him as our most eloquent spokesman, and as a man who did get things done, maybe not always [how] I wanted him to and maybe not always with the results I wanted but he did get things done." He said of King's death, "It was just like having someone in our family offed." Far from the irrelevant leader of Andrew Kopkind's portrait, King had many admirers, even among the violent crowds in Washington. The King of 1968 was a different leader than the man who entranced the nation at the 1963 March on Washington. "Everybody might not agree with him, I'm not non-violent myself. But King was definitely in touch with the people because he had changed his stand, he had become more militant and everyone could see this.... Because of this and all the other things he had done for us, just about everybody dug him whether they agreed with him or not." King's evolution—from interracial dreamer to democratic socialist and anti-imperialist—went a long way with many African Americans.[19]

Even the most disaffected of the riot participants still respected King. So it was with the third interviewee, an unemployed twenty-one-year-old. He particularly appreciated King's turn against the Vietnam War. "First he was Tommin' . . . but then he seemed to be coming around." This man knew that King espoused nonviolence, and he disagreed with King on that score, but King "was telling the white Americans that they're wrong for being over there in . . . Vietnam killing those Vietnamese . . . I was diggin' on what he was saying." King's anti-war message alienated many white Americans. "And then they hollered that he was a Communist. . . . And then this honky down there . . . shot the man. And he really had no business shooting the man." This interviewee wondered about the assassin. "Why you want to do something or other like this? This man is on their side, he's on their side." White Americans should have seen King as their strongest ally.[20]

On the night of April 4, his friends urged him to come outside, so he grabbed his hat and ran down to Fourteenth Street. Caught up in the crowd, he hurled objects and pillaged stores. "I threw rocks, grabbed shit, you know, ran, everything that goes down in a riot." Then on

Friday, April 5, he looted many businesses. As he was walking away from a liquor store with bottles of Chivas Regal, a plainclothes police officer placed him under arrest. He was taken to several different precinct houses, interrogated, and briefly jailed. In an interview with James Mosby in May 1968, this man explained his reasons for rioting. "This is black man's territory, and the honky, really, shouldn't be down here." He saw the riot as a battle between two enemies—black versus white. "As far as I'm concerned, it was a goddamn war."[21]

He also thought the promoters of nonviolence were mistaken. Roy Wilkins "was rapping about that's no way to remember Martin Luther King Jr." This riot participant believed Wilkins should have focused less on the looting in the cities and more on the original act of violence perpetrated against King. Wilkins "forgot to say that this shit wouldn't have happened, man, if the honky . . . wasn't up there shooting like a goddamn maniac." Furthermore, he explained how King's devotion to nonviolence made his assassination so dastardly. "King was not gonna hurt anybody. . . . But yet, he got fucked-around, man, and like, there's no excuse for it. . . . So whatever the honky gets after that, he's got it coming to him." He ultimately agreed that King's killing dashed all hopes for nonviolence. Stokely Carmichael "said that they just left room for him now, which I think is true." Indeed, in the coming days, militant leaders would fill the void King had left.[22]

Other participants would reinforce the views of these three men— the waiter, the Howard dropout, and the jailed looter. A *Washington Post* reporter later interviewed three other individuals who joined in the violent uprising. These men understood their actions variously as a form of political rebellion, a way of furthering Black Power, or a way to exact vengeance on whites. They rebelled against what they saw as a whole structure of oppression. They had been building toward such aggression for months; King's assassination was an excuse for their actions as much as a catalyst. King's death "came as a hell of a surprise," recalled Arsonist Number One. "It caught some of us off guard. But we were still able to do our thing." King's assassination made their violent actions more palatable to others. "We needed an incident that would make it justifiable even in the eyesight of the mass of the people that do not agree with the term 'Black Power.'" Because of King's death, even the detractors of Black Power might acknowledge its appeal.[23]

The riot participants disagreed about which of King's messages most incensed white Americans. Arsonist Number One explained, "Dr. King, the king of love, got killed because he preached love for all." The third arsonist argued that King was murdered because he had criticized American foreign policy. "He was also killed because he was one of the ones that attacked the militarism. . . . They didn't start hating King until he started coming out against the war in Vietnam . . . when he got international . . . this country just can't stand that shit." They all agreed that King's death itself had not driven them to violence. "My thing wasn't because of Dr. King's death," offered Arsonist Number Two. "I got a satisfaction. As long as I can destroy the beast in any form I can—you know, economically, physically or any other form." Arsonist Number One agreed: "I personally want to destroy the system." They had been prepared to act well before April 4.[24]

If the racist "system" had a face, it was the white storeowner. Merchants suffered overwhelming losses in the aftermath of King's assassination. More than nine hundred Washington businesses were damaged. On the night of April 4, some grocers and liquor storeowners hurried to acquire photos of King that they could display in the window. Others lowered their American flags or placed advertisements in the newspaper to honor King. But such actions produced complicated reactions. Some merchants reported that their white constituents complained about the tributes to King, and about the flags that flew at half-staff. And many white-owned stores were looted or burned regardless. A seventeen-year-old looted a drugstore on Division Avenue. "It had nothing to do with Dr. King's murder," she explained. "The manager was nasty and mean, and the bastard overcharged." One congressional report concluded that African Americans had reason to resent the local shopkeepers. The congressional committee had conducted its study

before the 1968 riots, and found that in Washington's black neighborhoods—as in black neighborhoods in many other cities—grocery
stores carried a lower quality of goods at higher prices. Another study
judged that merchants, in comparison with whites in other occupa-
tions, "were among the most unsympathetic to the plight of the ghetto
Negro." In Washington and across the country, merchants stood as everyday symbols of racism.[25]

ONLY A FEW other cities experienced the kind of violence that leveled
Washington. One of them was Chicago, where riots raged on the city's
West Side for nearly a week. The rioters attacked buses, and snipers
targeted firemen who attempted to save burning buildings. Along West
Madison Street, stores were charred for a twenty-eight-block stretch.
Power and phone lines went dead through parts of the city. By Sunday,
April 7, some 12,000 troops—National Guard and army combined—
were patrolling the streets.[26]

Across the country, cities large and small witnessed sporadic outbreaks. There were fires, broken store windows, and firebombings in
hundreds of cities—from Hartford and Philadelphia to Savannah and
San Francisco. By Palm Sunday, a tense peace hung over many parts of
the nation. But Baltimore and Pittsburgh had both just begun to erupt.
Violence broke out in Pittsburgh's Hill District on Friday night and increased through Saturday, by which time 3,000 National Guardsmen
had arrived. The Hill District endured some five hundred fires. Meanwhile, conditions in Baltimore careened out of control. Looters took
over parts of the city on Saturday evening as 8,000 National Guardsmen
rushed to Baltimore. Over the weekend, four residents were killed and
three hundred injured, while hundreds of fires lit the Baltimore sky.[27]

In some cities, observers could argue about whether chaos or order
reigned. The events in New York City posed for them the ultimate
test. In a comparative sense, New York emerged from the weekend un-
scathed. Peace and calm ultimately prevailed, and without the mobili-
zation of National Guard or army troops. Yet the experiences of New

Yorkers showed that even the supposedly tranquil cities teetered on the edge of destruction. If New York was an example of peace and order, then the nation truly stood on the brink.

After King was shot, crowds gathered along 125th Street in Manhattan and Fulton Street in Brooklyn. One Brooklyn resident described Fulton Street as "pure pandemonium." It was a mélange of fire engines and police cars, loud music and whiskey bottles, the sidewalks full of sprinting teenagers and older folk who could only shake their heads and watch. In Bedford-Stuyvesant, as well as in Brownsville and East New York, law enforcement officials reported sporadic incidents of rock-throwing, looting, and arson.[28]

Mayor John Lindsay, a white liberal and a Republican, had worked for two years to open up lines of communication with black New Yorkers. He formed the Urban Task Force, a loosely organized matrix of New Yorkers that he hoped could respond to just the type of news that rocked the city on April 4.

Lindsay traveled to Harlem that night, against the advice of the police and his staff. Sid Davidoff, an aide, remembered "thousands of people were coming on the street. It was a situation that could have sparked any minute. Both the police and I felt it was just too dangerous to bring [Lindsay] up. But Lindsay didn't care. He was going." Consultant David Garth arrived in Harlem with Lindsay. When Garth saw the crowds, "I thought my life was over." Lindsay promptly waded through those crowds, shaking hands and offering words of sorrow. Some Harlem residents welcomed Lindsay. But there was also great anger. "Harlem was alive," recalled Pablo Guzman, a member of the revolutionary Young Lords. "People were spontaneously going bonkers. There was a lot of running and yelling and smashing of windows and throwing of rocks." Hundreds of people surged down Eighth Avenue and onto 125th Street. The crowd swelled and began to swallow Lindsay. As the situation grew more ominous, Percy Sutton, the Manhattan borough president, arrived in a limousine. A bodyguard shepherded Lindsay into the car and whisked him back to Gracie Mansion.[29]

Harlem endured half a dozen major fires that night, though some African Americans attempted to keep the peace. A group of thirty young militants, all members of Harlem CORE, assembled in Jay's Bar and Grill on 125th Street and volunteered as peacekeepers. They walked the streets and urged others to stop looting. The local radio station WLIB held an all-night talkathon and replayed King's speeches through the wee hours. Still, the *New York Times* reported that "the looting and arson left a trail of destruction along main business streets" in Harlem and Bedford-Stuyvesant. "Stores were smashed as if hit by a hurricane or a tornado." Lindsay returned to 125th Street on Friday, April 5, and walked a busy thoroughfare. He took strolls in two separate parts of Bedford-Stuyvesant. He appeared on television late that night and declared the city was "relatively peaceful." He praised New Yorkers for keeping that peace.[30]

Neither the National Guard nor the army was mobilized. There were no snipers, gas masks, or bayonets, and few bloody confrontations between rioters and law enforcement. The violence in New York was aimed almost exclusively at property, the fires often targeting vacant buildings. Other *New York Times* reports called the outbreaks "relatively mild" and characterized the city as "generally calm." While riots in Chicago and Washington devastated entire neighborhoods, in New York only a handful of city blocks had been affected by the violence.[31]

In other cities, snipers attacked firefighters, neighborhoods were reduced to rubble, and only the armed forces could restore order. Clay Risen, author of *A Nation on Fire*, concluded that New York City experienced "nothing concentrated, nothing sustained." Risen noted that Mayor Lindsay was so determined not to have riots in New York, he would go so far as to "alter the very meaning of the term." The violence in New York was certainly consistent with any commonsense meaning of the word "riot." Yet as Risen points out, the situation was "nothing uncontrollable."[32]

Local merchants, on the other hand, had no difficulty in defining the events of 1968: riots destroyed their businesses. A group of storeowners, including Puerto Rican and African American merchants, asked Lindsay to declare parts of the city disaster areas. They charged that Lindsay had misrepresented the amount of damage. "Places in Brownsville look like they were bombed out," said Louis Hernandez, an official of the Bedford-Stuyvesant Puerto Rican Merchants Association. "You can see the shells of small stores . . . that are no longer in business." To Hernandez, this looked and smelled and felt like a riot. In Harlem, sixty-eight merchants closed their stores. But the *Amsterdam News* argued that some of them had it coming. Many of the affected merchants knew "that they have been singled out by the looters because of their past histories of avariciousness, trickery, overcharging and even plain robbery of the minority people living in these ghettos." The newspaper also congratulated Lindsay and his police force for their restraint. In contrast to Chicago, the police in New York did not shoot at or brutalize looters.[33]

Despite Lindsay's assurances that peace prevailed in the city, some white New Yorkers were consumed by racial terror. Pictures of black insurrection streamed across television screens. Journalist Bennett Kremen wrote that his friends and neighbors exhibited "a fear more intense than they had ever shown before." He had to persuade them that after reporting from Harlem, "I wouldn't come back in a coffin." The mother of a friend insisted, "This time they're really going to do it! It's like shooting their President. Imagine what a lot of whites would've done if a Negro shot Kennedy?" Yet the reality in New York City never fulfilled those fears. In the end, New York City displayed the whole range of experiences: expressions of black rage as well as African Americans' embrace of nonviolence, acute white fear along with grand public displays of interracial peace. Amid the fires and looting, the broken windows and surging crowds, New York was battered but unbowed.[34]

WHEN THE NEWS of King's death broke, many Boston residents assumed their city would burn. King had attended graduate school in Boston and met Coretta there. He returned in 1965 to lead a march for school integration, and spoke on Boston Common. King's assassination thus "hit Boston with a particularly heavy impact," recalled city councilor Tom Atkins, the first African American elected to that body. "There was a sense of loss that was very personal on the part of many people in the city." On the night of King's assassination, African Americans in Roxbury broke store windows and overturned cars. "People were crying and screaming," remembered local activist Ellen Jackson. "It became very chaotic at that point." Boston seemed on the verge of an explosion.[35]

Mayor Kevin White did not send the police in full force to neighborhoods like Roxbury and the South End. Instead, White encouraged Boston's black leaders to walk the streets and try to impose peace. Boston had tensed, but it had not yet snapped.[36]

On the morning of April 5, Tom Atkins phoned White with urgent news: James Brown was scheduled to perform that night at the Boston Garden, but Garden officials were canceling the show because they feared violence. Atkins first had to explain to the mayor who James Brown was. Then he described what would happen if the Garden canceled the concert: thousands of African Americans would arrive in downtown Boston on a Friday night, with no show to attend. And they would be angry. It was crucial that White persuade the Garden to proceed with the show. Atkins also hoped they could find a television station to broadcast the concert, so people would stay at home and watch. When Atkins picked up James Brown at the airport and explained the situation, Brown was livid. Some audience members already believed the concert was canceled, so they would not show up. Moreover, thousands of people would simply watch on television instead of buying tickets. James Brown asked the city to guarantee the gate, to the tune of $60,000. White told Atkins the city would never pay that kind of money. Atkins tried desperately to work out a deal, and White finally agreed to Brown's terms.[37]

Two thousand people ultimately showed up at the Boston Garden. Tom Atkins welcomed the audience and introduced Kevin White. Seeing that the mayor was visibly nervous, James Brown took the microphone. He called White "a swingin' cat" and urged the crowd to give him a big round of applause. White thanked James Brown and paid tribute to Martin Luther King: "Dr. King died for all of us, black and white, that we may live together in harmony. . . . Let us look at each other . . . and pledge that no matter what any other community might do, we in Boston will honor Dr. King in peace." Then the show began. The Godfather of Soul gave the audience what they had come to see, while thousands watched on WGBH, Boston's public television station. WGBH replayed the concert all night, as did radio stations. And it worked. "The concert was like magic," said Atkins. "The city was quieter than it would have been on an ordinary Friday night." James "Early" Byrd, a DJ at WILD radio, remarked, "If the concert had not occurred, we would have had the biggest problem in the history of Boston since the Tea Party." Tom Atkins's ingenuity, together with James Brown's performative genius, preserved the peace.[38]

James Brown's presence clearly helped to prevent explosions in Boston. More broadly, however, there was no clear pattern to explain why certain cities experienced major riots while others did not. Some scholars have attempted to pinpoint the factors that would produce such uprisings: high rates of black poverty, rigid segregation in housing and schools, and continuing police brutality. But the fact that cities like Philadelphia and Cleveland, which possessed all of those factors, stayed relatively calm is enough to weaken any overall theory.[39]

The distinction between riots and peace could actually appear quite blurry. In virtually every city with a substantial black population, there was some form of unrest, whether it was window-breaking and rock-throwing or looting and arson. No other cities witnessed the kind of violence that ravaged Chicago, Washington, and Baltimore. But everywhere, African Americans expressed their anger, and an increasingly larger segment of the black community rejected the tenets of nonviolence. Given this national reality, observers groped for language to fit the circumstance. A thin line separated what analysts described as "relatively quiet" from what they classified as "unrest" and "mayhem."

George Favre, a reporter for the *Christian Science Monitor*, reached this sort of ambiguous conclusion after he studied the situation in Newark, New Jersey. Favre noted that a hundred fires tore through

Newark on the night after King's funeral. "But the city kept its cool," Favre acknowledged. "That seems a contradiction in terms. But these are not ordinary times nor ordinary circumstances." The murder of Martin Luther King placed American cities in an extraordinary predicament. In such times, words could fail. A city could "keep its cool" amid dancing flames and shattered glass. The journalist "must improvise new benchmarks by which to draw the line between what is a bad situation and what is violence gone rampant." That was an important distinction—not between peace and riots, but between "a bad situation" and "violence gone rampant." Favre described how a few hundred black youths took to Newark's streets, bent on destruction. But five hundred other black youngsters, wearing orange community center badges, worked to minimize the outbreaks. This suggested to Favre that the situation was controllable. King's death changed the air of American cities. In this environment, Newark could simultaneously lose its mind and keep its cool.[40]

MARTIN LUTHER KING Jr. himself warned of these very types of eruptions. Days before his death, King drafted a letter to SCLC donors, appealing for funds for the Poor People's Campaign. He opened the letter on a striking note: "Our national government is playing Russian roulette with riots; it gambles with another summer of disaster." He was thinking of the riots that paralyzed the country in 1967, and he looked ahead fearfully to the summer of 1968. Shortly after Detroit exploded in July 1967, Lyndon Johnson formed a committee to study the riots. The Kerner Commission released its report in February 1968. It detailed the oppressive conditions in the ghettos, faulted American leaders for failing to combat those conditions, and warned that further government inaction would sentence the cities—and the country—to a grim future.[41]

President Johnson chose not to act on the report. King wrote to his allies, "Not a single basic social cause of riots has been corrected." The nation possessed the resources to lift up the cities, King argued, but was squandering that treasure in Vietnam. King had recently campaigned for the abolition of slums and proposed that every citizen ought to receive a living wage. If government bodies did not act, they would countenance the suffering, deepen the bitterness, and court more violence. "It was obdurate government callousness to misery that first stoked the flames of rage and frustration. . . . In the halls of Congress, Negro lives are too cheap to justify resolute measures; it is easier to speculate in blood and do nothing." King urged political leaders to act with temerity. He was telling them that it was still not too late to avert further violence in the cities, and to make the nation just and free.[42]

The policies of the federal government helped to create segregated and impoverished black neighborhoods in many American cities. Beginning in the 1930s, the Federal Housing Administration insured home mortgage loans. And in 1944, the Veterans Administration commenced with the same kind of lending. From the outset, these agencies encouraged housing segregation. It was far easier for a prospective homeowner to procure a loan if he was white and if he was buying in an all-white neighborhood. Whites who lived near racial minorities thus had every incentive to leave mixed-race urban areas for all-white neighborhoods and towns. The rare African Americans with the money to move to an all-white community had to face another deterrent: white residents often banded together in campaigns of intimidation and violence to drive out would-be black neighbors. African Americans were increasingly corralled in their own urban neighborhoods, many of which grew more and more segregated over time. Those were the kinds of neighborhoods that exploded in the wake of King's assassination.[43]

During that first weekend of April, after King's death, many American leaders proclaimed that the rioters were trampling on King's legacy. But King had already given his reply: "We cannot condone either violence or the equivalent evil of passivity." He often referred to riots as "the language of the unheard." Violence was an evil, but so was government inaction in the face of poverty and inequality. King proclaimed that the SCLC "cannot watch as the only systematic response to riots are feverish military preparations for repression." He anticipated the tanks that rolled through Memphis and the lights that shined on Clarence Coe's new Buick. Furthermore, he wrote, concerned Americans "cannot sit in appalled silence and then deplore the holocaust when tragedy strikes." King would have been horrified—though not surprised—to see the flames that enveloped America's cities in the days after his own assassination. But he was equally horrified by the living conditions that led to the riots, and by a white society that had created the urban black neighborhoods through redlining and housing discrimination, that had retreated to the suburbs, and then denounced those whom they isolated and left behind.[44]

King closed his letter by explaining the tactics and goals of the Poor People's Campaign, and he asked for contributions to the SCLC. By the time King's letter had reached the mailboxes of those donors, he was gone and the cities were in flames.[45]

AS KING'S DEATH acted as a catalyst for conflagrations in American cities, it also sparked confrontations among American servicemen who were stationed overseas. Up until that point, many military leaders had boasted that the troops in Vietnam showed no signs of racial conflict. In 1967, *Time* reported that "black-white relations in a slit-trench or a combat-bound Huey are years ahead of Denver and Darien, decades ahead of Birmingham and Biloxi." Into 1968, General Creighton William Abrams endorsed that rosy view. Abrams asserted, "Racial problems among our men in South Vietnam are for all practical purposes insignificant." Yet for those with open eyes and ears, the racial tension among the troops was clear. In concert with the "white backlash" at home, white soldiers abroad showed overt signs of racial hostility. They scrawled racist graffiti on their helmets and in the barracks, and flew Confederate flags from their buildings and bunks. In turn, African American soldiers displayed an increased racial solidarity. It was a combustible situation well before King's murder.[46]

Armed Services Radio brought word of King's death. As Richard Houser remembered, "It was as explosive a situation as you could possibly have." Houser had flown many sorties, yet he recalled the aftermath of King's assassination as "one of the scariest situations in Vietnam." While African Americans mourned and raged, some white soldiers exhibited a nasty racism. Brawls broke out at base after base.[47]

King's death prompted many black soldiers to question their own role in the war. After Don Browne heard about King's assassination, he had the intense desire to go home. He wrote a letter to President Johnson. "I said that I didn't understand how I could be trying to protect foreigners in their country with the possibility of losing my life wherein in my own country people who are my hero, like Martin Luther King, can't even walk the streets in a safe manner." For black soldiers like Browne, King's killing highlighted the absurdity of their mission overseas. "The most shocked and dumbfounded group of individuals over the tragic and wanton murder of Dr. Martin Luther King Jr. is the group of Negro servicemen serving 'freedom's cause' in Vietnam," Sergeant Dennis McIntosh wrote in a letter to *Ebony*. "In view of the circumstances which permit such acts to be perpetrated, we can only ask ourselves one question—'What the hell are we doing here?' If it's to gain freedom for the Vietnamese, then who will gain our freedom in the States?" McIntosh added that many black soldiers in Vietnam were part of the younger generation, and inclined toward Black Power. "We've disagreed with many of Dr. King's non-violent doctrines," and yet "we all believed in his sincerity and admired his eloquence, fortitude, and courage." McIntosh warned that in the jungles of Vietnam, the United States was schooling a generation of young black men in the ways of violence. "Only when all these Negro servicemen return to the States and get together will people realize the greatest contribution that Uncle Sam is making to the Negro's freedom—he is teaching him how to kill." The United States would soon reap what it sowed.[48]

Black soldiers in Vietnam drew closer together. "After the assassination of Dr. M.L. King you could also feel the malcontent," Private

Morocco Coleman wrote to *Ebony*. "Almost everywhere here you can see the unity which exists among the Negro soldiers." Charles Taliaferro recounted that King's death gave black soldiers in his unit "a feeling of unity and got them thinking about black issues." They perceived King's killing as a renewed attack on all African Americans. Many soldiers resolved to devote themselves more explicitly to the cause of racial justice in the United States. "We all got to dig in and fight for our race now," reflected Specialist 4 Reginald Daniels, a twenty-one-year-old from New Orleans. "We all got to help our people. If I can come over here and try to liberate these people, I sure as hell can liberate my own people." Specialist 4 Robert Sinclair, an Alabama native, came to a similar realization. "I suppose we got a cause in Vietnam, but we got a cause back there in the States too. These are our own people back in the States." Black soldiers began to cut through the layers of foreign policy bluster, challenge the Cold War logic, and reconsider their own sacrifices for those principles. Many decided that if their blood was going to be spilled, it was better to fight for the freedom of their own people than to advance the nation's dubious interests in a faraway place. From American streets to foreign theaters, King's killing radicalized African Americans.[49]

THE GROWTH OF the Black Panther Party became the most significant marker of the shift toward militancy. Founded in Oakland in 1966, the Panthers pledged themselves to active self-defense. They would defend the black community and police the police, using arms if necessary. The Black Panthers also developed an array of "survival programs" in urban black neighborhoods, providing services like health clinics and free breakfast. The Panthers had gained renown well before King's death. Yet by April 1968, they had established operations only in Oakland and in Los Angeles. After April 4, African Americans clamored to open Black Panther chapters across the country. By the end of the year, the Panthers had established chapters in at least seventeen other cities, from Bakersfield and Des Moines to Albany and Philadelphia. There was no riddle of causation to unwrap. King's assassination sparked the nationwide growth of the Black Panthers.[50]

Ironically, on the night of April 4, the Black Panthers helped to *prevent* violence in Oakland. Huey Newton, the founder of the Black Panther Party, was in an Oakland jail at the time—charged with murdering a police officer. Newton believed that after King's assassination "police across the country were prepared and expecting an uprising in the community. We felt that to protect the community from the kind of brutality that we anticipated, we would ask the community not to have an open rebellion." Newton directed Panther leaders to stave off riots. David Hilliard, the party's chief of staff, passed Newton's message along. Hilliard explained that the Panthers had already been discussing the futility of riots, and drew sobering lessons from recent examples of "unorganized rebellions." The 1965 Watts uprising and the 1967 Detroit and Newark riots all led to the deaths of African Americans and the devastation of black neighborhoods. They showed that riots could be suicidal.[51]

On the night of April 4, Hilliard and other leaders instructed the Panther rank and file to refrain from violence. But Eldridge Cleaver, the Black Panthers' minister of information, had a more combative message. Cleaver said, "We got to do something. . . . We got to prove we're the vanguard. Everybody's doing something around the country." Hilliard reminded him of Newton's warnings, and Hilliard prevailed— at least on that night. A report for the National Commission on the Causes and Prevention of Violence would credit the Panthers with "keeping Oakland cool after the assassination of Martin Luther King." The organization that preached armed resistance, and that would grow exponentially because of their stance, kept Oakland peaceful on the night the shot rang out.[52]

But that peace was fleeting. Cleaver recalled that on April 5, "everybody all day was talking about taking some action." A group of Panthers met in the evening, with Cleaver in charge. "The idea was we were just gonna go out and shoot up the town. Shoot up the cops." Still, Huey Newton's directive tugged at Cleaver. The group eventually decided "this is no way to go about doing anything. This is a spontaneous, irrational, and unorganized activity." Cleaver did not scuttle the idea of shooting cops; he only postponed it for one more day.[53]

Cleaver spent the afternoon of Saturday, April 6, in the San Francisco office of *Ramparts* magazine, where he began to dictate an article. Cleaver noted that many African Americans had long expected King's death. Both black militants and white racists harbored contempt for King. For his stubborn adherence to his ideals, King would surely pay with his life. "That Dr. King would have to die was a certainty." As Cleaver saw it, King's assassination was the jolt black people needed to finally renounce nonviolence. "That white America could produce the assassin of Dr. Martin Luther King is looked upon by black people— and not just those identified as black militants—as a final repudiation by white America of any hope of reconciliation, of any hope of change by peaceful and non-violent means." In the hours after King's murder, Cleaver talked with black activists around the country. Their reaction to the assassination was unanimous: "The war has begun." Cleaver predicted a national bloodletting. "Now all black people in America have become Black Panthers in spirit." Many more would become Panthers in name as well.[54]

Cleaver blamed white society in general for King's death. The slaughter of King seemed perfectly consistent with "what America demands by its actions." White Americans ought not consider King's death a tragedy, for "America worked so hard to bring it about." Cleaver thought that if white leaders had genuinely supported King while he was alive, rather than stirring up hostility toward him, perhaps the assassination would not have occurred. In Cleaver's eyes, the blame went all the way up to the White House. He could not believe that Johnson appeared on television on the night of April 4, asking for peace. Johnson had blood on his hands. The United States stood as the greatest perpetrator of violence in the world, as King himself had said; now the president hypocritically called for peace in the streets. "America is truly a disgusting burden on the planet," Cleaver fumed. "And if we here in America . . . " Then Cleaver received a telephone call. He stopped the essay in midsentence, hurried out of the *Ramparts* office, and drove to Oakland.[55]

The details of that telephone call remain unclear, and the details of that Saturday night remain contested. But it is clear that, just after nine o'clock on April 6, three carloads of armed Black Panthers pulled over to the curb at Union Street and Twenty-Eighth Street in West Oakland. Cleaver, who was driving the lead car, opened the door and stepped outside. A police car pulled up behind, and a firefight ensued. Writing from Vacaville prison two weeks after the incident, Cleaver maintained that the Panthers had been preparing for a fund-raising picnic the following day. They were shuttling people back and forth between restaurants, stores, and David Hilliard's home. In that version of the story, Cleaver claimed he was on his way to Hilliard's house when he stopped his car in order to relieve himself. In an interview more than a decade later, however, Cleaver described his intentions this way: "We basically went out to ambush the cops." When the police pulled up behind his car, it quickly became "an aborted ambush, because the cops showed up too soon." So the Panthers improvised. Cleaver explained, "We waited until the cop car got really in the middle of the three cars. Then we got out and just started shooting." Loads of police reinforcements arrived and unleashed a hail of bullets. The gunfight lasted for more than half an hour. "People scattered and ran every which-a-way." Panthers sought cover in nearby homes. Cleaver was shot twice. He fled into a basement along with a seventeen-year-old Panther known as Little Bobby Hutton. Hutton tore Cleaver's shirt off of him and searched for his wounds. The police shot firebombs and tear gas into homes to flush the Panthers out. Cleaver emerged naked from the burning basement, gave himself up, and was arrested. Bobby Hutton ambled into the street, unarmed and trying to surrender. Police officers opened fire on Hutton and shot him dead.[56]

Bobby Hutton's death would fuse with the killing of Martin Luther King to propel the Black Panther Party to new heights.

IN A SEATTLE jail, in those raw moments after King's death, Aaron Dixon seethed. Dixon, the Black Student Union leader who had been arrested for leading a protest at a local high school, did not share King's philosophy. Yet he was devastated all the same by the assassination. "Despite becoming impatient with his nonviolent, nonthreatening approach, we young organizers still greatly admired his courage," wrote Dixon. Like many young activists, he at once disagreed with King and worshipped him. "Martin had been heaven-sent . . . our Mahatma Gandhi, confronting America and its injustice as no other man had ever done, and doing all this with no malice, no anger, no hatred, just pure love and pure faith that someday we could all live in peace and harmony." Even young radicals like Dixon thought of King as "our modern-day savior."[57]

As Dixon sat in jail on the night of April 4, he contemplated King's life as well as his own. King's murder represented a turning point for Dixon. "For me, the picket sign would be replaced, and in its place would be the gun. . . . There would be no more unanswered murders." He eventually drifted off to a "painful sleep," and awakened the next morning for his bail hearing. His supporters filled the courtroom. To great cheers, the judge released Dixon without bail as well as his three fellow activists. On April 6, the *Seattle Post-Intelligencer* featured a photo of Dixon donning his "Stokely shades." Dixon acted the part. He met that night with a group of violent militants. Several members of the group went on firebombing expeditions, while Dixon and a friend kept armed watch over the house that acted as their base. "America was burning over Martin's death, and we wanted Seattle to burn, too." After that long night, Dixon kept his gun, snuck it into his parents' house, and hid it in his bedroom. Dixon thus committed himself to armed struggle. He would later write, "For me there was no turning back."[58]

Many young African Americans joined the Black Panther Party as a response to King's death. Bobby Seale, the chairman of the party, held a press conference on April 7. He declared, "Our brother Martin Luther King exhausted all means of nonviolence." Seale's declaration was a recruiting pitch, but he also believed he had accurately described the circumstance. Seale later reflected that King's murder "caused a lot

Spectators at the bail hearing for Aaron Dixon in Seattle on April 6. Dixon had been arrested for leading a protest at a local high school. In subsequent weeks, Dixon would help to found the Seattle chapter of the Black Panthers, one of the first Panther chapters outside California.

Fred Lonidier

of people who sided with Martin Luther King to say, 'The heck with it. Let's join the Panthers.' And they in effect tagged us as the vanguard of the revolution." Black communities across the country, particularly in the large cities of the Northeast and Midwest, underwent an unmistakable shift. Eldridge Cleaver also pointed to King's murder as the moment when African Americans moved toward armed resistance. "With us it was the death of Martin Luther King," Cleaver said in 1970. King's assassination "exhausted the myth that you could get what you want without fighting." Moreover, Huey Newton identified King's death as the event through which African Americans became disillusioned with nonviolence. Because of King's assassination, "the growth [of the Black Panther Party] was very heavy especially all over, but even more so . . . on the East Coast."[59]

The Panthers' appeal was obvious: they were bold and fiery, intelligent and confrontational. They wore black leather, brandished guns, and had no fear of the police. They developed a compelling ten-point program, equal parts self-determination and self-defense, and offered dignity to a people who for so long had their humanity questioned. But for all of that, the Panthers did not gain organizational footholds across the nation until King was slain.

King's assassination "changed the whole dynamic of the country," explained Kathleen Cleaver, the wife of Eldridge Cleaver and a prominent Panther in her own right. "That is probably the single most significant event in terms of how the Panthers were perceived by the black community." Many African Americans might have still preferred nonviolence, but that cause had lost its most powerful voice. King's message of peaceful change had been "violently rejected." Kathleen Cleaver pointed out, "The way he was assassinated so publicly, it shattered many, many people." The Black Panthers "were all of a sudden thrust into the forefront of being the alternative." One week after King's death, SNCC members helped to open a Black Panther Party chapter in Harlem. The Panthers also grew in Los Angeles, quickly becoming the dominant Black Power organization in that city. Meanwhile, Students for a Democratic Society offered its official support for the Black Panthers. All in all, Kathleen Cleaver concluded, "the effect of the death of Martin Luther King on the Panthers was overwhelming."[60]

The Panthers drew new members from the ranks of the devastated. William Calhoun, a leader of the Black Student Union at San Jose City College, was among them. He reflected: "They killed a man who walked through hell to try to get along with you, and you killed him?!" Calhoun became more enraged with white society, and after April 1968, that rage would never entirely subside. "You killed whatever hope I had in you. And I have no more use for you. None." White Americans had driven Calhoun to armed resistance. "They killed the last chance for me to be peaceful. They killed their last chance for negotiation." Hazel Mack saw it that way as well. A native of Winston-Salem, North Carolina, she was sixteen at the time of King's killing. After King's assassination, Mack recalled, "I parted with the idea that it was okay to let people beat you down in the street and put dogs on you. . . . The party became far more attractive. They said if you die, at least die fighting back." Mack joined the Winston-Salem chapter of the Black Panthers, where she focused less on the "fighting back" aspect of the party and more on its survival programs—including free breakfast, clothing, groceries, pest control, and ambulance services for the black community. Farther south, in New Orleans, King's death also made Malik Rahim a Black Panther. "After the King assassination—that's when I realized that we had to learn how to defend ourselves. That turn the other cheek wasn't working." Rahim, twenty years old at the time, decided "the Black Panther Party was the way for me." In 1970, African Americans formed a Black Panther chapter in New Orleans. Rahim and his wife joined immediately.[61]

The funeral for Little Bobby Hutton, the seventeen-year-old Panther who was killed by the Oakland police, became a launching pad for the national organization. On April 12, two thousand mourners packed into a Berkeley church. One hundred Panthers stood outside as the honor guard, in black leather jackets, berets, and pins supporting the party's imprisoned leader: "FREE HUEY." Aaron and Elmer Dixon were among those who attended. The atmosphere outside the church filled Elmer Dixon with "a feeling of both awe and pride." Decades later, he would describe the "magnificent and beautiful scene." Black people filled the streets "it seemed like for miles," Dixon recalled. "It looked like a black army." Inside the church, Rev. E. E. Cleveland led the two-hour service. Afterward, Panther members held an outdoor memorial service on Lake Merritt in Oakland. Bobby Seale told the lakeside crowd, "The black man wants nonviolence. We want the power structure to be nonviolent." Seale asked the nation to withdraw troops from Vietnam and demanded a black police force for Oakland's black community. But if white leaders would not commit themselves to nonviolence, neither would African Americans.[62]

It is difficult to overstate the importance of Hutton's death, in combination with King's assassination, to the rise of the Black Panthers.

Little Bobby Hutton was the Panthers' first recruit. "He was like my little brother that I never had," Huey Newton remembered. "He was the inspiration of the party." Hutton's killing was a kind of baptism for the Panthers. "Until he was killed," said Newton, "I really couldn't imagine—not really imagine—any of our party members being murdered." James Baldwin, Ossie Davis, Norman Mailer, Floyd McKissick, Susan Sontag, and others joined together to pen a letter to the *San Francisco Chronicle*, linking the murders of Hutton and King: "We find little fundamental difference between the assassin's bullet which killed Dr. King on April 4, and the police barrage which killed Bobby James Hutton two days later. Both were acts of racism against persons who had taken a militant stand on the right of black people to determine the conditions of their lives." King and Hutton—the leader of nonviolence and the Panthers' first recruit—perished together in the same struggle for black freedom.[63]

The Dixon brothers felt the profound impact of both killings. Aaron and Elmer were attending a Black Student Union conference in San Francisco on the weekend of Hutton's funeral, and they crossed the Bay Bridge to Berkeley to pay their respects. King's killing propelled them toward armed resistance; Hutton's funeral cemented their commitment to the Black Panther Party. After the funeral, Elmer Dixon recalled, "I knew that I was going to be a Panther for life."[64]

Bobby Seale delivered the keynote address at the Black Student Union conference. After the speech, the Dixons rushed up to Seale and announced that they wanted a Panther chapter in Seattle. Seale flew to Seattle the following week and oversaw the formation of the local chapter. Aaron became the defense captain.[65]

Aaron Dixon returned to Oakland for a crash course in Panther tactics and ideology. This included a visit to the Alameda County Jail for a face-to-face meeting with Huey Newton. Dixon then witnessed an epic standoff between armed Panther members and the police at Seventh and Wood Streets. The police ultimately retreated, which handed a thrilling victory to the Panthers and capped an exhilarating trip for

Seattle's Black Panther Party headquarters, in the Madrona neighborhood.

Aaron Dixon and Seattle Civil Rights and Labor History Project, University of Washington

Dixon. On his flight home to Seattle, Dixon reflected on a whirlwind month and on what lay ahead. "It was clear that when Martin Luther King Jr. was killed in Memphis, a change had occurred in the political consciousness of young Black America. The door of the nonviolence movement had been slammed shut, but a window was opened. Revolutionary thought was replacing the civil rights approach." Dixon was wholly committed, in body and mind.[66]

The Seattle chapter began to thrive while the Panthers extended their reach across the Northwest. In May, African Americans in Portland and Eugene, Oregon, started Black Panther Party branches. Both chapters came under Dixon's jurisdiction. And in Seattle, as Dixon recalled, "our little sleepy Madrona neighborhood had been transformed into a Black Panther fortress." The Panthers would march through Madrona Park and down Thirty-Third Avenue, rifles and shotguns aloft. In the summer of 1968, the Seattle Panthers unleashed their fury. They firebombed several local businesses that had developed reputations for racial discrimination. Dixon boasted that "the Panthers had put Seattle on the map."[67]

EVEN IF ONLY a small number of African Americans actually joined the Black Panthers or committed themselves to armed resistance, many adopted a more militant mind-set. They rejected the method of compromise as well as the larger goal of interracialism. The younger generation embraced this militancy most fully. An eighteen-year-old bank porter in Miami explained the rising radicalism. "There is more being militant, mostly not in action, but in talk, you know, trying to get across that we will not back down. . . . But not really as far as taking up arms." He referred not so much to the attraction of violence itself, but to the power of *talking* about violence. That "wakes up people—I mean they have to start to think what will happen." And he noted another phenomenon. This bank porter began to appreciate King more than he ever had during King's life. As the airwaves and streets hummed with talk of King's career, the porter developed a deeper understanding of his actions and achievements. "Everyone . . . has sort of seen the light." The assassination "opened a lot of people's eyes to what he was really trying to do." He gained a new respect for King, the prophet of nonviolence, just as he began to adopt a more militant perspective because of King's death.[68]

Thousands of younger African Americans experienced new ways of seeing. "I wasn't a militant before," said Franklin Scott, a black Atlantan and a student at Parsons College in Iowa. "I will become a militant now, and I want everyone to know it." Scott was back home in Atlanta on the evening of King's death. Angry and distraught, he trudged in the rain from the Southside to Five Points. While standing with a group of friends on Broad Street, he opened up to a white *Atlanta Constitution* reporter. "Now you go tell [Georgia governor] Lester Maddox he can't stop people from getting out in the streets with his 10,000-man army, because Negroes aren't afraid of the white man anymore." Scott treated the reporter as his mouthpiece to the white world. "White people are buying guns. Well, you tell them a lot of us have got guns and we know how to use guns. Even the ones who have been liberals are going to get into the streets, not only in Atlanta, but in every major city. There's going to be real trouble." Other black students underwent an evolution similar to Franklin Scott's.[69]

On the campuses of many black colleges, students seethed with anger. If black colleges acted as "forts in the great wilderness of the Old Confederacy," as Ta-Nehisi Coates has written, then the Atlanta University Center stood as a citadel in the heart of Dixie. The consortium included Morehouse College, Spelman College, and Clark Atlanta University. After learning of King's assassination, five hundred students marched toward downtown Atlanta in a cold, driving rain. A group of student leaders intercepted the marchers and steered them back to the Morehouse gymnasium, where 1,000 students had gathered. Findley Campbell, a Morehouse English professor, declared, "The blood of Dr. King has washed away 100 years of accomplishments." While Professor Campbell memorialized King—the most famous of Morehouse graduates—gloom and rage coursed through the crowd. Janie Rowe, a graduate student from Chattanooga, summarized the prevailing attitude: "Non-violence can no longer be effective. If you try to be non-violent, you'll end up dead." A Morehouse student agreed: "There is no other alternative for black people but to be more violent." The Atlanta University Center canceled all Friday classes, both to honor King and to stave off unrest.[70]

Anger surged at black colleges in North Carolina. At Shaw University in Raleigh, several campus buildings went up in flames on April 4. Groups of students from Shaw, along with those from St. Augustine's University (another black college in town), marched downtown on April 5, blocking a major intersection. National Guardsmen teargassed the students and drove them back toward the Shaw campus. In nearby Durham, students at North Carolina College gathered in the campus auditorium throughout the evening of April 4. The students planned to march through downtown Durham and to wreak havoc. Local black activist Howard Fuller, whom the students had invited to the auditorium, argued against the idea. Though Fuller had a reputation as a militant leader, he believed that a violent response would insult King's memory while inviting harsh police repression. He

convinced the students to delay. Still, violence took hold of Durham on
Saturday night, April 6. Eleven buildings were set on fire, including an
apartment complex owned by a slumlord and an A&P grocery store.
National Guardsmen were dispatched to fire stations while police officers in riot gear closed many businesses and patrolled the downtown
streets. Sporadic violence continued for the next week.[71]

Events at Tennessee A & I State University pitted those black students who still clung to nonviolence against others who wished to place
the placid practice in its coffin. Reports of gunfire drew 4,000 members
of the National Guard to Nashville on April 4. They sealed off the Tennessee State campus in North Nashville and fortified the capitol area.
Mayor Beverly Briley imposed a curfew and banned purchases of firearms and alcohol. Early on April 5, a peaceful group of 1,000 marched
downtown after attending memorial services for Martin Luther King.
They asked for an audience with Mayor Briley. The mayor refused,
claiming, "I don't like the idea of confrontation with irresponsible people." Civil rights leaders and ministers asked Briley to pull back National Guardsmen from the Tennessee State area, yet tensions there
only increased. On the night of April 5, sniper fire rang out from the
campus and pinned a group of policemen behind a stone wall. Police
officers and National Guardsmen descended on the campus in armored
personnel carriers, swept into dormitories, and forcibly searched students. On the night of Sunday, April 7, a large fire destroyed the university's ROTC building. It was one of twenty-five fires reported in
Nashville that evening. In response, some two hundred students and
faculty mobilized to try to prevent further violence. They organized
into groups that attempted to restore order. Among the peacekeepers
were seventy-three football players who traded their helmets for hard
hats and patrolled the campus. J. A. Payne Jr., the dean of students,
thanked the students for their help "in bringing tranquility in perhaps
the most tense situation the university has faced." Mayor Briley lifted
the curfew on April 10 as peace returned to Nashville.[72]

Even the Tuskegee Institute, which had a reputation as the most conservative of black colleges, witnessed pitched confrontations. In late March, students at Tuskegee had boycotted classes to express their grievances with the administration and to request specific reforms. The administration promised to implement these changes and students returned to class. But King's assassination spurred them back into action. On April 6, students locked twelve trustees in a guesthouse. Three hundred National Guardsmen and seventy state troopers rushed to the campus before a black sheriff persuaded the students to release their captives. Still, the college was closed for three weeks and ten students were charged with crimes. Historian Martha Biondi writes that Booker T. Washington, the founder of Tuskegee, "might have rolled over in his grave." This was a new era of student radicalism; King's assassination only accelerated the pace of protests and raised the stakes.[73]

The younger generation of black southerners was born in the early morning of the nonviolent civil rights struggle. But they were raised during the daylight of Black Power and radicalized amid the darkness of King's assassination. At Hamilton High School in Memphis, many students articulated not only a violent rage but also a specific loathing of white people. When Jimmy McIntosh heard about King's death, "I wanted to cry but I was all choked up and my surroundings seemed to have been closing in on me." After McIntosh regained his equilibrium, his anger flared. "Truthfully, I wanted to go out and shoot, mangle, or kill every white person I chanced to meet. I really wanted to go to City Hall to kill Henry Loeb because as far as I was concerned, he was the one that pulled the trigger that fired that fatal shot heard around the world." The sanitation strike had an "ever-lasting effect on me," McIntosh explained. It exposed the "inhuman" treatment of the workers, and of other African Americans in Memphis. The strikers' ordeal, combined with the killing of King, had changed McIntosh's views about "this once great, beautiful city of Memphis." Now his hometown "could sink into the current of the Mississippi River for all I care."[74]

Vengeance also took hold of some of his classmates. When James Wilson heard King had been assassinated, "I felt like burning the city down. I also felt like fighting every white person I saw because I blamed them for his death. I think many white people hated him." Alice Wright refused to believe her ears. She felt as though she had lost a member of her family. As she sat with the grim truth, Wright was startled by her own capacity for enmity. "I was so hurt when I heard about Dr. King's death, that I couldn't stand the sight of a white person. I didn't realize that I could hate anyone that much until the night Dr. King was assassinated." King's death introduced Alice Wright to a fury she had never known.[75]

As King's assassination produced such feelings of rage, it made his vision of an interracial America seem even less possible. Across the land, that spirit of anger was palpable. For many African Americans, King's death proved to be a turning point. They concluded that white racism and racial injustice would never wither in the face of peaceful struggle, and that aggressive self-defense was the best option. They finally discarded their attachment to King's own brand of nonviolence, and embraced a new militancy.

3

"HE KNEW THAT MILLIONS HATED KING"

W HILE DELIVERING KING'S eulogy, Benjamin Mays proclaimed, "The American people are in part responsible for
Martin Luther King Jr.'s death. The assassin heard enough condemnation of King and of Negroes to feel that he had public support." Mays
described the mind of James Earl Ray when he intoned, "He knew that
millions hated King." King's thirteen years in the public eye were thirteen years of bombings, jailings, and death threats. In a joint tribute,
Harry Belafonte and King adviser Stanley Levison added, "He was
stoned, stabbed, reviled, and spat upon." And the hatred of King persisted after his death.[1]

Many white Americans had long thought of King as a communist, a
rabble-rouser, and an agitator. They used the red brush in trying to discredit his many campaigns for racial equality. The FBI, under the leadership of J. Edgar Hoover, spied on King and harassed him. In 1964,
Hoover referred to King as the "most notorious liar in the country."
Presidents John F. Kennedy and Lyndon Johnson also fretted about
King's associations with former communists. In 1966, an opinion

survey found that 72 percent of white Americans held unfavorable views of King. Even if King seemed less frightening than Malcolm X or various Black Power leaders, his desired end—a "beloved community" of racial justice and interracial peace—was nothing short of revolutionary. He meant to transform the country. Many whites trembled before this vision. They feared his goals and begrudged him his fame.[2]

To explore whites' attitudes toward King in the wake of his murder is to plumb the depths of that hostility. It is also to understand one of the greatest transformations wrought by King's death: the revision of his image in the American mind. White antipathy for King certainly lasted even after his assassination. But over the years, King would gradually evolve from a controversial crusader, hated by many, to a national hero, beloved by all. King's murder began that evolution.

AS KING RAISED his voice against the Vietnam War and began to wage his Poor People's Campaign, white Americans responded in kind. David Halberstam's article about the radical King appeared in *Harper's* in the summer of 1967. Halberstam quoted King's call for a "reconstruction of the entire society." Later that summer, Halberstam attended a dinner party at which he encountered a housewife from suburban New York. She announced, "I wish you had spit in his face for me." The comment was no anomaly. It was the heyday of the white backlash against the civil rights movement. In 1968, Richard Nixon would stoke the anger of a "silent majority"—those white Americans who were enraged by antiwar protests and fed up with struggles for social change and racial equality. Halberstam observed that King had become "a recipient of an extraordinary amount of that hate." And the hatred seemed to intensify as the weeks and months elapsed. On March 14, 1968, King gave a speech in Grosse Pointe, Michigan. Right-wing protesters picketed outside the auditorium. As King spoke before an audience of 3,000, hecklers interrupted him by yelling, "Commie!" and "Traitor!" King remarked, "I have never received a reception on this level." It was "the worst heckling I have ever encountered in all my travels."[3]

King endured vicious criticism after violence broke out during his march in Memphis on March 28. The press charged that he could no longer lead a peaceful demonstration, and that his claims to nonviolence were deceitful. The *St. Louis Globe-Democrat*, working from a series of FBI talking points, printed an angry editorial. It asserted that the "real Martin Luther King" had been unmasked as "more dangerous than Stokely Carmichael because of his non-violent masquerade." A cartoon pictured King with a pistol in hand, shooting out the words "trouble" and "violence" and "looting."[4]

King planned a return to Memphis, determined to carry out a peaceful march—both to aid the strikers and to restore his own reputation as a leader of nonviolence. His detractors would have none of it. The *Dallas Morning News* labeled King a "headline-hunting high priest of nonviolent violence." This summarized the most frequent allegation leveled at King: that he created violence everywhere. When Bull Connor unleashed his attack dogs on black protesters in Birmingham, or when Jim Clark's posse fractured the skulls of marchers in Selma, whites blamed King and his followers for helping to produce that violence. So went the argument. And when the King-led march in Memphis turned to mayhem, many whites thought this legitimized their criticisms.[5]

Robert Byrd led the assault on the floor of the United States Senate. Byrd, a West Virginia Democrat, had belonged to the Ku Klux Klan in his younger days, though he had since renounced those activities. Byrd waxed apocalyptic about the events in Memphis, and asserted that if King went through with the Poor People's Campaign, anarchy and bloodshed would engulf Washington. He called King a "self-seeking rabble-rouser" who "undoubtedly encouraged" the violence in Memphis. King "gets other people into trouble and then takes off like a scared rabbit." Byrd dismissed as mere pretense King's language of love; King's rhetorical commitment to nonviolent resistance was a smokescreen for his pernicious intentions. "King lovingly breaks the law like a boa constrictor," Byrd charged. "He crushes the very life from it." King was a scared rabbit in one breath, a snake in the next. King's promises of

King led a march in Memphis on March 28 in support of the sanitation strike. Some marchers behind King erupted in violence. In response, many politicians and journalists sharply criticized King and questioned his standing as a leader of nonviolence.

Preservation and Special Collections Department,
University Libraries, University of Memphis

peace were nothing but "semantic gyrations" that the American people would see through. In Byrd's own semantic gyrations, he compared Martin Luther King Jr. to one of the great villains of the western canon: Shakespeare's Iago. Just as Iago had goaded Othello with sweet words, Byrd claimed, King had dragooned the American people.[6]

Members of the House were no less caustic. On April 1, Tennessee Republican Dan Kuykendall began his remarks by identifying King as "an internationally known figure, who by some unbelievable set of circumstances was at one time awarded a Nobel Peace Prize." He described the violence that broke out in Memphis and recounted how King "tucked his tail like a scared puppy and ran." Despite the ongoing sanitation strike, Kuykendall wanted his fellow congressmen to know "Memphis has a long and proud record of good relations between the races." He detailed the opportunities that were supposedly available to Memphis blacks in politics, education, employment, and housing. According to Kuykendall, King came to town and "destroyed" all of this progress. He accused King of "agitating destruction, violence, and hatred." He blamed King for the tension in Memphis and warned, "I hope this exposure will wake up people to the evil results of his activities before it is too late and freedom is destroyed in America for all." In this vision, King's campaign for the impoverished somehow imperiled the freedom of all Americans. One Memphis citizen, in a letter to the *Commercial Appeal*, offered another version of this bizarre argument: "King is determined to have a peaceful march if it kills us all."[7]

On April 4, hours before King was shot, Byrd returned to the Senate floor to warn that King would bring more violence to Memphis and to Washington. In the House chamber, Congressman Robert Michel of Illinois urged King to resign from the civil rights movement and return to private life. Political leaders thus amplified the hatred of a seething white populace.[8]

WHITE CONTEMPT FOR King knew no geographical bounds. It permeated Michigan and New York just as it did Georgia and Tennessee, infecting major cities and small towns alike. After King's assassination, the hatred did not abate. In Memphis, police officers traded jokes about King while local whites rejoiced over the killing of "Martin Luther Coon." One insurance salesman spoke for many local whites when he said, "King brought violence everywhere. I'm sorry it happened in Memphis, but I'm not sorry it happened." His only regret was that Memphis's reputation had been besmirched.[9]

In King's hometown of Atlanta, Maria Saporta was stunned by the hostility some whites displayed. Saporta, a Jewish girl whose parents had survived the Holocaust, counted Yolanda King (the eldest of the King children) as a close friend. The assassination devastated her. "I had never had that kind of intense pain and loss," Saporta recalled. Her family lived in the Burge Apartments near the Georgia Tech campus. Her mother did not feel up to cooking on the night of King's death, so the family headed out for dinner. As they departed the building, they passed a group of white men, including one of their neighbors. "They said, 'We're going out celebrating.' They were celebrating because Martin Luther King had been shot. I was incredulous. I never could talk to him again." In a place that touted itself as the "City Too Busy to Hate," there was enmity aplenty.[10]

This was the kind of racial hatred Miller Taylor had tried to escape. Taylor grew up among the "cotton fields and dusty roads" of Mississippi. He migrated north to Binghamton, New York, found work there, and settled in nearby Vestal. "Supposedly this area should offer a man peace and tranquility," he explained, "virtual freedom from all of that segregation, discrimination, racism." But Taylor was horrified by the way local whites responded to King's death. He relayed some sobering anecdotes in a letter to the editor of the *Binghamton Sun-Bulletin*. At a hospital on the night of April 4, a nurse rushed into a room full of people and exulted, "Oh, I'm so glad they got him." The following morning, at the Endicott-Johnson Shoe Company in Johnson City, a white woman held up the front page of the *Sun-Bulletin*—featuring King's photo—and began to laugh. Many of her coworkers shared her delight. Yet Miller Taylor warned, "The irony and grim tragedy of the whole issue is that these people, like so many other white people in this country, still don't realize that they have lost their best friend." He suggested that Stokely Carmichael, H. Rap Brown, and other black militants were waiting in the wings.[11]

On the day after King's assassination, Chicago seemed deserted. Frederick C. Stern, an English professor at the University of Illinois in Chicago, stopped at a diner for coffee, where his counter-mates indulged their stereotypes about violent African Americans. One man muttered, "Goddamn savages." On a bus, Stern heard a fellow passenger give voice to his racial fears. "I should have taken my little .25 along," offered the rider. "The monkeys better not fuck with me." The rider did not consider King's death to be a national tragedy, or any great loss at all. "This ain't no assassination. That's Kennedy and like that, not some goddamn nigger preacher. He wasn't so much." The unvarnished hatred shocked Stern, who was an immigrant from Austria. As he surveyed the streets of Chicago, he was transported in time and space back to his native Vienna. Stern was a child in 1934, when a group of Nazis assassinated Austria's chancellor. "Now it is Chicago, thirty-four years later," he wrote in *The Nation*. While martial law reigned in several American cities and whites eagerly expressed their loathing, Stern recalled with dread a similar mix of racial hatred and militarism.[12]

That same day, April 5, an Oklahoman named Margaret Grealy wrote a letter to Representative Carl Albert to inform him of ordinary citizens' attitudes toward King. "Martin Luther King was sanctimonious," she asserted, and she feared that "the whole world will make a martyr of him now." King was "not a non-violent saint," she assured Albert. "There are millions of whites who think this man asked for what he got." Many King haters were certain that the vast majority of white Americans shared their views. On April 10, one "listener and voter" wrote to NBC News anchor Edwin Newman: "We now live in a mad, mad world where a law-breaker and rabble rouser is suddenly acclaimed a saint." This individual was "sure that I reflect the views of many people."[13]

As word of King's assassination traveled around the country, two of America's leading journalists sat down at their typewriters: Mike Royko in Chicago and Ralph McGill in Atlanta. They reached similar conclusions, as revealed in their columns on April 5. An entire society had murdered King, regardless of which individual pulled the trigger.

Royko, a columnist for the *Chicago Daily News*, felt confident the FBI would soon arrest the assassin. But "they can't catch everybody," Royko wrote, "and Martin Luther King was executed by a firing squad that numbered in the millions." White Americans fed "words of hate into the ear of the assassin." The killer was simply following orders. "The man with the gun did what he was told. Millions of bigots, subtle and obvious, put it in his hand and assured him he was doing the right thing." It would have been all too easy, and none too accurate, to blame the "southern redneck" for this climate of racism. So Royko focused on white northerners: the law-and-order demagogues, the anti-busing crusaders, all of those Chicago residents who opposed King's struggle for open housing and pelted him with rocks in Marquette Park. "They all took their place in King's firing squad." Royko faulted Hoover's FBI for its smear campaign and denounced "every two-bit politician or incompetent editorial writer" who blamed King, rather than themselves, for rising racial tensions. The hatred directed at King was "ludicrous." King "came on the American scene preaching nonviolence. . . . He preached it in the North and was hit with rocks. He talked it the day he was murdered." But white Americans refused to hear King's calls for peace and freedom. "Hypocrites all over this country would kneel every Sunday morning and mouth messages to Jesus Christ. Then they would come out and tell each other, after reading the papers, that somebody should string up King, who was living Christianity like few Americans ever have." In a career full of blistering columns, this was one of Royko's angriest.[14]

Ralph McGill targeted the southern bigots. McGill, a leading southern liberal and publisher of the *Atlanta Constitution*, chose a title for his editorial that was sure to aggravate the haters: "A Free Man Killed by White Slaves." He wrote, "White slaves killed Martin Luther King in Memphis. At the moment the triggerman fired, Martin Luther King was the free man. The white killer, (or killers), was a slave to fear." Collectively, these hateful whites had killed King. McGill located many such "slaves" in Memphis. Loathing for the sanitation workers, and for King, had enveloped the Delta city. McGill beseeched all white Americans to root out racial prejudice and injustice. "The white South—the white population in all the country—must now give answer."[15]

McGill understood that his April 5 editorial would attract some vicious responses, and he was indeed showered with nasty letters and outraged phone calls from across the country. On the morning the editorial appeared, one man called up McGill's secretary to say, "The death of old King is the greatest news since the Second World War ended." In a follow-up column on April 6, McGill described this caller as "one of a very few" who harbored such hate. But a review of McGill's correspondence suggests there were many haters, and they betrayed little shame or hesitation. One unsigned letter to McGill read, "Many of us peace-loving, God-loving humans today unite in thanks to our God for delivering us and ridding humanity of one who has caused so much violence, bloodshed and discord." McGill received a threatening letter from a correspondent in Boston. And Douglas Williams of Toccoa, Georgia, claimed King had it coming. Williams wrote that King "reaped exactly what he sowed. He taught people to disobey laws, and his assassin simply disobeyed the law against murder." An anonymous Atlantan wrote to McGill, "Thousands of people would like to say why couldn't it have happened 10 years ago. But they are afraid to."[16]

Many whites were stunned and infuriated by the numerous tributes to King. Carl McIntire was a fundamentalist preacher who hosted a radio program and published a newspaper called the *Christian Beacon*. After King's death, McIntire denounced King for defending "draft-card burners." He added, "America has witnessed a strange spectacle with the mass media bringing out all of their eulogies and praises, while the multiplied millions of people do not believe it and have refused to accept it." Indeed, there were many who refused to believe the eulogies. A "responsible businessman" in Louisville wrote to McGill, "The eulogies of this man is one of the greatest hoaxes ever perpetrated." A Thomaston, Georgia, resident named Olin Miller also stood among the skeptics. Miller wrote a telegram to Ralph McGill, detailing his confusion and frustration at the tributes to King. "A large number of us can't understand why so many prominent people . . . went all out in eulogizing Dr. Martin Luther King Jr. We can't understand why President Johnson proclaimed . . . a national day of mourning for King." Miller titled his telegram: "King a Hero?" If Miller expressed confusion, then Shelbyville, Tennessee, resident Richard Brantley was revolted. "The leaders of the government pay homage to a rabble rousing, riotous insurgent," Brantley wrote to the *Nashville Tennessean*. "I am sick to my soul."[17]

One Sarasota, Florida, resident, Mrs. M. McKinney, called McGill's editorial "one of the most despicable I have ever read by a white man." McKinney was much less concerned with King's death than with the rioting in American cities, and she conflated the peaceful tributes to King with those violent uprisings. She denounced the "so called peace marchers who have turned into animals." McKinney ranted about those who "take the law into their own hands as King and many Negroes are doing. I think all should be punished (instead of eulogized)." She saw the encomiums to King as a "disgrace." McKinney claimed she had never before harbored racial hatred. But the repeated testimonials to King and the numerous urban rebellions began to fill her with a sense of hostility. "I have never felt any antagonism in any sense of the word toward Negroes before—but believe me I do now." Moreover, she insisted that she was not alone: "Everyone I know feels the same way." In a sense, she made McGill's case for him—she reinforced the argument that so many whites were "slaves" to racial fear.[18]

For each member of the media who memorialized King, a pile of hate mail awaited. Ralph McGill, who made a career out of skewering his fellow white southerners, might have anticipated such responses.

But Edwin Newman had done little to provoke the enmity. Newman anchored an NBC News Special that presented a panoramic view of the nation on Palm Sunday. In pulpit after pulpit, ministers turned their worship services into tributes to King. Newman's program interspersed clips of church services with eulogies, speeches, and public gatherings that showed Americans in mourning. Newman simply narrated the special and introduced each segment. For that he received angry letters from whites throughout the nation. E. A. McHale, a self-described "irate citizen" from Chicago, wrote to Newman, "Mr. King dead or alive was most certainly not the hero? martyr? people are trying to convince us." He added some choice words about the Great Migration and about the recent urban riots. "These negroes were sent up here to the North from the South like flies just to swell the votes for Mayor Daley, well they burned up his city." One letter writer from the Bronx described his initial reaction to King's assassination: "My first thought was 'Someone has done us a favor.'" Ed Lehrbass, from East Jordan, Michigan, agreed. "The man in the street, would say Amen to Dr. Martin Luther King Jr.'s death.... Wherever you look and wherever you stop to hear a comment the retort 'He asked for it' prevails." While Newman's television special revealed a grieving nation, citizens like Ed Lehrbass belonged to the segment of America that delighted in King's murder.[19]

Lionel Lokos, a conservative author from New York, attempted to cloak his spite for King in the guise of respectability. That he could find a publisher for his scurrilous attack says as much about white Americans' attitudes toward King in 1968 as it does about the politics of the publishing house. Arlington House, the leading publisher for the conservative movement, released Lokos's blatantly biased *House Divided: The Life and Legacy of Martin Luther King* only four months after King's death. Yet *House Divided* was not dismissed as mere lunacy. *The New York Times Book Review* took it seriously enough to print a review of the book, albeit an unfavorable one.[20]

A Brooklyn Jew and a navy veteran, Lokos was raised as a liberal Democrat. During the Korean War, he drifted toward conservatism.

Lokos then wrote two books: the first was an anticommunist rant about Irving Peress, one of Joe McCarthy's prime targets; the second savaged the critics of Barry Goldwater. On the book flap of *House Divided*, Lokos's author biography noted that he lived "in a heavily integrated neighborhood." Perhaps that detail was meant to excuse the book's five hundred pages of vitriol and slander directed at King.[21]

Fifty years later, Lokos's screed reads like a bizarro story of King's life. Lokos organized his chapters around many of the familiar episodes: the maids of Montgomery who walked defiantly to work, the Birmingham protesters who faced down Bull Connor and his vicious police dogs, the epic march across Selma's Edmund Pettus Bridge. But King appears unrecognizable. The King of *House Divided* is a demagogue who wrought violence and chaos, justified riots, and romanticized the Vietcong. King was the "high priest of selective lawlessness," according to Lokos. His tactics of civil disobedience produced destructive urban riots. King promised peace and justice to his people and his nation, yet he delivered only bloodshed, crime, and discord. Thus, King "should be ranked among the most colossal failures of all time."[22]

When riots swept across the nation in the summer of 1967, King spoke eloquently about the despair at the root of such eruptions. Lokos equated King's empathy with encouragement. Though no individual committed himself to nonviolence more sincerely than Martin Luther King, Lokos found that a trifling fact to dismiss. "King never hurled a Molotov cocktail, but he never stopped faulting society for those who did." Why not just throw the bomb himself? "King never hid on a roof with a rifle and sniped at the police, but he never stopped picturing the police department as a sort of home-grown Gestapo." In Lokos's hands, criticism of police brutality became the moral equivalent of shooting police officers. By 1968, the "forces of law and order" were on the defensive. For Lokos, that was Martin Luther King's "unhappy legacy."[23]

If anyone had hurled a verbal Molotov cocktail, it was Lionel Lokos. All of those who celebrated King's death could gain inspiration and justification from Lokos's words. Lokos had tapped into a set of views about King that many Americans shared. Arlington House took full advantage, and quickly churned out a second printing of *House Divided*.

ONE SEES HOW deeply the hatred penetrated when exploring the ways white children responded to King's death. They gave expression to the rage that consumed their parents and they parroted the criticisms of their political leaders. Among white students in Florida's public schools, for instance, 41 percent thought the assassination was King's own fault; 17 percent believed the killer ought to receive congratulations. In Staley, North Carolina, five seventh-graders wrote to the SCLC's Ralph Abernathy to report that they were "disturbed by the reaction of schoolmates and adults alike. There was such bigotry and prejudice displayed." But those five white children—Gordon Owen, Bobby Rogers, Billy Sutton, Steve Thompson, and Garry Dark—noted that they would "recognize the rights of all men, regardless of color." Among white southern students, they were clearly in the minority.[24]

At Millington High School in suburban Memphis, a teacher distributed a questionnaire to his class one week after King's death. Tom Beckner asked his students, "What was your reaction to the shooting of Dr. Martin Luther King Jr.?" Most of them answered with satisfaction or glee.

When whites looked at King, many saw a second-class citizen, or less. "I felt it was wrong for his life to be taken," wrote a fourteen-year-old girl, "as I would any animal." She believed that sentiment was charitable. To her, King was "two-faced" and "communistic." She considered King's 1964 Nobel Peace Prize "the biggest mockery of a Nobel prize that ever has been." In the end, "I have no sympathy whatsoever for he or his family." As the nation paused to mourn King, many of the Millington High School students recoiled at the public displays of grief. "They made King look like a saint or some kind of God or something," lamented a fifteen-year-old girl. "For days and days, all the T.V., radio,

and newspapers talked about was 'KING!'" Why mourn the passing of
an outlaw?[25]

Other Millington students hoped King's death would portend more
carnage. One girl wished that Stokely Carmichael or H. Rap Brown
had taken bullets instead, though she was careful to add that King's
murder "certainly did not upset me." She noted that the assassin still
remained at large. "So maybe Rap or Stokely will get it yet." A fourteen-
year-old boy expressed surprise that Coretta Scott King had escaped
harm. As Martin Luther King always provoked violence, it stood to
reason that he would have consigned his wife to the same grisly fate.[26]

Wherever King went, "violence followed." This was the criticism
most frequently articulated by the scribes at Millington High School.
One seventeen-year-old was "glad" when he heard about King's assassination. He asserted that King used "non-violence as a front only." Another student granted that perhaps King did not deserve death, but "he
should have been punished for inciting riots." King "was behind them
all." This student argued that King "should have been disposed of a
long time ago." Specifically, he suggested that King should have been
locked up in prison. He explained, "Everywhere he went he caused
riots and nothing but trouble." And a fourteen-year-old took this reasoning to its logical conclusion: "In a way his death was his own fault."[27]

These students repeated what they heard from America's elected
officials. Ronald Reagan, the governor of California, described King's
killing as a "great tragedy," which he qualified by referencing King's
own acts of civil disobedience. That tragedy "began when we began
compromising with law and order, and people started choosing which
laws they'd break." Strom Thurmond added that King "pretended to
be nonviolent." At a Methodist Church on April 7, Governor Lester
Maddox of Georgia referred to civil disobedience as "a sinful pastime"
that had produced "a harvest of riots, death and open defiance." Even
more outlandish, Maddox claimed that communists had killed King
in order to push the United States Congress toward passing an open
housing law. The white South was awash in such conspiracy theories.[28]

One seventeen-year-old Millington High student cited J. Edgar Hoover as his strongest influence. "I have more respect for what Mr. Hoover" said about King, noted this lifelong Memphian. "He [Hoover] said he [King] was the biggest liar and communist in this country." White youths picked up on the cues, and refashioned these messages as their own. Some hailed the assassin as a great patriot. One student described his immediate response to King's death: "I thought it was one of the greatest feats of Americanism I have ever heard of." Another explained that because of King's death, Americans would be "better off in the long run."[29]

The exercise in Tom Beckner's class unsettled some students, for it asked them to lay bare their racial attitudes. A fifteen-year-old girl explained that the questionnaire plunged her into a state of torment. Yet her written response betrayed little anguish. She detailed the depths of her own racism in a manner that portrayed it as unremarkable. This student's family had lived in Mississippi for generations. "I have always been taught to leave Negroes alone. Not to taunt or tease them. But I admit that I'm prejudice[d] against them." In particular, she loathed those African Americans who dared to rebel. "I hate colored people who incite riots, insult my country, my race, and my government. I consider them Communists." King fit into that category. "I have no feeling of regret for the death of Dr. King. I considered him a troublemaker who had the blood of many deaths on his hands." She acknowledged that some Americans idolized King. "Oh sure, people said he was great." But she found King appalling, and his program profoundly threatening:

> He was a nigger who wanted me to ask him into my home, to eat with him, to consider him as my social equal. . . . I resent them wanting to take over and control this nation. And that's what Dr. King wanted. Don't get me wrong Mr. Beckner. There are many, many good Negroes in this world. And they deserve to be equal. But you see, they are the ones who know who and

what they are, and they are staying in their own place and don't
ask to be my personal friend. . . . Another thing Mr. Beckner, I
know it's wrong to kill anyone or anything, *regardless*. But I have
no sympathy for Dr. King's family in his death.

The response was breathtaking both in its callousness and in the
matter-of-fact way it conveyed such contempt. Three years after the
passage of the Voting Rights Act, the crowning achievement of the
southern civil rights movement, the Millington High responses
showed that racism remained fierce.[30]

A different tone prevailed on the floor of the United States Senate—
at least at first. On the morning after King's assassination, majority
leader Mike Mansfield called the Senate to order. Mansfield, a Montana
Democrat, paid homage to King and asked the other senators to keep
their speeches to less than three minutes. One by one, the senators rose
to honor the slain civil rights leader. Many of the leading liberals—
including Jacob Javits, Walter Mondale, Philip Hart, Ted Kennedy, and
Edward Brooke—urged the Senate to pass meaningful legislation to
bring King's dream of racial justice closer to reality. They hailed King's
acts of nonviolent disobedience and praised his commitment to the
civil rights struggle. Then Robert Byrd of West Virginia asked if he
could have fifteen minutes, to which nobody objected. Byrd expressed
"great sorrow at what happened yesterday in Memphis," and "sorrow"
for King's family. But Byrd had little interest in honoring King. He suggested that King's life was no more valuable than any other individual's. He lectured about "the lesson to be drawn from what happened in
Memphis": that mass protests led to violence and bloodshed. According to Byrd, "Those who advocate such methods often become, themselves, the victims of the forces they themselves set in motion. This, in
a manner, is what happened to Dr. King." When senators spouted such
theories on Capitol Hill, it was little wonder so many white teenagers
in Memphis followed their lead.[31]

AFTER KING'S DEATH, public officials in many cities and states debated whether to lower the American flag in King's honor. Some whites also raised the Confederate flag to show their hatred for King.

On April 5, President Lyndon Johnson ordered the lowering of American flags on all federal buildings. He also ordered the flag to fly at half-staff at all embassies abroad and military facilities. Local officials differed widely in their responses. The officers at Memphis's National Guard Armory defied Johnson's order. On Palm Sunday, the national day of mourning, Rev. Dick Wells drove past the armory and saw American flags flying at full staff. Wells asked a colonel why the flags had not been lowered. "I thought that was yesterday," the colonel replied, and drove off. In contrast, Henry Loeb lowered all of the flags at Memphis's city offices. Mayor Richard Daley of Chicago also lowered his city's flags to half-staff. On April 5, a local right-wing leader raised a flag outside a Chicago school to full staff; he was promptly arrested. In Louisiana, King's assassination prompted a literal tug-of-war. One of Edwin Newman's friends wrote him a letter to describe the chaotic scene in Baton Rouge. On the morning of April 5, "someone went out and pulled down the flag to half-mast. Soon it went up again and so it has been ascending and descending all morning." Emotions ran high at Ole Miss. African American students insisted that university leaders lower the American flag. But as rumors spread that the flag would be lowered, another round of rumors surfaced that armed whites were speeding toward Oxford in order to raise the flag back up. In the end, the flagpole was left empty.[32]

In Durham, North Carolina, whites raised the flag on April 9, not only to demonstrate hatred for King but also to insult local blacks. African Americans in Durham keenly felt King's absence. Before King escalated his involvement in the Memphis sanitation strike, he had originally planned to visit Durham on April 4. He had agreed to campaign with Reginald Hawkins, an African American who was running for governor of North Carolina. On April 3, King phoned Hawkins to say that he needed to stay in Memphis. Hawkins was "crestfallen," as were many blacks in Durham. And if they were crestfallen on April 3, the following evening brought a pain far more intense. Then on April 5, an interracial crowd marched peacefully through the city. The march concluded on the steps of city hall, where black leaders eulogized Martin Luther King and someone in the crowd lowered the American flag to half-staff. Mayor Wense Grabarek, a white liberal, came outside to greet the marchers and to receive their demands. He told the crowd that he had already planned to fly the flag at half-staff. The flag remained in a lowered position for several days. At noon on April 9, the day of King's funeral, a group of local whites gathered at city hall and raised the American flag back up as they joined in a chorus of "Dixie."[33]

At the Ford Glass plant in Nashville, white workers banded together to protest the lowering of the American flag. Ford officials lowered the flag to half-staff on April 8. The following day, workers approached their United Auto Workers (UAW) representatives to express their anger. They complained that the flag had not been lowered at the death of Pope John XXIII, and they guessed it probably would not be lowered if Billy Graham died. They felt King did not deserve such an honor. The workers threatened to walk off their jobs if the flag was not raised. Don Corn, president of the UAW local at Ford, informed the workers that the union did not support such a strike. In the end, the flag remained at half-staff and the workers stayed on the job.[34]

The events in Atlanta would have seemed farcical if they had occurred under less painful circumstances. Ben Fortson, Georgia's secretary of state, lowered both the American flag and the state flag to half-staff immediately after King's assassination. Georgia's state flag consisted of the Confederate battle flag alongside a small image of the state seal.* A Confederate symbol was thus lowered to honor Martin

---

* Georgia added the Confederate symbol to its flag in 1956, as a response to the rising civil rights movement.

Luther King. On April 8, Governor Lester Maddox called Fortson to register his objections. The next morning, as King's funeral service began, Maddox sheltered himself in the Georgia statehouse and surrounded it with 160 state troopers in riot gear. Maddox marched over to the flagpole and began to raise the flags. He suddenly realized that television cameras from the major networks were tracking his every move. He ultimately left the flags where they were and retreated into his office. Maddox later explained, "I didn't think we oughta use our flag to honor an enemy of our country." Opinion polls showed that roughly half of white Atlantans supported Maddox's first instinct to raise the flags.[35]

In Blacksburg, Virginia, Harry Golden awakened on April 5, the morning after his debate with Strom Thurmond, to a local controversy over the flag. A group of Virginia Tech students had asked the university's president to lower the American flag to half-staff. The president demurred, so the students promptly walked outside and lowered the flag themselves. Golden noticed that they also lowered Virginia's state flag. "If they can lower the flag for Martin Luther King in a state which once closed its schools rather than integrate them," Golden reflected, "maybe his life wasn't in vain." The actions of those white southern students filled Golden with hope for the future.[36]

In Vietnam, American servicemen jousted over the prevalence of the Confederate flag. That argument took on higher stakes after King's assassination. Lieutenant Eddie Kitchen, a career soldier who had risen to the commissioned ranks, arrived in Vietnam in January 1968. An African American from Chicago, Kitchen was disgusted to find Confederate flags on many military vehicles. He wrote a letter to his mother in February, asking her to alert President Johnson as well as the NAACP to the presence of these offensive symbols. Kitchen insisted black soldiers should not have to "serve under the Confederate flag, or with it. We are serving under the American flag and the American flag only." Other soldiers wrote similar letters home. "After you in the field," explained Richard Ford, a member of the 25th Infantry Division, "you took the flag very personally." The Confederate battle flags waved as serious affronts. Eddie Kitchen wrote again to his mother in early March and promised to send a photograph of the flags. He lost his life three days later.[37]

In an effort to ease racial tensions after King's death, all US Marine units banned the display of the Confederate flag. Army headquarters followed with similar orders. Yet on the national day of mourning, April 7, as patrol boats in Cam Ranh Bay harbor flew American flags at half-mast, a group of white servicemen raised a Confederate flag in front of navy headquarters.[38]

Some white soldiers celebrated King's death. John Brackett recalled the "overt joy expressed by some of my white colleagues that this 'troublemaker' had been eliminated." Staff Sergeant Don Browne, an African American from Washington, DC, who was serving in the air force, remembered that several whites groused about the tributes to King that beamed across the television and crackled over the radio. A few days after King's assassination, an image of King appeared on the television screen. One white piped up, "I wish they'd take that nigger's picture off." A fistfight broke out in response. White soldiers exhibited everything from outright hatred toward King to quiet callousness. A military policeman in Saigon couldn't understand all of the attention his country was paying to King. "We have 300 Americans dying here each week," he told reporter Bernard Weinraub. "King was one man. What about the people out here who are dying?" Specialist 4 Elwood King registered his indignation at the national day of mourning as well as the lowering of the American flag. Martin Luther King "marched with the draft card and flag burners," Elwood King wrote in a letter to the *Nashville Tennessean*. Martin Luther King "expressed no sorrow" for wounded American soldiers, yet his "heart bled" for the Vietnamese victims of napalm. Elwood King concluded his letter: "Honor those who deserve it."[39]

The controversy over Confederate symbols in Vietnam would not die. After the armed forces imposed a ban on rebel flags, white servicemen simply began to fly southern state flags, many of which featured the Confederate symbol. Commanders then forbade the state flags as well. White soldiers expressed outrage that in the days after King's assassination, they could not adorn their bunks with the insignia of the slave South. They complained to their congressmen, who then appealed to the Pentagon. Representative W. S. Stuckey, a Georgia Democrat, reported to his House colleagues that one of his constituents was ordered to take down the state flag. In mid-May, the Pentagon announced that it would permit the southern state flags. White soldiers were once again empowered to insult the African Americans in their company.[40]

THE LOATHING OF King continued well beyond the spring of 1968. But the haters would eventually lose the battle over how Americans remembered him. The assassination made King a martyr. His death spurred a gradual evolution in which the polarizing dissident was reshaped into a national hero, ultimately worshipped and claimed by Americans of all creeds. His legend grew over the days and weeks of official proclamations, public tributes, marches and protests, songs and sobs. King's message would come to seem less threatening when compared with the alternatives that presented themselves in the following months and years, like the Black Panthers or the Weathermen, an offshoot of Students for a Democratic Society that embraced violence. In this volatile atmosphere, King looked ever more appealing. Still, in the early days after his assassination, a significant number of Americans proved reluctant to honor him.

The skirmish over King's legacy began almost immediately after his death. On April 8, 1968, Congressman John Conyers of Michigan offered a bill that would make King's birthday a national holiday. The US House of Representatives declined to pass Conyers's measure. This became an annual ritual: Conyers offered the motion every year for the next decade (except 1972), and Congress rejected it.[41]

At the local level, cities and towns considered proposals to honor King. In Chicago, Mayor Richard Daley attempted to shape King's legacy to his own ends. Daley was determined to host a successful Democratic National Convention in August 1968. To try to ensure racial peace, he posed as an advocate for black equality and an ally of King's. Just two years prior, Daley had clashed with King over open housing. But once King was dead and gone, he no longer presented a threat. In June 1968, Daley strengthened the city's fair housing laws. Then in early August, he introduced a resolution to rename a Chicago street for Martin Luther King. Alderman Leon Despres, an independent, proposed naming a street in the Loop (in downtown Chicago) after King. But Daley showed little interest in gracing downtown with King's name. Instead, Daley offered to rename South Parkway, a street made famous during the years of the Great Migration. Sam Theard sang about it in 1938: "I'm going to the sweetest place in the world / That cool breeze blowing on the Michigan Lake / Everybody's happy and there's no more heartache / You ask, they call it heaven, but it's South Parkway." It ran for thirteen miles through the South Side, the heart of the city's black community, and only through the South Side. Independents on the city council thought Daley disingenuous, but they could do nothing to alter his proposal. The resolution passed unanimously. One week before the Democratic National Convention, Daley presided over the ceremonies to dedicate Martin Luther King Drive. Over the years, hundreds of other cities followed Chicago's lead and situated King streets in black neighborhoods.[42]

While King's name beckoned from more and more street signs, and legislatures considered bills for King holidays, the haters held on. Many efforts to memorialize King ran into resistance. In 1969, Coretta Scott King organized a plan to build a monument to King. She tried to garner federal funding for the project, but the Nixon administration balked.

Conservative author William F. Buckley criticized her endeavor. Buckley sniped at Martin Luther King for advocating civil disobedience, which Buckley considered "mortal to civil society." Through the decades, Buckley and his fellow conservatives would continue to criticize King for breaking laws and for his connections to leftists.[43]

In the coming years, white Americans' attitudes toward King would undergo a total change. But because he had been so hated, the debates over his legacy would become bruising struggles. This made his eventual sainthood a complicated and painful process.

4

ROSES FOR
MY SOUL

A S WHITES EXPRESSED their hatred toward King and rioters
took to the streets, King's dream of racial harmony seemed to
crumble. King's assassination brought racial hostility to the surface
of American life and ultimately helped to usher in a world harsh and
angry. But that broader impact was not always apparent in the early
days after his death. At the time, many Americans hoped the assassination might have the opposite effect. They joined together, determined
to keep the possibility of interracial amity alive. Artists unfurled their
brushes, working people stopped working, and thousands of Americans strapped on their marching shoes. They saw King's death as a
call to action. From ordinary white southerners and longtime political
conservatives to old black laborers, many participated in social activism for the first time in their lives. In a series of grassroots protests
that unfolded after King's assassination, marchers tried to give life and
meaning to King's own ideal of the beloved community.

The effect of his assassination resonated most powerfully on college campuses. In 1967 and early 1968, most student protests, especially
among white students, focused on Vietnam. King's death lent an urgency to issues of racial injustice and helped to spark the massive student uprisings that would define 1968.

Across the country, students mourned, seethed, and marched. In Madison, Wisconsin, 20,000 students paraded from the campus to the downtown area on April 5. The chancellor of the University of Wisconsin, William Sewell, led the procession. Deep in the South, the University of Texas suspended classes for the day. Five thousand people gathered on the university mall in Austin for a memorial service, then marched to the state capitol for a rally. In Kalamazoo, Michigan, students from Western Michigan University joined with those from Kalamazoo College to take over a campus building at Western Michigan. They demanded more scholarships for black students, and increased recruitment of black faculty. Edwin Taliaferro was a Kalamazoo student who participated in the takeover. He soon changed his name to Chokwe Lumumba and joined a black separatist group. Lumumba eventually became a civil rights lawyer; in 2013, he won election as the mayor of Jackson, Mississippi. King's murder had vaulted him into a life of political activism.[1]

King's death not only prompted public protests but also forced personal realizations. At Hobart and William Smith Colleges in Geneva, New York, students and community members—white and black—marched from the Mt. Calvary Church to city hall on Friday, April 5. Then they attended a memorial service for King. "It was good," reflected Stocky Clark, a white student from Washington, DC, "because our expression came from our emotions. Our sadness was genuine." But for Clark, there was also something more. He returned to Washington that weekend, where he saw a city devastated by the riots. King's assassination pushed Clark to reckon with the fact that "the structure puts my people on top. . . . It took the death of a great leader to make me stop and really look at myself."[2]

On several prestigious campuses, King's assassination plunged college presidents into uncharted waters.

Princeton had a small number of African American students, many of whom belonged to a campus organization called the Association of Black Collegians (ABC). Alfred Price, a junior in 1968, remembered that King's death "went through all of us like a knife." Two thousand people attended a campus memorial service on April 5. ABC members then issued a mild request: Princeton should cancel classes on April 9, during King's funeral, in order to hold a day of discussion and reflection. President Robert Goheen declined to cancel classes. The students' request "just fell on deaf ears with him," Price recalled. Goheen claimed that King would have wanted students and faculty to press on with their studies. Education "may well be the best tribute we can pay this great man," Goheen declared. He called only for the Princeton community to observe a moment of silence at noon on April 9.[3]

The leaders of ABC caucused in a dorm room on Sunday night, April 7, and resolved to act. Thirty-three students marched down Nassau Street until they reached the president's residence. "And there we were," Price recalled, "the entire black student body of the university, standing on his porch." As Goheen opened the door, "his eyes were as big as saucers." It was eleven o'clock at night, and "there was a black mob on his front porch. . . . And we said, 'You're closing the university.' And he started bubble gumming. And we said, 'You don't understand. You're closing the university and we're going to have a memorial service. And we think there ought to be a day of discussion about race relations in America.'" One ABC member made clear the stakes. "This may be the last time a group like this will come to talk to you," he told Goheen. "Tempers are so high now some of us would just as soon tear this place down. Let's use this day to set up a dialogue between blacks and whites." Given the tense atmosphere in the nation, and the rise of Black Power groups and Students for a Democratic Society (SDS) chapters on many college campuses, the least Goheen could do was to grant the day of discussion.[4]

He ultimately acceded. Dr. Carl Fields, assistant director of the Bureau of Student Aid and the highest-ranking African American at Princeton, helped to work out the arrangements. Activities began with a chapel service on the morning of April 9. In the afternoon, students attended smaller forums on race in America. ABC members led the discussions, assisted in some cases by members of SDS. Alfred Price led one of the conversations in a McCosh Hall room that was filled to capacity. At the end of the day, all of the discussion leaders gathered on the steps of Nassau Hall. Carl Fields urged the students to join hands. He led them in a prayer and used the experience as a teaching moment, asking the students to consider why they had not all joined hands sooner.[5]

WHILE PRINCETONIANS TALKED and grieved, students at Duke waged a silent vigil that overtook the campus for a week and eventually attracted 1,500 participants.

The university's president was Douglas Knight, a literature scholar whom a Durham newspaper described as "Yankee-born and Yale-educated." He was attempting to remake Duke in the image of Ivy League institutions—more forward-looking, progressive, and high-powered. The corporate executives who sat on Duke's board of trustees, and the wealthy southerners who composed its alumni, were already skeptical of Knight long before the evening of April 5, 1968—when hundreds of students trooped to his home.[6]

Duke had begun to enroll black undergraduates only in 1963. Into the mid-1960s, maids continued to clean the students' rooms and make their beds. As student activist David Henderson recalled, "Duke was still . . . a Southern institution content to be a Southern institution, with its attendant provincialism and institutionalized racism." Bertie Howard, an African American who enrolled in 1965, recalled a "hostile environment" at Duke. The campus had seen civil rights and antiwar protests in 1967 and early in 1968, but they drew few participants. Still, Duke had a small and dedicated cadre of activists. Among the student body as a whole, a placid façade concealed the fact that many harbored a concern about the social issues of the day and a dissatisfaction with the lack of political passion on campus. King's death brought all of that to the surface.[7]

On the night of April 4, word of King's assassination rippled across the Duke campus. Jack Boger, a senior, was attending a Religion

Department symposium when a student walked down the aisle and announced that King had been shot. "The theology of hope seemed instantaneously irrelevant," Boger remembered. He left immediately, stunned and upset. A report by the university administration would characterize the mood on campus as "a mixture of sadness, fear, guilt, and frustration, undergirded by a conviction that our world had turned a corner . . . and could never be the same again." But President Douglas Knight remembered that on the Duke campus and throughout the city of Durham, "there were a good many white people rejoicing." A man erupted in cheers at an on-campus dining facility called the Cambridge Inn, and one student on Kilgo Quad leaned out of his window to exult, "Martin Luther King is dead!" Some alumni reacted with a cold ambivalence. "There were a great many members of the Duke constituency who didn't care whether Martin Luther King lived or died," Knight recalled. "They felt he was disruptive." The Duke community had within it "real stress lines." Those stress lines would break into open fractures.[8]

Douglas Knight had spent the evening of April 4 at a dinner in Winston-Salem. He traveled there with Wright Tisdale, the chairman of Duke's board of trustees and vice president of Ford Motor Company. On the way back to Durham, Knight and Tisdale engaged in "one of our customary abrasive conversations about student unrest," Knight later wrote. They were speaking generally about the campus protests of the late 1960s. Tisdale had a blunt message for Knight: "Not here and not now." George Gilmore, an African American, chauffeured the men to and from the dinner. They dropped Tisdale at his hotel, then Gilmore told Knight that Martin Luther King had been killed.[9]

Late that night, Duke students gathered in a dorm room to discuss a collective response to the assassination. "An air of shock and disgust" pervaded the discussions, recalled student activist David Henderson. They resolved to march through Durham. A young professor named John Strange grew involved in the planning. He steered the students away from their idea to march to the conservative enclave of Hope Valley, and advised them to focus their energies on the faculty neighborhood of Duke Forest. "I figured they might get 50 people," Strange recalled. At seven o'clock on the night of April 5, 450 students and faculty gathered in the alumni lounge. "I was surprised by the number who showed up," remembered David Henderson. "When I saw how many we were, I knew we had seized a moment in history." They walked through the rain to the president's home.[10]

President Knight welcomed the students to University House and spoke briefly about the tragedy in Memphis. Two hundred fifty students streamed out of the rain and into the house, while the others stood outside and listened to Knight. The students left the campus with a list of six demands. By the time they reached Knight's home, they had whittled the list down to four. They asked Knight to sign his name to an ad that would appear in the *Durham Morning Herald*, calling for a day of mourning and urging Durham citizens to work for racial justice. The students also asked Knight to relinquish his membership in the segregated Hope Valley Country Club. The most substantive demands centered on Duke's treatment of its maintenance workers, most of whom were African American and earned far less than the federal minimum wage. (Duke University, as a nonprofit organization, was exempt from federal minimum wage laws.) The students suggested Duke pay its workers the federal minimum wage, $1.60 per hour, and that accumulating the resources for such a raise should "take first priority of all fundraising efforts." Finally, they asked Knight to establish a university committee to study plans for collective bargaining. Knight assured the students that he sympathized with them. "I'm glad you came," he told them. "You express what all of us both think and want to express—a deep concern, shock, outrage, and hurt." Knight noted that he would address some of their issues at a campus memorial service, scheduled for the following day. The protesters had little interest in his vague gestures of good faith.[11]

Knight met in his study with three student negotiators, hoping to reach some sort of compromise. Hundreds of others remained in the house and on the lawn. They were orderly and peaceful, but they would not budge from their demands. After two hours of discussion, Knight and the student negotiators had made no headway. The mass of students began to chant, "Hell no, we won't go!" This "shook the house," wrote David Henderson, and left Knight "visibly shocked." At eleven o'clock, a rattled Knight took a break for a bite to eat. Then he addressed the students. "All of us are trying to find ways to keep our society together ... I don't think pushing one another is the answer to it." From the ranks of the protesters emerged an eloquent voice. Jack Boger stood to face Knight and proclaimed, "An old order has changed in the United States. We will not allow amoral institutions to trap good men. In the new order we have to stand against amoral institutions. ... I have no doubt of your deep concern, but we have come here non-violently as students of this university to say we must do something important now. ... We are non-violent, but we will not be moved." The students erupted in wild applause that echoed for ten minutes. Knight said he was retiring for the night. The students vowed to remain at his home until he answered their demands. Knight invited them all to stay as his guests. Reflecting the civilized nature of the Duke protest, some of the women at Knight's home grew concerned that they would be punished for failing to sign out from their dorms. They asked Knight to waive that requirement, which he did. Two hundred fifty students and faculty stayed for the night. Amid the thick carpets and fine china of the president's home, the protest continued.[12]

When the students first departed the campus earlier that evening, few of them had revolution on the mind. They saw themselves as members of the university community who were presenting a reasonable set of requests. For many people at Duke, as Alan Ray wrote in the *Duke Chronicle*, Martin Luther King's death was "the first experience that made them consider the consequences of their own inaction." They initially joined the march "for the cathartic effect." They expected President Knight would comply with their demands concerning the newspaper ad and the country club, and hoped for a "'consideration' of the others." Margaret "Bunny" Small, a senior and one of the lead student negotiators, explained, "We didn't see ourselves as radical. We were challenging universities to play the role universities in liberal societies are supposed to play."[13]

When Jack Boger decried "amoral institutions" that "trap good men," he perfectly described Douglas Knight's dilemma. Knight underestimated the passion and the resolve of the students who marched to his home. In turn, the students overestimated Knight's ability to cooperate. Many of them had viewed Knight as "a visionary, a liberal leader," as Robert Creamer later recalled. But they did not realize the extent to which Knight would defer to the trustees. Regarding the *Durham Morning Herald* ad, David Henderson explained, "Dr. Knight said he could not sign the advertisement because it said 'we are all implicated in the assassination of Dr. King.' He felt that some of the Trustees of the university did not feel implicated." Neither would Knight yield on the matter of his country club membership. He said that he wanted to work from within the club to desegregate it. On the labor issues, Knight stressed that he had no authority to enact such changes himself. Knight later wrote, "I had to explain that I could not take such a step even if I would." All of this frustrated the protesters, and further eroded their faith in Duke as an institution. Jack Boger remembered, "There was a feeling that if we couldn't get a rich, prosperous, progressive school like Duke to do something as modest as talking about the president ending his membership in a segregated country club, or calling for modest wages for black employees, then there was not much hope for our society." Knight remained caught between the outraged students and the reactionary trustees.[14]

Knight had breakfast with Jon Kinney, another of the student negotiators, on the morning of Saturday, April 6, while other students busily cleaned the president's home. Knight then addressed the group. He admitted that he hadn't realized how deeply they felt about his country club membership; he said he would set up a committee to discuss labor issues; he also indicated that he might sign the newspaper ad with a slight change in wording. Then he left to meet with other university administrators before the one o'clock memorial service for King. At the service, Knight spoke obliquely about exploring the issue of collective bargaining. He later confessed, "I satisfied no one—including myself." After the service, 350 additional students, faculty, and workers marched to Knight's house to show support for the protesters. The students, further angered by Knight's weak words at the service, viewed him more and more as a stooge of the trustees. At the same time, the events on campus enraged many alumni and trustees. As those alumni interpreted the situation, Knight had welcomed hundreds of rabble-rousers into his home and encouraged the mayhem. They wanted law enforcement to forcibly remove the students. In their eyes, Knight had enabled a band of lawless protesters to make a sorry mess of Duke.[15]

All of the tension took its toll on Douglas Knight. He had recovered from hepatitis just months earlier. His physician, fearing a relapse, advised Knight to withdraw from the negotiations. On the evening of April 6, Knight left the campus for his lake house. The students saw less reason to remain in his home. On Sunday morning, April 7, they departed the president's house and took their protest to Duke's campus. That decision carried some risk. "None of us were sure that we could hold the group together if we went to the quad," Henderson explained, "and none of us expected the kind of support when we got there."[16]

They moved onto the main quad with their sleeping bags and books. The students decided they would speak only during meals and during song. Bertie Howard, who had some prior experience with civil rights demonstrations, helped to come up with the idea of a silent vigil. While many black students at Duke stood aside from the protest, Howard was a leader from the beginning. The students also agreed to focus their energies on obtaining economic justice for Duke's nonacademic employees, and they heightened those demands. While they had initially requested that the federal minimum wage for employees "take first priority of all fundraising efforts," now they proposed that the university begin to implement a $1.60 per hour minimum wage for all employees. In addition, they would no longer be satisfied with the mere formation

In the days after Martin Luther King's assassination, students at Duke University waged a silent vigil. They demanded changes at Duke, asking the institution to raise the wages of campus workers and to enter into collective bargaining with the labor union that represented those nonacademic employees. The vigil lasted one week, April 5–11. As many as 1,500 students and faculty participated.

The Chanticleer, Duke University Archives

of a committee to study collective bargaining. They now asked that the university engage in collective bargaining with the employees' union, Local 77. Approximately 250 students and faculty spent that Saturday night at the president's home. On Sunday night, nearly 550 people slept on the quad. The original members awoke with the Monday sunrise to discover their ranks had swelled. "I still have a feeling of awe when I think about waking up that first morning on the quad," Bertie Howard later recalled. "I did not believe the numbers of students who had joined the vigil during the night."[17]

Throughout the day on Monday, April 8, hundreds more students would join them on the quad to bear silent witness. By Monday night, the vigil included more than 1,000 students and faculty. Until then, the majority of the student body seemed unconcerned with labor matters.

The editors of the *Duke Chronicle* estimated that "student support of the union before King's death was probably at an all time low." The protest not only sparked widespread student interest in local union issues, but also launched the union itself into action. That evening, the dining hall workers voted to go on strike. They demanded a raise to $1.60 per hour as well as collective bargaining rights for their union. Local 77 called for a student boycott of the West Campus dining halls.[18]

Workers set up picket lines on West Campus, and the vigil voted to support the strikers' demands. Oliver Harvey was instrumental in strengthening the ties between the union and the vigil. Harvey, a janitor and an African American, had in the past served as the union's first organizer. David Henderson remembered, "From the first time he spoke to the vigil, he won the hearts of the participants." On Tuesday morning, King's funeral was broadcast live to the crowd. The maids and janitors at Duke joined the strike later that day, and the number of vigil participants grew to 1,500. "There was no way any of us could have predicted what happened," recalled Professor John Strange. "It was serendipitous; as it evolved it was magic, it was beyond any one of us. People who took part were really moved and touched." The participants had forged a new relationship between students and employees at Duke, and they were trying to change the character of the university itself.[19]

Samuel DuBois Cook was John Strange's colleague in the Political Science Department, and the only African American on Duke's faculty. In addition, he had been a classmate of Martin Luther King's at Morehouse. At first, King's death threw Cook into despair. "The ultimate tragedy is that Dr. King's death will not be redemptive," Cook said on the night of the assassination. "Racism will be the order of the day as usual. This country, I believe, will not learn from the tragedy." Cook then traveled to Atlanta for King's funeral, accompanied by student activist Jon Kinney and the university's chaplain. When he returned to Duke, the size and intensity of the vigil lifted his spirits. Cook spoke before the vigil on the afternoon of Wednesday, April 10. As much as

Cook found it hard to believe that King was actually gone, "it is equally difficult to believe that a movement for social justice and equality, a movement to create the beloved community, is alive at Duke." Cook rejoiced: "This is a great moment!" By that point, the students had endured three cold nights on the quad. "I do not know if you fully realize the ultimate significance of what you are doing," he told the students. "I haven't seen anything anywhere comparable to this. You would, of course, expect the victims of oppression to sacrifice, to take the hot sun, to take the rain, to sleep at night in the open and cold air, to expose their health, to do everything possible to remove the yoke of oppression and injustice. But you do not expect people born of privilege to undergo this harsh treatment." Cook told the students, "You are making profound history." He assured the protesters that decades in the future, they would look back with pride on their actions. And he reassured them, "Our cause is right." Cook's speech electrified the protesters camped out on the quad.[20]

In turn, the vigil eased Cook through a painful time. He admitted that King's funeral had been difficult. But as he looked upon King's casket from his place in the Atlanta crowd, Cook was "sustained by the knowledge of a thousand or more bodies, full of life, vision, and integrity, here carrying on his legacy." The energy of the vigil made King's funeral "more bearable." Cook confided, "Your vigil wiped my tears and helped to sustain me. You provided, at a tragic moment, roses for my soul."[21]

That same day, the executive committee of the board of trustees met to finalize its response. Wright Tisdale presided over the meeting. He had arrived in Durham on Sunday night and placed a call to inquire about logistics in bringing the National Guard onto the campus. Provost Taylor Cole and Frank Ashmore, the vice president for institutional advancement, supported the idea of clearing the vigil off the quad. In addition, Tisdale suggested the possibility of closing down the university. Charles Heustis, the vice president of business and finance, thought it a terrible idea. "I remember saying in essence, 'Wright—will you explain to me why it is necessary that Duke University be the first university in the United States to close in the face of a . . . peaceful student protest?'" In the ensuing hours and days, Tisdale held a series of discussions with top Duke officials, many of whom resolutely opposed the use of force against the protesters. William Griffith, the assistant to the provost for student affairs, acted as a liaison between the student protesters and the trustees. Griffith recalled, "We had our resignations in our hip pocket—if someone came in and told us there was going to be force used." Griffith tried to reason with Tisdale, pointing out that the demonstrators had acted peacefully throughout the ordeal. Tisdale was indeed heartened by the fact that the students had moved out of Knight's house on Sunday, and he soon backed away from his most extreme suggestions. The more time Tisdale spent on the campus, the more he came to appreciate the nonviolent and disciplined character of the vigil.[22]

At the meeting of the executive committee, Tisdale began by praising the students for their civility and restraint. The executive committee resolved not to call in law enforcement to clear the quad and began to consider the students' demands. They agreed to a gradual pay raise for the nonacademic employees and pledged to establish a committee to explore the university's relationship with those workers. The vigil had moved the trustees, if only by inches.[23]

At five thirty on Wednesday evening, two hours after Samuel DuBois Cook's soaring speech, Wright Tisdale stood on the quad to address the protesters and announce the trustees' decision. "I realize your deep concern with respect to the human issues which have now so intensely been brought into focus," Tisdale told the students. "I personally share this concern with you . . . I am confident that we can find ways to work together with mutual confidence and respect." Tisdale promised to begin to raise wages, and that by 1969 all employees would earn at least $1.60 per hour. He said nothing specific about Local 77 or collective bargaining. Tisdale was conciliatory in spirit, even if his promises seemed insufficient.[24]

Charles Heustis had tried to prepare Tisdale for what would happen next. In the meeting of the executive committee, the Duke officials told Tisdale the students would probably respond to his statement by singing "We Shall Overcome." Heustis and the other officials encouraged Tisdale to sing along, as a gesture of good faith. Heustis remembered, "When it was suggested that it would mean a lot to the students if he joined in, Wright gave a long, level, cold stare and said, 'I'm not sure I can do that.'" Out on the quad, the protesters did indeed greet the end of Tisdale's speech with a rendition of "We Shall Overcome." To everyone's surprise, Tisdale was moved by the moment. Heustis remembered, "I was suddenly aware that here was Wright, booming out the song in his baritone voice, and he knew the words!" Wright Tisdale stood on the rainy quad, grasped the hands of those next to him, and raised his voice in song. The *Duke Chronicle* featured on its front page a photo of the scene. The caption read, "The power structure sways to the strains of 'We Shall Overcome.'" It was a stunning sight.[25]

That night, the protesters gathered in Page Auditorium and discussed how to proceed. John Strange advised that the vigil formally drop its demands about the newspaper ad and the Hope Valley Country Club. He also suggested that the students suspend the vigil and implement a ten-day moratorium; this would allow the trustees more time to present a proposal regarding collective bargaining. Strange argued that it was crucial for the protesters to maintain the support of the faculty. A moratorium would enable students to return to class, which would indeed hearten their professors. After hours of debate, the group adopted Strange's proposals. They agreed to emphasize collective bargaining as the critical issue. And the moratorium began.[26]

Tisdale learned of the moratorium in the middle of the night. A religious man, he decided to visit the Duke Chapel at two o'clock in the morning, with Heustis, Griffith, and Ashmore in tow. He prayed quietly, then headed out of the chapel. A group of students recognized Tisdale and began to pepper him with questions. Tisdale explained that he was not prepared to negotiate with the union, as "a union can get nothing for these workers that we will not give them." He promised to meet workers "as individual employees" but not "as union representatives." David Henderson recalled that Tisdale was "absolutely adamant that Duke would never have collective bargaining." The silent vigil had paused, but the battle over collective bargaining raged on.[27]

The students moved off the quad, though thousands continued to attend rallies and strategy sessions. The largest rally of all occurred on Thursday, April 11, the first day of the moratorium. Three thousand people gathered on the quad to affirm their support for collective bargaining. The faculty's academic council also passed a resolution in support of collective bargaining and formed a committee to explore its implementation. The boycott of West Campus dining halls continued.[28]

On April 16, six days into the moratorium, the board of trustees released a proposal. John Strange read the details aloud on the vigil quad, where 2,500 people had gathered. It spelled out the logistics of the wage increase, which would raise workers' wages to $1.60 per hour by July 1969. The board also called for a committee of trustees and Duke officials, which would "look into the adequacy of the relationship between the university and its non-academic employees." In addition, the trustees had the gall to invite striking workers to return to their jobs. The vigil leaders termed the trustees' proposal "disappointing and inadequate."[29]

The Special Trustee-Administrative Committee on labor matters included three Duke administrators and six trustees. Many of those trustees happened to be corporate executives who had spent their careers crushing the labor movement. Henry Rauch headed the Duke committee, and was chairman of the board of directors of Burlington Industries, the largest textile manufacturer in the nation. For decades, Burlington had prevented its employees from unionizing. Furthermore, many employees had contracted "brown lung disease" from exposure to cotton dust in Burlington's mills. Duke's committee also included the vice president of R.J. Reynolds Tobacco as well as the senior vice president of Shell. In addition, P. Huber Hanes, president of the Hanes Corporation, agreed to serve. The Hanes Corporation compiled a particularly sorry labor record. In a recent example from March 1967, Hanes had fired a worker who tried to organize a petition for higher pay. For many of the executives who sat on Duke's committee, this was the way they had always conducted business. To appoint such men to a committee on collective bargaining was to stack the deck against workers. It was like filling a civil rights committee with white southern sheriffs.[30]

This made the committee's statement on April 20 especially surprising. The committee expressed a desire to work with representatives of the nonacademic employees: "It is clear that inadequacies in the relationship of the university and its non-academic employees do exist and we intend to work as rapidly as possible to remedy them." The committee also offered an accelerated timetable for workers' pay raises. The student protesters welcomed this statement, as they had expected much less from the committee. Henderson described "an atmosphere of general elation" at a strategy session later that day. "Everyone seemed to feel that we had won a significant victory." The students believed the university was finally moving in the right direction, and that their actions had steered Duke onto that course. On the night of April 21, a vigil rally became a victory celebration.[31]

The members of Local 77 were likewise buoyed by the latest statement and expected the trustees to work toward collective bargaining. The laborers decided to return to their jobs on April 22. They agreed to a three-week moratorium of their strike. Yet in the following weeks, the trustees failed to formulate any specific proposals. Douglas Knight later explained that many trustees feared a domino effect. If they implemented collective bargaining at Duke, they thought "it might lead to a kind of union ascendancy which could have repercussions on other labor situations."[32]

The nonacademic employees did eventually earn a pay raise. And the following year, in response to escalating activism among black students, Knight resigned from the Hope Valley Country Club. Yet the trustees took no immediate steps toward collective bargaining.

Many students and faculty nonetheless believed the vigil had transformed Duke forever. It roused the student body from its apathy, galvanized campus activism, fashioned an alliance between white students and black workers, and attained for students a voice in how their university was run. The editors of the *Duke Chronicle* rejoiced in the fact that thousands of silent students had moved "an enormous institution to social action it hardly considered before." An April 12 editorial expressed a giddy sense of disbelief over what had occurred. "We have seen things happen here that seemed inconceivable less than a week ago. . . . The school will never be the same." They saw previously conservative students boycott classes and man picket lines. And they heard Wright Tisdale bellow the words to "We Shall Overcome." In response to King's death, students generated a new spirit on the campus and dragged Duke into the 1960s.[33]

The vigil sparked a period of protest that soon swallowed Douglas Knight. Early in 1969, a group of African American students occupied the Allen Administration Building. In the eyes of the trustees, this was the final proof that Knight no longer had control of Duke. He was forced to resign in April 1969.

AT COLUMBIA UNIVERSITY, President Grayson Kirk would meet a similar fate. While Duke's vigil flew below the national radar, the student uprising at Columbia became one of the iconic events of the era. Students took over administration buildings for several days in late April, before New York City police officers swarmed the campus and brutalized students and professors alike. The bold student occupation and its bloody results were seared into the national consciousness. Those dramatic events tended to overshadow the original reasons for the students' actions. The conflict had its roots in a debate over the university's treatment of the local black community. King's assassination

delivered a catalyzing jolt at a crucial moment, adding to those grievances and accelerating the student uprising.

The Columbia rebellion and the Duke vigil, though born of the same
tragedy, revealed some striking contrasts. One protest occurred at an
Ivy League university thoroughly comfortable in its prestige, the other
at an institution that dripped with wealth and privilege yet still aspired
to national and international renown. Columbia also had an active SDS
chapter, a vibrant antiwar movement, and a strong contingent of student
radicals. At Duke, many of the students were engaging in social action
for the first time. Among the thousands of protesters at Duke, almost
all of them were white. Though Columbia had only a small number of
black students, the Society of Afro-American Students came to play a
decisive role in Columbia's uprising. The participants in Duke's silent
vigil mostly thought of themselves as part of the Duke family, asking the
leaders of the university to enact thoroughly reasonable reforms. The
Columbia protesters saw their institution as rotten to its core. They did
not push for a few minor adjustments, but wished to topple the entire
edifice. At Duke, students sat quietly on the lawn and occasionally sang
songs—not only "We Shall Overcome" but also "America the Beautiful." The Columbia rebellion was full of fury. While one group of protesters tempered their demands with a spirit of southern gentility, the
other breathed with the brashness of New York City. One group seemed
to embody the harmonious spirit of the early 1960s. The other pulsed
with a fiercer radicalism, a kind of radicalism that the manifold events
of 1968—King's death among them—would unleash.[34]

The confrontation at Columbia was ten years in the making. In 1958,
Columbia administrators hatched a plan to build a new gymnasium.
They targeted a two-acre patch of land in Morningside Park and nego-
tiated a sweetheart deal with New York City to rent the parkland. In
a hulking structure built along the slope of the park, Columbia would
erect one gym for the Ivy League undergraduates and another for the
residents—mostly black and Latino—of Morningside Heights and
Harlem. This plan was consistent with Columbia's recent expansion

into adjoining neighborhoods, in which it had used eminent domain to relocate Puerto Rican and African American residents.[35]

As the details of the gym plan began to emerge, local leaders sounded the alarm. Blueprints showed that only two floors out of ten would be open to local residents. The gyms would have two separate entrances, designed to keep the patrons apart. The citizens of Morningside Heights and Harlem would be treated to a final humiliating blow: their entrance was down at the bottom of the building, while the Columbia students would enter at the top. In May 1966, Percy Sutton and Basil Paterson, two black legislators known for their moderation and interracial approaches, introduced bills to repeal the 1960 law that originally granted the land to Columbia. The bills died quickly in the state legislature. But opposition to the gym plan was mounting.[36]

During the "long hot summer" of 1967, many New Yorkers worried that riots would erupt in upper Manhattan. Columbia's Grayson Kirk, who played perfectly the role of the callous Ivy League president, threw the local residents some sops: a swimming pool and a locker room for the community gym. Basil Paterson welcomed those additions, but noted they did nothing to resolve the basic issue. New York Congress of Racial Equality members, Black Power activists, and black elected officials all denounced the gym proposal. Paterson said, "I would stand with anyone against that racist gym." Early in 1968, flyers appeared on the Columbia campus and in the surrounding neighborhood: "STOP GYM CROW."[37]

On February 19, 1968, one week after the garbage workers in Memphis had begun their strike, bulldozers rolled into Morningside Park. The next day, protesters staged a sit-in before the construction crews. Police officers arrested six Columbia students and six community residents. Demonstrations grew in the following weeks as an unlikely coalition emerged: black and white student activists came together, while neighborhood groups embraced the students. Community organizations led several rallies in the park, including a nighttime candlelight procession on March 20. Four days later, Columbia students marched to the gym site and chanted together with the residents, "Gym Crow Must Go!" Policemen arrested a dozen protesters. Grayson Kirk announced that construction of the gym would continue.[38]

Before the gym controversy intensified, Columbia's branch of SDS focused on opposition to the Vietnam War. Students denounced Columbia's involvement in defense-related research and its membership in a twelve-university consortium called the Institute for Defense Analyses (IDA). In the fall of 1967, Kirk banned all indoor demonstrations. Then the Dow Chemical Company, which supplied the military with napalm, began to enlist Columbia scientists and opened a recruiting office in Dodge Hall in February 1968. SDS staged a protest at Dodge Hall and demanded Columbia withdraw from all IDA projects. By early April, Columbia's SDS was waging a two-front battle against the administration's war-related activities and against its construction of the gym.[39]

On April 4, King's death reverberated through New York City. Mark Rudd, the chairman of Columbia's SDS chapter, stood that night at the corner of Morningside Drive and West 116th Street, across from Grayson Kirk's home. Rudd gazed north and watched the smoke billow over Harlem. He could hear the wail of sirens. He and a friend ran through Morningside Park to Harlem. They watched African Americans loot stores and face down cops. King's death had conjured another ghost. "Malcolm X . . . was alive that night on the streets of Harlem," Rudd later wrote. The uprising made a deep impression on this aspiring revolutionary.[40]

King's assassination jolted Columbia's student body. For several days after King's death, Rudd remembered, "every conversation had to do with the persistence of racism in our society and in our own lives." Until then, many in the Columbia community were unaware of (or at least unconcerned with) the controversy surrounding the gym. According to Rudd, "Few white people at Columbia had paid attention to the issue before the King assassination put institutional racism right into their faces, where they could no longer ignore it." For SDS, opposition to the war and to the IDA had long stood as the most important issues. But by the second week of April, so central was the gym to campus life that the bulldozers may as well have positioned themselves right in front of Butler Library.[41]

Columbia held a memorial service for King at St. Paul's Chapel on April 9, the morning of King's funeral. The chapel overflowed with students, faculty, and administrators. Grayson Kirk opened the service with the observation that "the entire country has been diminished" by King's death. Dr. Moran Weston, a Harlem minister and Columbia graduate, read excerpts from King's writings and speeches. He not only read from "I Have a Dream," but from more recent—and more radical—offerings about war and poverty. Weston linked hands with John Cannon, the university chaplain, and led the mourners in "We Shall Overcome."[42]

When the song was complete, Columbia vice president David Truman walked toward the speakers' platform to deliver the eulogy. Mark Rudd rose from his seat, cut in front of Truman, and took the microphone. Rudd did not originally plan to do so. SDS members had even contemplated walking out before Kirk's opening speech. But when Rudd heard the "revolutionary" content of King's recent addresses, he felt compelled to speak. Rudd, "trembling inside with fear," proceeded to deliver his broadside. "The university administration is committed to a policy of racism," he charged. David Truman looked toward John Cannon to intervene, but the chaplain sat still. Rudd proclaimed, "We feel that Dr. Truman and President Kirk are committing a moral outrage against Dr. King's memory. We will therefore protest against this obscenity." The microphone went dead, but Rudd raised his voice and pressed on. He asked, "How can the leaders of the university eulogize a man who died trying to unionize sanitation workers when they themselves fight the unionizing of their own black and Puerto Rican workers?" He referred to Columbia's cafeteria workers, who were attempting to unionize. Rudd then spoke about the gym project and the ban on demonstrations. "How can these administrators praise a man who fought for human dignity when they have stolen land from the people of Harlem? How can they praise a man who preached nonviolent disobedience while disciplining their own students for peaceful protests? . . . If we really want to honor this man's memory, then we ought to stand together against this racist gym." Rudd walked out of the church and into the April sunshine, trailed by forty SDS members. Some in the audience clapped. Others cried, "Shame!" John Cannon stood and affirmed the right of "any student who is moved by the spirit of the truth" to speak in the chapel at any time. David Truman then walked to the platform and read his prepared remarks as though nothing had happened.[43]

On April 22, SDS published a four-page magazine entitled *Up Against the Wall!* One article explained what motivated SDS members to walk out with Rudd: they wished to "force the people at the service to perceive the contradiction between Columbia University's rhetorical affirmation of Dr. King's ideals and its practical repudiation of these ideals." SDS did not just despise the university's actions toward the Morningside community. "What outraged us," Rudd recalled later, "was the sheer hypocrisy of holding the memorial. It was so phony and sanctimonious." Bob Feldman echoed this sentiment in an article for the SDS magazine. "To silently permit the decision-makers of Columbia University to eulogize Dr. King," Feldman wrote, "was to silently permit an act of blasphemous hypocrisy to occur." Feldman noted that hundreds of the mourners in the chapel identified with King's causes: racial equality, social justice, and world brotherhood. Yet they could not admit that Columbia's policies flagrantly flouted those ideals. Or even if they recognized the dissonance, they declined to challenge the university's leaders. In the wake of King's death, SDS wanted the Columbia community to understand that disconnect and to mobilize against the administration.[44]

Columbia's SDS members were true radicals. They harbored little interest in reform, and disdained mainstream institutions and leaders—whether it was Columbia University or the US Department of

Defense, Grayson Kirk or even Robert Kennedy. The whole system reeked of injustice, incapable of transforming from within. SDS's four-page magazine was most famous for its cover, which featured an open letter from Mark Rudd to Grayson Kirk. "You call for order and respect for authority," he told Kirk. "We call for justice, freedom, and socialism. There is only one thing left to say . . . it is the opening shot in a war of liberation. I'll use the words of LeRoi Jones, whom I'm sure you don't like a lot: 'Up against the wall, motherfucker, this is a stick-up.'" Between Mark Rudd and Grayson Kirk, there was no common ground.[45]

King's death not only handed to SDS the perfect example of the administration's hypocrisy. It also radicalized Columbia's Society of Afro-American Students (SAS). Before 1968, SAS was known as an "apolitical if not slightly conservative" organization. Days after King's death, the group elected a new president, Cicero Wilson. He committed SAS to an agenda of more active protest. SAS and SDS quickly came together to oppose the construction of the gym. They planned a joint protest for April 23.[46]

Three hundred students, black and white together, marched from the campus to the gym site and back. They entered Hamilton Hall and staged a sit-in. The students soon took over the hall, barricading a dean in his office. Their demands included a cessation of the gym project and a lifting of the ban on protests. The students stayed through the night, as tensions erupted between SAS and SDS. In the early morning, SAS expelled the white students from Hamilton Hall. SDS members then broke into Low Library and occupied President Kirk's office. From April 24 to April 26, various groups of students seized Avery Hall, Fayerweather Hall, and Mathematics Hall. Columbia was occupied territory.[47]

The students held the buildings until the morning of April 30, when New York City police officers descended upon the campus. The police forcibly cleared the buildings, beating students and professors who stood in the way. They injured 150 people and arrested 700, creating bloody images that appeared on front pages across the nation. Still, the protesters achieved some of their goals. On April 26, the university suspended construction on the gym. Grayson Kirk resigned in August. And Columbia eventually canceled the gym project for good. King's death helped to spark a string of events that consigned the "racist gym" to a death of its own.[48]

WHILE CAMPUSES BECAME crucibles of activism, protest marches clogged the streets of major cities. Americans gathered in public squares, parks, and grand boulevards all across the country to express their collective sadness, shock, and shame—and to mobilize for racial justice.

In New York City on April 7, 3,000 people marched from Harlem to the Central Park band shell, where they joined a crowd of 12,000 mourners. Nearby, a "Walk for Understanding" in Newark, New Jersey, drew 25,000 people. In a city devastated by the 1967 riots, and scarred by fires and looting after King's death, a large interracial crowd assembled. The marchers were approximately 60 percent white, including suburbanites as well as city dwellers. They walked thirty blocks through downtown Newark to the Essex County Courthouse, calling for unity and peace. In Milwaukee on April 8, Father James Groppi led the largest civil rights demonstration in the city's history. Fifteen thousand people marched through downtown. The march in Tuscaloosa, Alabama, was smaller but no less affecting. More than 2,000 people, black and white, joined for a memorial service at First African Baptist Church and then marched eight abreast to the county courthouse. Four hundred people marched in Portland, Maine, and another 3,000 marched in Louisville, Kentucky. Hundreds gathered at Grace Episcopal Cathedral in San Francisco and then marched through Nob Hill. For several days, it seemed the whole country was marching. This lifted the spirits of Alma Baker, a resident of Toms River, New Jersey. "Fifty years from now, when kids are studying history, the good of all this turmoil will be apparent," Baker wrote to NBC's Edwin Newman. "Dr. King's death will be known as a turning point—the marches will be known as the period when we took the ear plugs out of our ears and paid heed to the cries; when we took our blinders off and saw the inequities we had been aware of all our lives." She thought King's death had not in fact shredded all hopes for interracial progress, and that perhaps the peaceful processions might force much-needed epiphanies.[49]

Some of the marches occurred on the same streets King himself had so memorably walked. Five thousand people marched in Montgomery on April 5, and thousands of others in Birmingham and Selma. These Alabama cities were the sites of King's most famous protests. King had also led a march in Boston in 1965, from Roxbury to Boston Common. He had stood at the Parkman Bandstand and spoken about the need for school integration. On April 8, 1968, a crowd of 30,000 filled the Common and surrounded the bandstand. A parade of speakers—religious leaders, Black Power activists, and the lieutenant governor of Massachusetts—offered tributes to King. From Boston to Birmingham, many vividly remembered King's presence in their cities. He had recently championed their causes. Now these places became shrines to King, where people massed by the thousands in search of ways to honor his legacy.[50]

To pay tribute, laborers organized work stoppages. On April 5, longshoremen shut down ports on the Atlantic and Pacific coasts as well as the Gulf of Mexico. Some 200,000 longshoremen participated in the largest stoppage since the assassination of John F. Kennedy. And in the garment district of New York City, black and white laborers abruptly walked off their jobs. Leaders of the Retail, Wholesale, and Department Store Workers Union then called for work stoppages throughout the garment industry; laborers followed through on the day of King's funeral. In forty different states, some 470,000 garment and department store workers stopped working. King's commitment to the Memphis strikers made him a hero to many union members. Cafeteria workers at Duke University felt that connection as strongly as did the garment workers in New York, and the longshoremen everywhere from Portland, Maine, to Oakland, California.[51]

WHILE KING'S DEATH inspired large-scale protests and work stoppages, it also brought change at the individual level, prompting shifts in attitudes and actions. After King's assassination, Norm and Kathy Kohn longed to somehow offer a hand. They were young white parents living in the Atlanta suburbs who had never been involved in civil rights. When thousands of mourners flocked to Atlanta for King's funeral, the Southern Christian Leadership Conference put out calls for assistance. There were simply too many mouths to feed and too many guests to house. The Kohns heard the appeal on the radio on Saturday, April 6, and responded immediately. On a whim, they packed their station wagon with groceries (and with their children) and drove to the SCLC office. The Kohns grew nervous as they approached Auburn Avenue, foreign terrain to many white suburbanites. But they were put at ease when SCLC staffers sent them to their own church, Central Presbyterian, which had become the center of operations. Norm Kohn stayed at the church to volunteer, while Kathy drove the kids back home. Norm remained at the church for the next three days, serving meals and setting up cots and sleeping bags. Kathy envied his place in the middle of the excitement. Buses pulled up to Central every few hours, dropping off tired and hungry mourners. Throughout the Atlanta area, restaurants had endured massive cancellations, so owners came to Central and dropped off food they could not use. On the morning of the funeral, Kathy Kohn relieved Norm at the church and helped to serve breakfast to 5,000 people. From that point forward, the Kohns became dedicated community activists.[52]

King's death pulled many African Americans into social activism as well, some for the first time in their lives. The assassination not only accelerated the rise of radical groups like the Black Panthers; it also made civil rights marchers out of lifelong black laborers.

On April 8, W. M. Horton marched in the sea of silent mourners. Horton was seventy years old and had worked in the fields all his life. He was a nomad of a laborer. "I generally just follow the harvest," Horton said. He had never participated in any sort of political action. "I guess I always favored Dr. King's program and the things he worked for," said Horton, but he was not interested in protests. When "all this business of marches and demonstrations started, I just let the young ones hold up my end." But the sanitation strike changed W. M. Horton. In late March, he donated five dollars to a striker. "In all my life," he remarked, it was the biggest thing he had done for his people. Then King's death changed Horton even more. In the hours and days after the tragedy, Horton wrestled with how to respond. He finally decided to enlist in the silent march. A friend gave him a ride to Clayborn Temple that morning. Horton marched for several hours, a straw hat perched atop his head and chewing tobacco inside his cheek. After the march, Horton reflected on what brought him out that day. "I been hearing for a long time about all the things Martin Luther King has done for us. And then this sanitation trouble. I got friends who's suffering over it. It ought to be settled. . . . I'm here for those reasons and lots more." In the end, the old man's actions brought him peace. "This is the first time I ever did something like this. If I don't ever do it again at least I'll say I did it right my time." By midafternoon, the marchers had been on their feet for hours. When the speeches began at city hall, many took seats on the grass or leaned against railings. Not Horton. He stood at attention, straight as could be.[53]

In Memphis, King's assassination changed some opponents of the civil rights struggle into allies of the sanitation workers. One citizen, identified as "DWA" in a letter to the *Commercial Appeal*, felt "disgusted" back in 1964 when King was awarded the Nobel Peace Prize. King "just goes around causing trouble and then running away," DWA had concluded, "which was, I told myself, what he did in the garbage strike march here." When King was killed in Memphis, DWA initially dismissed the assassination as the work of a lone lunatic. Then he got to thinking that perhaps the assassin believed he had done a favor for the "decent white citizens of Memphis." DWA was appalled at the violence committed in his name, and experienced a drastic shift in his attitudes. King's assassination brought a reckoning. "The choice is open to only one group—decent white America. Will we continue in our complacent acceptance of old hatred? Will we continue to sit in our houses and pretend that things are not so bad? Will we forget next week or next year the martyrdom of Martin Luther King?" In a matter of days, his views on King underwent a total revision.[54]

For Jarell Watkins, King's death laid bare the cost of his silence. A Mississippi native and a longtime Memphis resident, Watkins had always thought of himself as a good white southerner. He believed in racial equality, though he never dared to speak or act on that conviction. "The real tragedy of my living here and now is that I, along with countless of thousands of other 'good white southerners,' have remained silent." It took King's murder to "realize how out of tune we really are." This was a gradual awakening, Watkins reflected. Good white southerners were "alarmed at our own conscience" in 1962, when they found themselves quietly rooting for James Meredith in his quest to integrate Ole Miss. They were ashamed when Medgar Evers was gunned down in his own driveway, "yet we quickly looked away." When a group of Klansmen murdered three civil rights workers in Philadelphia, Mississippi, Watkins and his ilk reacted with shock. "Yet we somehow managed to blame it on a few sick people rather than a society that allows such sickness to remain untreated." There were always excuses. But now the prophet of nonviolence had been slaughtered in Watkins's city. He could no longer avoid his own responsibility. "Blood is on our hands," he wrote to the *Commercial Appeal*. "God help us if that same bullet does not kill our indifference and our cowardice. Our silence must be broken. Our fears of social and economic reprisal must be buried with him." King's assassination had tipped the scales. It finally forced in Watkins a most painful realization: to remain silent in the face of such horrors was to condone them.[55]

The story of Jerred Blanchard was an especially powerful demonstration of how King's assassination brought personal and political change. Blanchard was born in Missouri and moved to Memphis in 1932, at the age of fourteen. He attended college at Yale, law school at the University of Missouri, and enlisted in the army during World War II. Then he returned to Memphis to practice law. He served for several years on the county election commission. In 1967 he ran for a seat on the city council. Blanchard described himself as a right-wing Republican, adding, "I have never liked labor unions." Though both labor and civil rights groups opposed Blanchard's candidacy, he won the election. He joined the city council as a strong ally of Mayor Henry Loeb. The garbage strike would prompt Blanchard to rethink his views on racial politics, his attitudes toward unions, and his allegiance to Loeb. And the death of King would change him further.[56]

When the sanitation strike began in February 1968, Blanchard stood "100 percent with the mayor." But as issues of civil rights and racial justice moved to the center of the struggle, Blanchard pragmatically adjusted his thinking. He became convinced that if city leaders could not reach an agreement with the union, Memphis would erupt in violence. Blanchard concluded that "a dues checkoff was a small price to pay" to avoid such a fate. Henry Loeb dug in against the workers and vowed he would never negotiate. The other white councilmen either backed the mayor or evaded the issue. But Blanchard tried to mediate an agreement. For that, he would earn the scorn of his fellow white Memphians.[57]

As Memphis grew ever more divided over the strike, Blanchard embraced the role of peacemaker. When violence broke out during the King-led march on March 28, Blanchard rushed to the scene. He walked through the downtown streets and tried to restore calm, a handkerchief shielding his eyes from the tear gas. The city council met the following morning. Councilman Lewis Donelson proposed a resolution that committed the council to take "affirmative action" in recognizing the union. Donelson was a conservative businessman who had undergone a similar change of heart. Earlier in March, Donelson denounced "Negro racist groups" that engaged in "violent talk" and issued "ridiculous demands." But Donelson became enraged by Loeb's stubbornness and arrogance. In the wake of the violence on March 28, some white leaders gloated that police officers and National Guardsmen had cracked down on the city's African Americans. Donelson was appalled. On March 29, Donelson tried to amass enough votes to pass his motion. He tried for hours to persuade his fellow councilmen. Blanchard voted for the resolution. So did the three African American councilors as well as the council's chairman, Downing Pryor. But the council ultimately deadlocked at 6–6, and the motion failed to pass. Looking back on that day, Blanchard reflected that if the councilors had passed the resolution, they might have kept King alive.[58]

With that vote, Blanchard solidified his status as an ally of the striking workers. He received hate mail and threatening phone calls, and lost friends. "This thing was getting to be a burden, a real burden," Blanchard recalled. His wife, Eugenia, would answer the phone in the middle of the night only to hear menacing voices. Jerred lamented, "When they call you at four o'clock and say 'your husband's a nigger-lover,' ain't nothing you can do." The Blanchards needed to get away from Memphis.[59]

They took a trip to Houston, where Blanchard entered a golf tournament. He finished a practice round late on the afternoon of Thursday, April 4, and headed back to the clubhouse. There he learned that King had been assassinated. Blanchard used the phone at a friend's house and frantically attempted to reach his daughters in Memphis. He stayed on the line for hours until the operator was able to connect him. Next he spoke with Downing Pryor, who reported there was nothing the council could do. Blanchard decided to stay in Houston and to play out the golf tournament. That decision suggested that Blanchard's support of the strikers only went so far; he had not completely effaced his identity as a southern conservative. While Memphis reeled and the nation burned, Blanchard opted to pitch and putt. The tournament ended on Saturday. Later that day, Blanchard learned of plans for Monday's silent march.[60]

The Blanchards agreed that Jerred would fly back to Memphis in time for the march, though he had not decided whether he would join in the demonstration. He departed Houston late on Sunday night, landed at the Memphis airport at one o'clock on Monday morning, and took a cab home. He could not sleep. He was deeply torn about whether to march that day. Blanchard had never participated in such a demonstration. He also knew his presence at the march would further inflame his white constituents and alienate his friends. He drank some whiskey, bought an early edition of the *Commercial Appeal*, and tossed and turned in bed for a couple of hours more. "I really didn't want to be alive that day. I guess it's really about that simple." Blanchard felt that he couldn't march, but he couldn't not.[61]

The day dawned gray and ominous, and Blanchard rose in a mood to match. He woke at five o'clock in the morning, "stewing and fretting." He went to his downtown office but was in no state to practice law. "The temple was calling, and I knew it." Blanchard left the office and walked toward Clayborn Temple through a gauntlet of National Guardsmen. Tanks so choked the streets that "you could scarcely get to that temple." Finally, "I got down there and shuffled around, can't make up my mind whether to go home and cry." Clark Porteous, a reporter for the *Memphis Press-Scimitar*, pressed Blanchard: "Well, you gonna march?" Blanchard did not see himself as taking any sort of great moral stand. But his better angels triumphed. "On that great, tired weary hung-over Monday morning, it was my mother speaking and my wife, and I'm not trying to be dramatic or anything else but . . . decency said, 'You get your old south end in that march, bud, and go on . . . to hell with the country club.'" Blanchard followed that inner voice into the streaming throng.[62]

Once he made his decision, the fear left him. He latched onto Odell Horton, an African American who was the city's director of hospitals, and the two walked arm in arm. Blanchard was impressed with the discipline of the event. He praised Bayard Rustin for his organizational skills. "I knew there was a genius up there," said Blanchard, noting the rows upon rows of people, all marching eight abreast, with nary a word among them. He surprised even himself. "If you had told me last December 31 that I would have taken part in such a march, I would have told you that you were crazy." Blanchard's first civil rights march made a lasting impression. "I've learned a lot in the past few weeks. I think maybe we all need to re-examine our personal feelings."[63]

Blanchard noted that the city council had undergone a "remarkable change." He and Lewis Donelson were both conservatives who came to support the union. Downing Pryor was also a Republican who had been vehemently anti-union for many years. But he became outraged by Henry Loeb's handling of the strike and swung to the union's side. Blanchard was the only one of them who voted with his feet as well, a conservative Republican among Bayard Rustin's silent thousands.[64]

One week later, the city and the workers reached an agreement. The US undersecretary of labor, James Reynolds, worked with local mediator Frank Miles to bring the two sides together. A Memorandum of Understanding was ratified on April 16. The terms included official recognition of the union, a dues-checkoff system, a grievance procedure, and a pay raise. The city council voted in favor of the agreement, and Henry Loeb finally accepted it. Jerry Wurf, the head of the American Federation of State, County, and Municipal Employees, brought the terms to the local union members. At Clayborn Temple, some 1,300 strikers approved the agreement. After two long months off the job, the men swarmed the speakers' platform in a moment of jubilation. "Dr. Martin Luther King must be beaming in his grave," wrote the editors of the *Tri-State Defender*, Memphis's black newspaper. "The Memphis pact, therefore, is a graven monument to the slain civil rights leader."[65]

The SCLC's Andrew Young did not know that Jerred Blanchard marched behind him in Memphis. But Young had people like Blanchard in mind when he reflected, "Martin Luther King's death was something of a turning point, of white people suddenly being willing to come around. I think a lot happened in white America that's never been recorded, in the wake of the death of Martin Luther King . . . I sensed then that whites wanted to help, but didn't know how."[66]

In hindsight, one sees how King's assassination helped to create a harsher racial dynamic in the land—deepening the divide between the races, sending young African Americans further toward militancy and whites toward an embrace of "law and order." But in those first days after King's assassination, such racial division did not seem fated. Many Americans drew together. Jerred Blanchard's story was evidence that King's death created a vast amount of goodwill among some whites, prompting them to undergo profound transformations and to work for an interracial America.

MANY ARTISTS RESPONDED creatively to King's assassination. Dolph Smith, a white Memphian, often used watercolors to capture the flavor of his native South, depicting shacks and barns and the accumulated residue of the region's agrarian past. But on the night of King's death, Smith did not pick up his paints. Instead, he grabbed an American flag and tore it in two. Then he began to patch sections back together and glued the ripped pieces of the flag onto a large canvas. Though he never worked with canvas, he had previously stretched several canvasses just in case. "Somehow I just want to have some around," Smith later explained. That medium "just seemed appropriate to the act." Down the center of the flag, gaping holes emerged between the stripes of red and white. Smith pasted photographs into those spaces. He entitled the work *The Veil of the Temple Was Rent in Two.*[67]

Smith did not consider himself a political person, though he admired and supported King. He was heartened when he first heard that King would be coming to Memphis. He had hoped King would "bring his non-violent meanings, attitude here . . . and make it work." On the night of April 3, Smith sat in his home with his wife and children and listened on the radio to King's "Mountaintop" speech. The next night, a friend called the Smiths to tell them King had died. Smith remembered, "We were standing on the deck of our carport and watching the fires burn in three directions in Memphis. I looked down and my little 6-year-old girl was in tears. And I picked her up and we both just stood there weeping." Smith felt an almost physical response to hurry into his studio. "Without any thought, I was just compelled to go and do that." This was a new experience for him: "I don't all of the sudden feel great urges to rush into the studio." Smith worked on the collage for five days straight, listening all the while as radio stations played King's speeches. Smith would later downplay his achievement. It was "just an outburst," he insisted, the frenzied artistic result of an emotional trauma. He finished the work on the day of King's funeral.[68]

At the top of the collage, Smith attached a print of his own son holding a cap gun, to symbolize the white assassin. Then he worked his way down. He used proof sheets of photos he had taken in Memphis and in nearby parts of Mississippi. In one image, a group of young black children stood on a shabby couch upon a front porch. In another, two old black men shared a bench in a public square. Other prints showed a white official at his desk, an integrated schoolroom, and snapshots of life on Beale Street. One image featured a classroom with broken windows. Smith took that photo at a school in Mississippi from which white families had withdrawn their children after integration. There was also a post office in a small Mississippi town, a pawn shop, an old train depot, a cluster of abandoned buildings. Many of the images dealt with race and poverty, but none of them—other than the image of his son—referred to any specific person or event. "I wanted it to be more honest than that," Smith said. "I wanted it to be the sense of my own personal growth" in attempting to overcome racial prejudice, "and dealing with it as a member of the community." At the bottom of the flag, red strands hung down like flowing blood. Smith's calligraphy exclaimed, "I've been to the mountaintop! Mine eyes have seen the glory of the coming of the Lord—Coretta! Oh God! Oh God! God God God!"[69]

Smith's artwork expressed "what Memphis citizens were feeling at that moment," said Carol Lynn Yellin, an author and researcher who conducted hundreds of interviews with Memphis residents after the sanitation strike. King's death had torn them all asunder, and filled so many with a longing to engage in something meaningful. Smith's work was a prayer for the city and the nation.[70]

Sam Gilliam was another artist who reacted to King's death with a creative outburst. He was working in his Washington, DC, studio on

Dolph Smith, an artist in Memphis, responded creatively to King's assassination. After King's death, Smith withdrew into his studio. He tore up an American flag and attached it to a canvas. In the rips of the flag Smith affixed various photographs. He titled the resulting collage *The Veil of the Temple Was Rent in Two.*

Dolph Smith

the evening of April 4. Gilliam watched from his window on Johnson Avenue NW, mere blocks from the epicenter of the riots, as the city erupted. Over the coming months and years, Gilliam, a Mississippi native and an African American, worked on a group of six paintings he called the Martin Luther King Series. Gilliam would experiment with diluted acrylic paints, applying the watery colors to untreated canvasses. On April 4, 1969, Gilliam stood in the same Johnson Avenue studio and worked on a painting he would title *April 4*. The resulting piece was enormous, filling a canvas nine feet by fifteen feet. It overwhelmed the viewer with colors of purple, lavender, and yellow. It almost suggested a sunrise that brought with it a new day. Gilliam used uplifting and regal hues, reflecting the hope and inspiration King had provided to so many. But the stains bled together and produced a splattering of bright red. Those red circles could be bullet holes, dripping with blood. When the National Museum of African American History and Culture opened on the Washington Mall in 2016, it featured Gilliam's *April 4*.[71]

King's death inspired many different kinds of artists, from the abstract painting of Sam Gilliam to those who more directly shaped the nation's popular culture. It led cartoonist Charles Schulz to eventually create a new character, and to thereby embrace a multiracial vision of America's future. Schulz had to be pushed in that direction. On April 15, a housewife and former schoolteacher in Sherman Oaks, California, wrote the illustrator a letter. "Since the death of Martin Luther King," Harriet Glickman began, "I've been asking myself what I can do to help change the conditions in our society which led to the assassination and which contribute to the vast sea of misunderstanding, fear, hate, and violence." Glickman had been thinking about the images disseminated in the mass media, and she believed that the propagators of such images could do more to bring about a truly interracial society. She regaled Schulz with tales of how much her three children loved his comic strip. Glickman and her husband kept *Peanuts* cartoons on their desks "as guards against pomposity." As she put it, "We are a totally Peanuts-oriented family." Glickman urged Schulz to consider introducing black characters in *Peanuts*. She understood that Schulz could not make such a change without some grumbling from the syndicates. But she was confident Schulz had the stature to withstand any such criticism. Glickman mailed the letter and awaited the cartoonist's reply.[72]

She also wrote to several other cartoonists. Allen Saunders of *Mary Worth* was initially receptive to her suggestion and engaged in a substantive exchange with Glickman. Ultimately, Saunders worried that the syndicate would drop him if he dared to integrate his cartoon. Charles Schulz offered Glickman a somewhat different reply, which came on stationery adorned with drawings of Charlie Brown and Snoopy. He appreciated Glickman's idea, "but I am faced with the same problem that other cartoonists are who wish to comply with your suggestion." Though many illustrators might like to add black characters, Schulz explained, "each of us is afraid that it would look like we were patronizing our Negro friends." Schulz ended the letter on a note of resignation: "I don't know what the solution is." He preferred an all-white *Peanuts* to one that contained condescending depictions of African Americans.[73]

Glickman took Schulz's response as a challenge. She showed his letter to some friends. One of them, an African American named Kenneth Kelly, wrote to Schulz and tried to assuage the cartoonist's fears. "Though I doubt that any Negro would view your efforts that way," Kelly assured Schulz that "an accusation of being patronizing would be a small price to pay for the positive results that would accrue!" Kelly proceeded to explain such possible results. The inclusion of a black character in *Peanuts* would "ease my problem of having my kids seeing themselves pictured in the overall American scene." It would "suggest racial amity in a casual day-to-day sense." Too often, films and television shows depicted African Americans in ominous and violent settings, and excluded them from "quiet and normal scenes of people just living, loving, worrying."[74]

On July 1, Schulz wrote Glickman a follow-up letter. He informed her that at the end of the month, the comic strip would address her concerns. "I have drawn an episode which I think will please you." That episode began with Charlie Brown at the beach, looking typically forlorn. A black boy came up behind Charlie and asked, "Is this your beach ball?" A delighted Charlie offered his thanks. Then the two boys headed for a sand castle—slightly deformed—that Charlie had been trying to construct. On July 31, 1968, after eighteen years as an all-white comic strip, Schulz introduced millions of Americans to *Peanuts'* first black character, Franklin.[75]

Franklin eventually became Charlie Brown's most loyal friend. This ruffled the editor of the *Meridian Star*, in Mississippi, who objected to the portrayal of black and white children together. "We would appreciate it if future 'Peanuts' strips did not have this type of content," he wrote to his syndicate. At the same time, Franklin provided the kind of lift for which black parents had hoped. As Clarence Page wrote in the *Chicago Tribune*, Franklin "did us proud. He discussed philosophy with Linus, talked about his grandfather and played terrific center field." Yet he never developed any character flaws. Schulz never opened the window into his fears, longings, or obsessions. Franklin was completely normal, far too normal. Schulz wagered that his audience was not ready for a black character with real human complexities. Still, Clarence Page, along with many other African Americans, found it meaningful that Schulz "put a black face on the ideal American dream child." It took the death of Martin Luther King, and the cajoling of Harriet Glickman, to bring Franklin into so many American homes.[76]

Glickman, like thousands of other Americans, was moved to action in the aftermath of King's murder. Collectively, they reaffirmed their dedication to a multiracial America at the very moment when that vision had become most endangered.

5

THE WORLD
STANDS AGHAST

A T THE TIME of his death, King was beginning to conceive of the Poor People's Campaign as a first step in a nonviolent revolution that would encircle the globe. On the afternoon of April 4, 1968, King talked with Bernard Lafayette outside his room at the Lorraine Motel. "In the next campaign," said King, "we'll have to institutionalize non-violence and take it international." Lafayette, plenty weary from the Memphis sanitation strike and the Poor People's Campaign, "blinked in disbelief." King smiled and went back into his room.[1]

Because of King's support for democratic socialism in his last years as well as his opposition to the Vietnam War, he faced a deepening en-mity among white Americans. Overseas, however, such stances made him that much more of a hero. From England to Kenya, and on both sides of the Cold War, many global citizens had long seen King as their champion.

King's death was front-page news everywhere. The *Times of London* called it a great loss "to a world that had come to love and respect him." To many across the world, King's murder reinforced their image of the United States as a land rife with racial injustice. While citizens in a va-riety of countries grieved for King and denounced American racism,

they also began to mold King's legacy to fit their particular circumstances and to aid in their own struggles.[2]

To APPRECIATE WHY King's death struck with such force abroad, one
must understand his evolving connection with the rest of the world.

During King's life, an inverse relationship developed between his
global standing and his popularity at home. His Nobel Peace Prize,
awarded in 1964, was proof of his glowing international reputation. As
King opposed the Vietnam War more forcefully, foreigners lionized
him further, even as he attracted ever more ire within the United States.
He was one of the first prominent Americans to call the war what it
was: an exercise in imperial barbarism, foolish and catastrophic. King
also formulated plans for the Poor People's Campaign. He asked Congress to guarantee an annual income for each American, provide a job
for every individual who wanted one, and commit federal funds for
at least 500,000 units of low-cost housing per year. Overall, he asked
for $30 billion annually in antipoverty spending. To many Americans,
this sounded like communist lunacy. In most European nations, such
ideas were lauded as common sense. By the end of his life, the Baptist preacher was showing his "European" side. There was always this
sort of tension within Martin Luther King. He was a southerner with
homegrown tastes who was most comfortable in the black church. At
the same time, he could enthrall high-minded intellectuals and win the
affections of Parisians and Britons and Scandinavians.[3]

Not only in Europe but throughout Africa and Asia, he was viewed
as a part of anti-imperial, anticolonial, and antiracist struggles that were
global in scope.

King's first trip overseas in 1957 made a deep impression on him.
He was twenty-eight years old and fresh off the triumph of the Montgomery bus boycott when he traveled to Ghana to attend the nation's
independence ceremonies. In Accra, the Kings dined privately with
Prime Minister Kwame Nkrumah. King also spoke with Vice President Richard Nixon after failing to gain an audience with Nixon at
home. King absorbed some powerful lessons. While he was considered

an agitator in the Jim Crow South, the trip demonstrated his growing international stature. In addition, he saw firsthand the striking similarities between racial segregation in America and colonialism abroad.[4]

King visited India two years later. He explored Mahatma Gandhi's homeland and further immersed himself in the history of nonviolent resistance. As much as King learned from his trips to foreign lands, he also had a profound impact on others overseas. While King gradually embraced a broader international perspective, he became an inspiration to oppressed people—and to lovers of democracy—across the globe.[5]

From Ghana and India to Germany, many looked to King as a freedom fighter. They viewed King's career as relevant to their own plight, and often shaped King's messages to fit with their specific causes. That was nowhere more apparent than in Berlin. Divided by a wall built in 1961, Berlin stood as the world's prime example of how the Cold War had fractured humanity. Three years later, King thrilled audiences in both East and West Berlin.

King landed in West Berlin on September 12, 1964. Mayor Willy Brandt had invited him to participate in a memorial ceremony for John F. Kennedy. On the afternoon of September 13, a crowd of 20,000 packed the open-air Waldbühne stadium to hear King speak. He compared the racial chasm in the United States to the division of Berlin and offered a spiritual message of brotherhood. King later visited the Berlin Wall.[6]

At seven o'clock that night, King attempted to cross to East Berlin. He arrived at Checkpoint Charlie without his passport. Apparently he simply misplaced it—this was not the first time King had "mislaid" his passport. The East German border guards initially ordered his group to turn back to West Berlin, but one guard recognized King. The guards conferred with their superiors and agreed to let him through. They asked whether he had any proof of identity. King presented an American Express card, which became his ticket to the East.[7]

While King's group was negotiating at the border, thousands of people waited outside St. Mary's Church in the heart of East Berlin. The East German government had not announced King's visit, but word

spread nonetheless. "We didn't know for sure if he was coming," recalled Irmtraut Streit, the twenty-one-year-old daughter of a Baptist
minister, "but we all showed up just in case. . . . No one had a telephone,
but the rumor spread like wildfire." The church, teeming with more
than 2,000 souls, had to close its doors two hours before the event. Religious leaders hastily scheduled another speech at the nearby Sophia
Church.[8]

East Berlin's communist leaders offered no official recognition of
King's visit. Still, they allowed him to speak. They did so because he
had been a longtime critic of the United States. Communist leaders
wasted no opportunity to publicize American hypocrisy, and King
highlighted his nation's great flaw: racial injustice. Yet King was also a
hero to those East Germans who wished to oppose their own oppressive system. Young Germans worshipped him as a symbol of resistance.
"My friends and I heard that he was going to speak in Mitte and we
knew we had to be there," recalled Hans-Joachim Kolpin, who was fifteen years old at the time. "The Wall had been built three years before,
leaving us effectively imprisoned. We felt forgotten by the world, insignificant. . . . No one ever showed any interest in us—but the great Martin Luther King was coming to East Berlin—we couldn't believe it!"
The East German government allowed King into the country for one
reason; ordinary Germans flocked to his speeches for quite another.[9]

A van ferried King from the Berlin Wall to St. Mary's Church on
Alexanderplatz. He rode with two Americans who were living in Berlin at the time: Ralph Zorn, a pastor whose parish was in the Wedding
neighborhood, and Alcyone Scott, a twenty-five-year-old graduate of
the University of Chicago who had come to work with Zorn. As their
vehicle approached the church, the crowds proved overwhelming. "I
could not get out of the van because people were pressing against it,"
Scott remembered. "They all wanted either to touch him or to get an
autograph. . . . It was just phenomenal!" Scott felt as though she was
traveling with an international rock star.[10]

The atmosphere inside the church was just as extraordinary. "Spell-bound—it can hardly be described any other way—the thousands sitting at his feet listened," wrote Dieter Hildebrandt in the *Frankfurter Allgemeine Zeitung*. King presented an overview of the civil rights struggle in the United States and spoke of nonviolent resistance. "You could hear a pin drop," recalled Alcyone Scott. "These people are in a kind of prison not of their own choosing. . . . And he's talking to them about passive resistance. . . . And that was radical." With the Cold War at its height, few East Berliners imagined conditions would change. "For him to talk about hope in this situation was electrifying. I don't think I've ever been present where all of those things one wants to believe in and desperately hope for are given expression with such resonance. This was, however, the case for East Berliners in that church at that moment." The choir finished the service with "Go Down Moses," ending on the line, "Let my people go."[11]

That King spoke at St. Mary's Church was particularly remarkable. In general, as Alcyone Scott observed, "the church was probably the only arena in which he could have spoken in the East and been able to say what he did." Yet organized religion, and St. Mary's Church specifically, had become a target of state repression. The provost of St. Mary's, Heinrich Gruber, occupied that position in name only. He had been living in the West and was denied reentry to East Berlin because of his critical attitudes toward the state. When King arrived, St. Mary's was missing not only its provost but also a pastor. Martin Helmer, a former pastor, had fled to the West in 1963. The East German police had arrested and imprisoned his successor, Werner Arnold, for criticizing the building of the wall. The East German state had thus banished all potential critics from St. Mary's. But on the night of September 14, one of the world's great political rebels took the pulpit.[12]

After King concluded his speech at St. Mary's, he headed to the Sophia Church, which was packed with another 2,000 Germans. They stood in the aisles and crowded around the altar. At the end of the speech, people rushed to King, shook his hand, and hugged him. Hans-Joachim Kolpin got King's autograph on a napkin. "It was an uplift-ing experience," Kolpin remembered. "He made us feel better about ourselves." King was that rare individual who appealed to leaders and citizens alike in both East Germany and West Germany. In turn, King was emboldened by the reception. He remarked, "When I go back I will know that we do not struggle alone, that millions are with us." Millions stood with him indeed, on both sides of the wall.[13]

King's experience in Berlin furthered his understanding of how the African American struggle could advance by opening to the interna-tional stage. "The past few days here in Europe have brought me face to face with the most powerful ally that the Negro struggle made," King wrote from Europe on September 17. That ally was "the Court of World Opinion." King realized just how fully "the world is in sym-pathy with the Negro." He was "amazed at the knowledge which one finds of the United States racial situation here in Europe." And he left convinced that inequality could no longer withstand "the light of world exposure."[14]

King traveled from Berlin to Munich, and soon flew to Rome. There he met with Pope Paul VI. The FBI tried to prevent the meet-ing by feeding information on King's supposed subversive activities to Roman cardinals. In the end, Vatican leaders brushed off the FBI's ef-forts. J. Edgar Hoover wrote incredulously, "I am amazed that the Pope gave an audience to such a degenerate." For King, however, the visit showed his expanding international reach, widened his perspective, and enhanced his global status.[15]

In October 1964, King, exhausted and fighting a virus, checked him-self into an Atlanta hospital for a physical and a chance to rest. He lay in bed at St. Joseph's Infirmary on October 14, when Coretta called with the news that he had been awarded the Nobel Peace Prize. He was thirty-five years old at the time, the youngest person to receive the award. It completed his evolution from a southern preacher into a world leader.[16]

African Americans and civil rights supporters swelled with pride at the news while white southerners seethed. Virgil Stuart, the chief of police in St. Augustine, Florida, called King's Nobel Prize "the biggest joke of the year. . . . How can you win the Peace Prize when you stir up all the trouble he did down here?" Birmingham's Bull Connor was terse but vague: "Shame on somebody."[17]

On the front page of the *Atlanta Constitution*, Ralph McGill urged King's detractors to reassess. "It would be helpful if even those who oppose Dr. King would now attempt a quiet, honest evaluation of the man." The "calumny, abuse, and danger" that trailed King throughout his life showed how white Americans had become "befogged by emotions and prejudices." Perhaps Europeans could see the future in a way Americans could not. "Europeans understand what is not clear to all Americans—namely, that Africa and Asia have watched Dr. Martin Luther King and seen in him manifestation of the American promise."[18]

In December, King traveled to Oslo to accept the Nobel Prize. He stopped first in London, where he gave three days of speeches and was treated like royalty. Four thousand people packed St. Paul's Cathedral on December 6 to hear King, the first non-Anglican to occupy that pulpit. In another speech, King called for economic sanctions against South Africa and condemned apartheid. In Oslo, adoring crowds braved the heavy fog and rain to welcome him at the airport. King had "long deserved the Peace Prize," said the Swedish reverend Ake Zetterburg. His "unarmed struggle" would "inspire colored people all over the world." At a press conference, King denounced colonialism in the Congo. Then on December 10, hundreds of dignitaries filled the auditorium at Oslo University for the Nobel Prize ceremony. King accepted the prize on behalf of the freedom movement. He bemoaned racism and violence throughout the world, and pledged his "renewed dedication to humanity." King left Oslo with a heightened awareness of his new responsibilities to the entire world.[19]

King flew back to New York, where crowds greeted him with a hero's welcome. New Yorkers cheered King at a ceremony in the city council chamber, then treated him to an evening reception at the Waldorf-Astoria. Later that night, he attended a rally in Harlem. For ten days he had been "talking with kings and queens," he told the crowd of 9,000 that had gathered at the 369th Artillery Armory. "This isn't the usual pattern of my life, to have people saying nice things about me. Oh, this is a marvelous mountaintop. I wish I could stay here tonight. But the valley calls me." He was already turning his thoughts to Selma, Alabama, where he would wage his next crusade—the struggle for voting rights—in just a few weeks.[20]

King was met with an icy reception in Atlanta. What should have been a moment to celebrate a native son turned into a public relations disaster. Shortly after the initial Nobel Prize announcement, a group of local leaders—led by Benjamin Mays, Rabbi Jacob Rothschild, and Archbishop Paul Hallinan—had begun to organize a public ceremony for King. Few prominent whites supported their efforts. Businessmen were still angry with King for leading a sit-in at Rich's department store in 1960, and their ire increased when King lent his support to striking workers at Atlanta's Scripto factory in 1964. They saw little payoff in an integrated affair to honor an agitator.[21]

In mid-December, Rothschild, Hallinan, Mays, and Ralph McGill sent letters to more than one hundred prominent Atlantans, asking them to sponsor a banquet for King. The letter said in part, "This is the second Nobel award that any Southerner has received." (William Faulkner's was the first.) "We believe, it reflects on the South, and, particularly, on our state and city. It is with this pride in mind that we join in this undertaking." They received few responses. One bank executive vowed that Atlanta "ain't having no dinner for no nigger." But Mayor Ivan Allen spent all of his political capital to make that dinner a reality. He knew that further resistance would tarnish Atlanta's image as the "City Too Busy to Hate." Allen stepped up his efforts to convince Robert Woodruff, the head of Coca-Cola, to sponsor the dinner. Allen gathered twenty business leaders at the Piedmont Driving Club and explained that Atlanta's reputation hung in the balance. They ultimately agreed to sponsor the event, scheduled for January 27 at the Dinkler Plaza Hotel. Few of the businessmen actually wished to celebrate King, but all of them feared the uproar that would accompany their inaction.[22]

Ticket sales flagged. None of the corporate sponsors made plans to actually attend. On December 29, the *New York Times* published an article about white Atlanta's ambivalence. NBC News aired a segment about the controversy. Facing the condemnation of the rest of the country, city residents finally began to arrange themselves on the right side of history. In the days after the NBC segment, 1,500 tickets were sold. On the night of the dinner, hundreds more people were turned away at the door. Inside the ballroom, the Morehouse glee club performed before the integrated crowd. King thanked those in attendance and confided that the dinner presented "quite a contrast to what I face almost every day." At the end of the evening, the audience stood and sang, "We Shall Overcome." Robert Woodruff did not attend.[23]

During the previous month, limousines had chauffeured Martin Luther King through the streets of London, Oslo, and Stockholm. In Europe, he was the cynosure of all eyes. Back in his hometown, it took every bit of cajoling to stage a dinner in recognition of his Nobel Prize.

WHILE IT IS tempting to applaud Europeans for their racial tolerance and progressiveness, the contrasting perceptions of King at home and abroad can be explained by one basic fact: white Americans had skin in the game. When King promised a "radical reconstruction of society," it was American society he proposed to reconstruct. When King criticized the Vietnam War, he was denouncing a war in which American soldiers had lost their lives. Europeans could safely embrace King's cause from afar, comforted by the belief that he did not mean to upend their lives. Indeed, foreign support for King only rarely amounted to support for a global movement for human rights and economic equality.

In South Africa, whites perceived King as a genuine threat. King criticized apartheid as early as 1957, when he was one of more than one hundred world leaders who signed the "Declaration of Conscience." That document urged people around the world to protest against the "inhumanity of the South African government." Then in 1962, King coauthored an appeal for economic sanctions against the apartheid regime. In a speech in London on December 7, 1964, King said that American blacks felt a "powerful sense of identification with those in the far more deadly struggle for freedom in South Africa." King urged leaders on both sides of the Atlantic to cease buying goods and gold from South Africa, and to withdraw their investments.[24]

Whites in South Africa displayed their disgust for King. When an Amsterdam university conferred upon King an honorary degree in 1965, white South Africans erupted with rage. A Cape Town newspaper printed a series of letters to the editor that might just as easily have appeared in any number of publications in the American South. "It is to be hoped Dr. King will not be allowed to come to South Africa to stir up trouble," stated one letter to the *Cape Times*, "and to instruct African extremists and their White allies (mostly communists) in the art of 'freedom marches,' organized demonstrations, and sit-down strikes. This is not the way to help Africans." Little did this letter writer know that a group of college students were indeed working to bring King to South Africa. The National Union of South African Students invited King to address the organization's annual conference at the University of Natal. King wrote back quickly to express his "tremendous admiration for the students, leading churchmen, and African leaders who have been able to maintain a nonviolent spirit in the present situation." And he accepted the invitation.[25]

As King entertained a speaking request from another group of South African students, he delivered his most audacious address on the apartheid regime. He spoke at Hunter College in New York City on December 10, 1965, which was Human Rights Day. King asserted that Africa possessed savages and brutes—and they had white skin. South Africa's white rulers were "modern-day barbarians." They had revived the ideology and the practices of the Nazis. The United States remained an ally of this "monstrous government," providing support through its friendly economic policies and assistance with South Africa's nuclear technology. King declared that the world could not stand by while South African leaders pushed white supremacy toward its brutal end. He called for "massive" nonviolent action: a worldwide boycott of South African goods.[26]

Students at the University of Cape Town had asked King to deliver the Davie Memorial Lecture. King accepted that invitation as well, and in February 1966, he wrote to the South African consular office in New Orleans to apply for a visa. He explained that he would speak at Natal and in Cape Town. "My visit would be purely as a lecturer," King wrote. The South African officials promptly denied his visa request.[27]

While King would continue to speak out against the apartheid government, events in Southeast Asia soon became his focus. Early in 1966, a movement against the Vietnam War began to coalesce. In January, the Student Nonviolent Coordinating Committee announced its opposition to the war and encouraged resistance to the draft. That same month, Senator J. William Fulbright, chairman of the Senate Foreign Relations Committee, commenced a series of televised hearings on the war. King had spoken critically of the Vietnam War as early as March 1965, and proceeded to issue steady, though often quiet, criticisms. At that point, Coretta Scott King was a more vocal antiwar activist. In February 1967, he finally voiced his full-throated opposition with a speech at the Beverly Hilton Hotel entitled "The Casualties of the War in Vietnam." King charged that the United States had blatantly violated the United Nations charter. By continuing this misadventure in Vietnam, American policy makers would "turn the clock of history back and perpetuate white colonialism." America had betrayed its own professed principles. In a deeper sense, the nation had lost its way. King insisted that he opposed the Vietnam War "because I love America" and "because I am disappointed with America." This scathing address launched King into the antiwar movement and acted as a preview of his forthcoming speech in New York City. It would be more wide-ranging, more damning, and far more publicized.[28]

On March 25, 1967, King led 5,000 people in an antiwar march down State Street in Chicago. Then on April 4, exactly one year before King's death, 4,000 people packed into New York City's Riverside Church while a line stretched outside for two blocks. Speaking from the pulpit, King linked together all of the varied injustices that had come to consume his energies and occupy his mind. He decried the "giant triplets of racism, materialism, and militarism," articulated the precise connections between those forces, and proposed how the United States might find its way again.[29]

King tried to view the war not only with American eyes, but also from the perspective of other nations. "I speak as a citizen of the world," he told the crowd, and "for the world as it stands aghast at the path we have taken." With every dead body that piled up in Vietnam, the reputation of the United States took another beating. King quoted one of Vietnam's Buddhist leaders: "The image of America will never again be the image of revolution, freedom, and democracy, but the image of violence and militarism." King charged that the American government was "the greatest purveyor of violence in the world today." Twenty years after the United States had rebuilt Europe under the Marshall Plan, it frittered away much of its international legitimacy.[30]

And King pried deeper. The Vietnam War was not only mistaken foreign policy, it was "a symptom of a far deeper malady within the American spirit." Only a sick country would spend more on napalm to be used in Vietnam than on food and shelter for the impoverished citizens in its own cities. With its values confused and its image in ruins, America was approaching "spiritual death."[31]

To right itself, the nation needed to undergo "a radical revolution of values." American society was an "edifice which produces beggars," King added, and that edifice "needs restructuring." This was not only about transforming economic policies. It was also about seeing beyond

oneself, one's neighbors, one's community, and beyond one's own borders. To foster a revolution of values would entail a wholesale revision
of America's place in the world. As King put it, "Our loyalties must become ecumenical rather than sectional." He imagined a world without
national boundaries. He called for a "world-wide fellowship that lifts
neighborly concern beyond one's tribe, race, class, and nation." King
did have a dream: he envisioned a global brotherhood of humanity.[32]

That dream did not entrance many American leaders. Elected officials lined up to denounce him. President Johnson fumed. Newspaper editors flayed King in their pages. The *New York Times* and the
Washington Post both excoriated him while *Life* labeled his speech "a
demagogic slander that sounded like a script for Radio Hanoi." Several
civil rights leaders also criticized King for his foray into US foreign policy. They felt he would damage the civil rights cause by further alien-
ating powerful politicians as well as mainstream Americans. Indeed,
many Americans thought King was unpatriotic to sympathize with the
Vietnamese and to claim that the nation was headed toward "spiritual
death." In James Baldwin's view, this speech sealed King's fate: "At the
point, precisely, that he connected American domestic morality with
America's role in the world, he became dangerous enough to be shot."
King was no longer toiling just for the basic rights of his people, but was
challenging America's leaders on the world stage. With this critique,
King posed his greatest threat to the powerful.[33]

As the antiwar movement gained in popularity, King assumed a
more prominent role. On April 15, 1967, hundreds of thousands demonstrated against the war, across the country and the world. In New York
City, King led 400,000 marchers from Central Park to the United Nations. Another 100,000 people marched that day in San Francisco, and
thousands more in cities as far away as Rome.[34]

In other parts of the world, King's antiwar activism only reinforced
his reputation as a hero. Matthias Mirschel, the student body president
at Kirchliche Hochschule (a divinity school in West Berlin), wrote to
King on June 10, 1967. During King's visit to Berlin in 1964, the school

had granted him an honorary degree. "It is not only for this reason that we feel bound up with you," Mirschel wrote. "Like you we consider the American intervention in Vietnam as cruel, unjust, senseless, un-christian." Mirschel assured King that European students stood with him in his opposition to the Vietnam War. He exhorted King to press on. "May many in the USA and all over the world hear your voice and support your campaign." When King looked across the seas, he could glimpse a nonviolent army behind him.[35]

Into his last days, King deepened his commitment to the global struggles for nonviolence and for racial justice. The concluding chapter of his book *Where Do We Go from Here?* focused on "The World House." His final book, *The Trumpet of Conscience*, was devoted largely to issues of war and peace. And in his final speech, he employed a de-cidedly global perspective. On April 3, he told the crowd at Memphis's Mason Temple, "The masses of people are rising up. And wherever they are assembled today, whether they are in Johannesburg, South Africa; Nairobi, Kenya; Accra, Ghana; New York City; Atlanta, Geor-gia; Jackson, Mississippi; or Memphis, Tennessee—the cry is always the same—'We want to be free.'" Given these activities, Bernard La-fayette should not have been taken aback when King told him—at the Lorraine Motel—that the next campaign would take nonviolence international.[36]

Together, all of these stories—the trips to Accra and Oslo, the speeches in Berlin and Los Angeles, the campaigns against South Af-rican apartheid and the Vietnam War—help to explain the worldwide reaction to King's assassination. At that moment in April 1968, many people across the globe felt the blow just as fully, if not quite as person-ally, as did African Americans.

ON EVERY CONTINENT, throngs of people gathered in public squares and places of worship to honor Martin Luther King. At St. Andrews Presbyterian Church in Nairobi, Tom Mboya, Kenya's minister of planning, read King's "Mountaintop" speech to an overflow crowd that

included members of parliament. A visiting church worker from Indianapolis taught the audience the words to "We Shall Overcome." In
Madrid, Spaniards packed a church service for King while some 1,500
people huddled outside, prying open windows and doors to hear the
tributes. In Mexico City's Chapultepec Heights, several hundred people
attended a memorial service for King. One thousand marchers trooped
through the streets of West Berlin and into John F. Kennedy Square.
Two thousand Genevans marched to St. Pierre Cathedral for a memorial. In some places, mourning services produced affecting moments of
brotherhood. In Perth, Australia, Archbishop George Appleton urged
his countrymen to reconsider their treatment of Aborigines. Catholics
and Jews prayed together in Turin, Italy. The London headquarters of
Christian Action received more financial donations than it was prepared to handle. King's death seemed to have united the world house.[37]

Tributes to King mixed with denunciations of America. In Rome,
hundreds of people gathered outside the US embassy and staged an
anti-American protest. Nearby, on the Via Veneto, a small group of
Roman youths threatened three American sailors. Italian policemen
intervened to prevent violence. But the fact that Italians menaced
American sailors highlighted the irony of the moment. Many foreigners condemned America for slaughtering its own gift to the world:
Martin Luther King.[38]

J. Lowrie Anderson, a white American missionary working in Nai-
robi, sat down to tea with a Kenyan friend. "We hate you Americans,"
Anderson's African friend told him. "You killed our Martin Luther
King."[39]

King was assassinated at a time when America's global image already lay in shambles. As bombs rained down on civilians in Vietnam,
the rest of the international community expressed its outrage. Yet in
those first weeks of spring, a thaw seemed possible. In January 1968, the
Tet Offensive had helped to strengthen the antiwar movement within
the United States while President Lyndon Johnson's popularity plum-
meted. On March 31, Johnson delivered a speech that began with some

striking words about Vietnam. He said he was ordering a halt to the bombing in much of North Vietnam, and he called for peace talks. At the end of his forty-minute address, Johnson dropped the real bombshell: he would not seek reelection. Johnson's "twin jolt," as historian Taylor Branch described it, "lifted the whole country into euphoria." It lifted the world's spirits as well. From NATO headquarters in Brussels, the *Christian Science Monitor*'s Carlyle Morgan reported, "American prestige has been running high in the last few days because of President Johnson's new stand on Vietnam." Given those hopes for peace in Vietnam, King's assassination seemed doubly awful. Europeans worried that the fallout from his death might derail any momentum toward peace.[40]

The assassination only further demonstrated that America was a brutish nation. The *Frankfurter Rundschau*, a left-leaning paper in West Germany, offered a representative opinion: "America's prestige, damaged as it is already through her brutal warfare in Vietnam, must slip further when her prominent personalities can no longer be sure that they cannot be hunted down and killed like rabbits." *France-Soir* was more concise. "America is a brutal country," the editors observed. "Now she is afraid." A cartoon in the West German newspaper *Die Welt* suggested that King's assassination had dealt a death blow to America itself. This cartoon pictured the angel of death sitting atop Martin Luther King's coffin. The angel held a shattering tombstone that was designed like the American flag. The Soviet newspaper *Izvestia* mixed horror with glee. A headline on April 5 proclaimed, "United States is a Nation of Violence and Racism." *Izvestia* also asserted, "The killing must have had a political motivation," implying that American government officials were responsible. Other communist newspapers seized the chance to denounce the United States. *Neues Deutschland*, the organ of the East German government, predicted King's assassination would prompt "hundreds of thousands to join the international front against the barbaric imperialism of the US and its allies."[41]

Mourners assembled in Paris on the night of April 9. The Mouvement Contre le Racisme, l'Antisemitisme et Pour la Paix, known as MRAP, organized an homage to King. Political activists, union leaders, intellectuals, and concerned citizens gathered at the Cirque d'Hiver, where an illuminated portrait of King looked out from the dais. Pierre Paraf, head of MRAP, spoke of the "double crime" American leaders had perpetrated against African Americans in the United States and against the people of Vietnam. Charles Palant, general secretary of MRAP, criticized American racists for standing as "opponents of all human progress." The evening's most celebrated speaker was Jacques Monod, a Nobel Prize–winning biologist who was also a hero of the French resistance during World War II. Monod linked King with Gandhi. In King, "Gandhi's soul had found a body," Monod declared. He spoke of King's commitment to nonviolence, and praised King for provoking confrontations in the name of justice. Yet he also cautioned his fellow Frenchmen against castigating Americans in general: "Let us beware of betraying his thoughts and of using his death to humiliate the great American people who are victims today." Monod thus pushed back against the Europeans' tendency to condemn Americans. The event ended with the screening of a film about the 1963 March on Washington.[42]

On Palm Sunday, thousands gathered for Mass at St. Peter's Basilica in the Vatican. After reading the Passion of the Christ, Pope Paul VI spoke of King's death. "We cannot omit to mention here also the sad remembrance which weighs upon the conscience of the world, that of the cowardly and atrocious killing of Martin Luther King. We shall associate this memory with that of the tragic story of the Passion of Christ." The pontiff's voice broke with emotion as he described his meeting with King several years before. Pope Paul told the crowd he hoped King's assassination might prompt citizens to work for justice and to realize a global beloved community. He prayed that King's sacrifice would not be in vain.[43]

On April 9, hundreds of Parisians gathered for an homage to Martin Luther King. Political activists, union leaders, intellectuals, and citizens came together at the Cirque d'Hiver. Speakers not only grieved for King but also denounced American leaders for their treatment of African Americans and for waging the war in Vietnam.

Keystone-France/Getty Images

Other nations memorialized King in less rarefied ways. A bevy of foreign governments printed commemorative postage stamps. One day after King's assassination, the Congo announced it was issuing a stamp in King's honor. On April 11, the postal department in Mexico commissioned a stamp hailing King as the "apostle of nonviolence." Many countries followed suit: Mali, Liberia, Yemen, Rwanda, Guinea, and Paraguay. A joint stamp was issued by Anguilla, Nevis, and St. Kitts. Haiti produced a King stamp featuring the Nobel Prize. The Republic of Dahomey, later known as Benin, printed a King stamp with

REPUBLIQUE DU CONGO
50ᶠ
POSTE AÉRIENNE
PASTEUR MARTIN LUTHER KING
Prix Nobel de la Paix
(1929-1968)

After King's assassination, the Congo printed this stamp in King's honor. Many foreign nations did the same.

From the exhibition Blacks on Stamp, *curated by Dr. Akin Ogundiran and presented by the Dept. of Africana Studies, University of North Carolina, Charlotte. Courtesy of Dr. Esper Hayes*

the words, "WE MUST MEET HATE WITH CREATIVE LOVE," written in three different languages: English, French, and German. One year later, in 1969, India and Ghana both unveiled stamps for King. So did Chad, Togo, Cameroon, and Venezuela. It took ten more years for the United States to do the same.[44]

King stamps proliferated especially in Africa, South America, the Caribbean, and South Asia, reflecting his lasting influence on the Third World. Since his initial exposure to Mahatma Gandhi's teachings, King had felt a strong connection to the people of India. And Indians embraced him as a worthy heir to Gandhi. On April 5, Prime Minister Indira Gandhi spoke before parliament. "Dr. Martin Luther King followed Gandhi in life and has now followed him in death, sacrificing himself for a great cause." She called King's assassination "a setback to mankind's search for light." In a rare tribute to a foreign citizen, members of parliament stood for a one-minute silence.[45]

Indians could not look at King without seeing the Mahatma. As Indira Gandhi recalled, "When news of his assassination came, our thoughts instinctively turned to Gandhi." Days before King's death, the Inter-State Cultural League of India was formed to promote amity across regions, cultures, and classes. The Inter-State Cultural League then collected tributes to King and published more than a dozen of them in the fall of 1968. That he followed the "Gandhian method of truth and non-violence," remarked B. Gopala Reddi, the governor of Uttar Pradesh, "endeared him to all Indians." N. G. Goray, the chairman of the Praja Socialist Party, observed that King "appears to us to have a typically Indian aura."[46]

Some Indians tried to keep their faith in the United States. Suraj Bhan, the vice-chancellor of Punjab University, hoped King's death could somehow revive the American promise. "People all over the world share the hope that his death will succeed in saving the soul of the American nation—and as an end-result make this world safe for a multi-racial and multi-creed society." G. Nagarajan had staked his livelihood on that vision of America as a multiracial democracy. He had emigrated from India to the United States and became a physics professor at Allen University in Columbia, South Carolina. Nagarajan delighted in his ability to lay claim to both Gandhi and King. King's career had helped him to develop a love for his new country. After King's murder, Nagarajan wrote to Coretta Scott King:

> When we came from India, we thought our Gandhi did not die because his principles of nonviolence were carried out for the cause of poor people by your husband, a great man. Though your husband physically disappears, his philosophy and principles exist here. Many Kings and many Gandhis will come forward for the cause of poor people. It is really a great loss to your family and the whole humanity.

In the face of tragedy, G. Nagarajan still believed that the world could produce another nonviolent hero.[47]

The most self-serving tribute to King emanated from Haiti, a nation ruled by the dictator François Duvalier. As the self-proclaimed "leader of the black world," Duvalier sensed an opportunity in King's death. He moved quickly to wrap himself in King's mantle. Duvalier created a narrative that featured a triumvirate of black freedom fighters:

Toussaint L'Ouverture, King, and himself. After King's assassination, Duvalier directed Haitians to observe an official period of mourning. He closed all theaters and places of amusement for five days; he lowered the national flag to half-staff on all buildings; and he instructed radio stations to play only music "suited to the occasion." On April 9, Haiti held a memorial service for King in Port-au-Prince. Duvalier delivered the eulogy. Each time Duvalier spoke of King, he linked the American civil rights movement with his own leadership and with the struggle of black people in Haiti. While extolling King, Duvalier described Haiti as "a knight of liberty in the Americas," which "wishes to remain under my leadership the sacred bulwark of the ideal of Negroes the world over." In the coming decades, streets across the world would be renamed for Martin Luther King. Haiti led the way. On April 15, Duvalier declared the Ruelle Nazon would thenceforth be called Martin Luther King Avenue. That street intersected with John Brown Avenue.[48]

While Duvalier embraced King's legacy, many other despots saw in King a threat to their own rule. After King's death, whites in South Africa continued to denounce him. J. D. Vorster, the brother of South Africa's prime minister, claimed that King's murder was part of a communist plot to create chaos and civil war, and to disrupt the "established order." The state-controlled South African Broadcasting Corporation announced King's death with a news bulletin on the morning of April 5. The station did not mention King's career of activism or his dedication to nonviolence. "With barely concealed relish," as scholars John Daniel and Peter Vale recalled, the broadcast proclaimed, "Widespread rioting has broken out in the United States following the assassination of the Negro civil rights agitator, Martin Luther King." Apartheid leaders found other like-minded demagogues in a surprising place: Northern Ireland.[49]

Protestants in Belfast criticized King because they were fighting against resistance movements within their own country. To them, King had set a fearsome example. Street protests intensified in Belfast in 1968, and some of the Catholic demonstrators explicitly modeled themselves on the American civil rights movement. Ian Paisley, a fundamentalist reverend and editor of the *Protestant Telegraph*, denounced Catholic insurgents in Northern Ireland and African American protesters in the same breath. In the weeks after King's death, Paisley's newspaper maligned King while praising the white supremacist regimes in South Africa and Rhodesia. King had "loaded the gun of his own destruction by making himself the symbol of resistance to law and order," wrote Paisley. "Only the brainwashed or deluded really believe there is such a thing as 'non-violent' or 'passive' resistance to law and order." Paisley blamed King for his own death. On April 27, Paisley's *Telegraph* declared, "We give to our readers what the press and ecumenical leaders have kept from the people of this province—the fact that King's preaching and life led to violence. His so-called 'non-violence' produced the worst sort of violence." Newspapers in Rhodesia focused on the riots in American cities, proof of the supposed savagery of black people. The aftermath of King's death thus revealed an unlikely coalition of reactionaries, linking brutal white supremacists in South Africa and Rhodesia with Protestant leaders in Northern Ireland.[50]

AFRICAN LIBERATION STRUGGLES had unfolded alongside the American civil rights movement. Black Americans drew strength from the independence movements that rippled across the African continent. In turn, King helped to foster a "new consciousness," observed the South African writer Allan Boesak, that "powerfully influenced black people in South Africa and all over the world." King had inspired black people to discover "an unassailable and majestic sense of their own value."[51]

Africans displayed two basic reactions to King's assassination. Many felt as though one of their own had been murdered; at the same time, King's death reinforced their harshest critiques of the United States and its abhorrent racism. King "was an inspirational leader to many Africans as well as Americans," George Shepherd Jr. wrote in *Africa Today*. "The loss to Africa of Martin Luther King is second only to the loss of America." One Kenyan citizen would not concede to Americans even that much. He believed Africans had an equal claim to King:

"The American Negroes almost forgot that anyone else could be as close to him as they felt." The *Johannesburg World* called King a "son of Africa" and lamented that he "died when needed most." Many black South Africans echoed that sentiment in their letters to the *World*. B. S. Mofokeng, a resident of Mapetla, detailed his grief and anger. The "world as a whole, has lost one of its moderate leaders, Dr. Martin Luther King," wrote Mofokeng. He called King "a real symbol of peace and freedom," and believed the "light of freedom" had been "switched off." Mofokeng wrote that King's "influence and action were of desperate need" to Africa and the world. He too regarded King as a "Son of Black Africa." D. M. Molemo of Elandsfontein agreed: "The death of this dear man has left the world in the field of fear and confusion."[52]

Other Africans sharpened their criticism of American racism. The government of Ghana issued a statement calling it "a matter for world concern that it is necessary in the 20th Century for human beings to die in a struggle for human dignity in a country they helped to build." Ghana's *Daily Graphic* went further. America's "affluent society" was actually "a fraudulent society," wrote the editors, "a human jungle wherein the black man is the target for destruction, even extermination." They expressed the fury of a continent.[53]

From South Africa to South America, political dissidents found in King a kindred spirit. Chilean Ariel Dorfman had known little about King during much of the 1960s. But he would remember with "ferocious precision" the moment of King's death. Just a week before King's assassination, Dorfman and his family had moved from Chile to California, where he began his graduate studies. The Dorfmans were sitting in the living room of their temporary home, high in the Berkeley hills, when the television carried a report on King's assassination. "It was only then that I began to realize who Martin Luther King had been" and "what we had lost with his departure." Dorfman sat transfixed as the networks played excerpts from King's "I Have a Dream" speech. At the time of that speech, in 1963, Dorfman was not even aware the March on Washington was taking place. He only came to absorb King's dream in 1968, as he learned of King's death.[54]

Dorfman returned to Chile late in 1969, one year before Salvador Allende was elected president. Allende attempted to build a socialist polity through democratic and peaceful means. Dorfman served as a cultural adviser in Allende's administration. Chile's right-wing leaders, aided by the United States, engineered a military coup to overthrow Allende. General Augusto Pinochet ordered the torture and execution of suspected leftists. Dorfman and his family fled the country, fearing for their lives. In that atmosphere of terror, Dorfman "first began to seriously commune with Martin Luther King." He watched from afar as Pinochet continued to commit atrocities in Chile, and a resistance movement grew. "King's voice and message began to filter fully, word by word, into my life." Brave Chileans would gather in the streets of Santiago to protest against the military regime. It was a strategy they shared with King. Dorfman recalled, "I never felt closer to Martin Luther King than during the 17 years it took us to free Chile of the dictatorship." In both countries, protesters practiced civil disobedience, subjected themselves to grave danger, and lifted their voices in song. Decades after his death, King's impact stretched to the tip of the hemisphere.[55]

IT TOOK YEARS for some Chilean protesters to "commune" with King's legacy. But in West Germany, the effect of King's death was immediate and profound.

In the days after King's assassination, the German press fixated on the riots in American cities. Those urban rebellions drove the German media to crass caricature. One cartoon in *Die Welt* depicted the Statue of Liberty raising the chalice in her right hand while using her left arm to cover her eyes. She could not bear to watch as the cities burst into flames. The cartoonist added another reason for Lady Liberty's fright: the image included eighteen small figures surrounding her. A *Der Spiegel* writer described these as "furious monkey brats, leering, only recognizable upon further inspection as subhuman, black faces." The cartoon suggested that monkey-like black rioters were destroying the land of liberty. The *Kieler Nachrichten*, or *Kiel News*, printed a cartoon just as alarming. Under the headline, "Black Power," an African American took a gun and torch to Martin Luther King's coffin.[56]

These sinister images were responses to the circumstances in Germany as much as to the riots in America. A radical student movement had begun to shake West Germany. Students protested in the streets through 1967 and 1968, railing against the Vietnam War and allying themselves with the Black Power movement. Elected officials as well as right-wingers angrily criticized the students. So when riots erupted in Washington and Chicago after King's death, many Germans viewed them through the lens of the protests that had jolted Berlin, Frankfurt, and Hamburg.

The most prominent student activist was Rudi Dutschke. Weeks before students in Paris brought France to the brink of revolution, the *New York Times* had described "Red Rudi" as "Europe's leading student revolutionary." A Brandenburg native, Dutschke fled to West Berlin in 1961 at the age of twenty-one, shortly before the wall was built. He enrolled at the Free University in Berlin, became a leader of the German Socialist Students League (also known as SDS), and in 1966 he married an anthropology student from Chicago. Dutschke embraced Marxism, but not the Soviet Union or East Germany. He looked to Che Guevara and Ho Chi Minh for inspiration, but refused to advocate violence. Dutschke preferred what he called "permanent discussion," a method of activism in which protesters interrupted everything from faculty meetings to church services.[57]

Although a large number of West Germans opposed the Vietnam War, many viewed the student protesters as lawless rabble-rousers. Political officials generally supported the United States. Berlin mayor Klaus Schütz denounced the radicals at Free University while the West German newspapers helped to incite a backlash against the student movement. On Christmas Eve, 1967, Martin Luther King preached a sermon for peace from the pulpit of Ebenezer Baptist Church. In Berlin, Rudi Dutschke disrupted a service at the Kaiser Wilhelm Memorial

Church. He stood at the chancel and spoke against the Vietnam War. An angry congregant assaulted Dutschke and struck him in the head.[58]

In February 1968, activists from around the world poured into West Berlin for an international congress on Vietnam. More than 5,000 students marched through the city and unfurled the banners of the North Vietnamese and the Vietcong. Dutschke riveted the crowd: "Tell the Americans the day and the hour will come when we will drive you out unless you yourselves throw out imperialism." Mayor Schütz had tried to ban the march, but it proceeded. Schütz organized a rally in support of the United States. The counterdemonstrators attacked students and chanted, "Throw Dutschke out of West Berlin!" Several student protesters suffered brutality at the hands of the police. Students held demonstrations against the Vietnam War in a host of other German cities. One thousand students in Hamburg marched on America House, and in Frankfurt, a group of students demonstrated at the US consulate. Protesters also clogged the streets of Freiburg, Munich, Bremen, and Kiel.[59]

King's assassination intensified the conflict between West German officials and student protesters. In several cities, including Berlin and Frankfurt, students not only mourned King but also condemned the United States for its racism and imperialism. In Frankfurt, Mayor Willi Brundert led a silent march on April 9. Demonstrators waved banners that read, "To mourn the death of Martin Luther King means to oppose Bonn's support of the U.S. war in Vietnam." In West Berlin, Schütz led a march for King in which US officials also participated. In that same crowd, students carried banners that said, "Memphis is burning—when will the Pentagon burn?" As the group arrived at city hall, students chanted, "Black Power now!" Though political leaders and student radicals had joined to mourn King's passing, they were marching for very different causes.[60]

On the afternoon of April 11, one week after King's death, Dutschke left the offices of the students' federation and hopped on his bicycle to head home. A twenty-three-year-old named Josef Bachmann waited outside the building. He stepped toward Dutschke, pointed a revolver, and fired three shots. Dutschke was hit twice in the head and once in the chest, but he survived. Investigators later questioned Bachmann. He explained, "I read about Martin Luther King, and I said to myself, 'You must do this too.'" He had resolved to "bump off" Dutschke because the student leader was a "Communist." King's death thus inspired the assassination attempt on Rudi Dutschke.[61]

Doctors worked to save Dutschke's life while students took to the streets of Berlin. They marched to the headquarters of Axel Springer, a conservative publishing magnate. The police fired water cannons at the crowd. The following day, 2,000 students attempted to march through John F. Kennedy Square to Berlin's city hall. They waved red flags and chanted "Ho Chi Minh!" and "Ru-di Dutsch-ke!" Police officers wielded billy clubs and bloodied the students. Protests spread beyond Berlin as some 10,000 students across the country joined in.[62]

West German students saw parallels between King's assassination and the shooting of Dutschke. Many student groups had aligned themselves with the Black Power movement in the United States and viewed King as too moderate. Yet they still admired his career of activism and were drawn to his antiwar message as well as his increasing commitment to democratic socialism. After King's assassination, German officials honored him as a champion of nonviolence and brotherhood. But even then, student activists needed a more radical King. Berlin protester Ekkehart Krippendorff identified King as "the first great leader, spokesman and organizer of the extra-parliamentary opposition." Krippendorff declared, "We are the ones who must satisfy his demand for a truly revolutionary change of our society. . . . The legacy of Martin Luther King is, for us, the continuation of his social-revolutionary struggle with his—but also with our—methods, here in our own country." The two shootings, just a week apart, encouraged German students to view King and Dutschke as allies in the same struggle: they were both rebels who battled imperialism and racism. King's legacy was thus shaped to fit the hands of the sculptor.[63]

The twin shootings further spurred the student rebellion. The students focused on a specific target: Axel Springer and his publications. Springer was a fervent anticommunist. His headquarters, nineteen stories high, stood a mere fifty yards from the Berlin Wall—a gleaming testament to capitalism within easy sight of the East. Springer controlled 70 percent of the press in West Berlin, and almost 40 percent in West Germany overall. *Bild Zeitung*, a tabloid-style newspaper with a circulation of 4 million, was the largest of his fourteen publications. *Bild Zeitung* vilified the student protesters. "Stop the Young Reds' Terror Now," blared one headline after Dutschke's shooting. Another read: "We Shouldn't Leave All the Dirty Work to the Police and Their Water Cannons." *Die Welt* was the most respected of Springer's organs; it had also printed the cartoon of the Statue of Liberty encircled by snarling black figures. Many of Springer's papers actually criticized the Vietnam War, but they more vehemently condemned the antiwar protesters. After the shooting of Dutschke, student radicals asserted that the Springer press had helped to create a climate in which the attack could occur.[64]

Students demanded the breakup of Springer's media empire and called for the resignation of President Heinrich Lübke. On the night of April 12, throngs of protesters surrounded the Springer headquarters. Some sat on the sidewalk or idled their cars in the road, attempting to block the path of the delivery trucks. Police squads unleashed tear gas, but they failed to thin the crowd. Students massed at printing plants throughout the country, in Essen, Cologne, Frankfurt, Hamburg, and Esslingen. They halted the delivery of about 1 million copies of *Bild Zeitung*. Protests developed across the continent. One thousand students gathered in Rome, hurling explosives at the West German embassy and smashing windows. Austrian students demonstrated outside Vienna University and carried anti-Springer posters. In Amsterdam, students blocked traffic and chanted, "Viva Dutschke!"[65]

On that same day, April 12, protesters in West Berlin held a different kind of demonstration. The Berlin Komitee Black Power organized a gathering at Lehniner Platz in the American zone. In advance of the event, activists had distributed flyers that proclaimed, "GUNS FOR BLACK POWER." The Black Power struggle in the United States "is also our resistance. This is why the American negroes do not need words, but guns. Only this language . . . Burn, Baby, Burn can be understood by the white *Herrenmensch*." The German students had integrated Black Power into their own ideology. And after the shootings of King and Dutschke, their radicalism only intensified.[66]

German officials chastised the activists. Franz Josef Strauss, West Germany's finance minister, likened the aggression at the printing plants to Nazi attacks on the Jews during the 1930s. Chancellor Georg Kiesinger denounced the "leftwing extremist forces" bent on "destruction of our parliamentary democratic order." The ranks of student protesters grew. On April 13, they blocked traffic on West Berlin's Kurfürstendamm. Police officers swarmed the street in armored vehicles and on horseback, arresting 230 students. Demonstrators gathered in at least ten other German cities. At Frankfurt's St. Peter's Church, students drowned out the Good Friday hymns with the "Internationale," the classic socialist anthem. As Dutschke recovered in the hospital and as more protesters were bloodied in the streets, sympathy grew for the students.[67]

The continued police brutality helped to shift public opinion. Heinrich Albertz, the former mayor of West Berlin, had thanked the police in 1967 after they shot and killed a student protester named Benno Ohnesorg. But in April 1968, Albertz declared that police aggression was no way to deal with the students' demands. He wished Dutschke well and called him "a man who will be needed in the future." Dutschke received a deluge of get-well wishes from leaders in Bonn and West Berlin. These were "embarrassing telegrams," remarked Albertz, noting that political officials had condemned Dutschke for years. Yet they all professed a sudden change of heart after the shooting. Albertz lamented, "It seems as if only a wounded Dutschke is a good Dutschke." Albertz himself was guilty of precisely this kind of shape-shifting. Just as many American politicians performed an about-face after King's

The murder of Martin Luther King inspired a copycat assassination attempt in West Berlin, where student activist Rudi Dutschke was shot on April 11. Students staged protests throughout West Germany. At many such marches, like the one in Stuttgart on April 14 (Easter Sunday), participants both honored King and railed against the conservative publisher Axel Springer.

DPA/Alamy

assassination, German leaders altered their views of Rudi Dutschke seemingly overnight.[68]

On April 15, Easter Monday, 5,000 West Berliners gathered peacefully at a rally in honor of Dutschke. But violence erupted in other cities. Hamburg police set up "fortress-like defenses" at a Springer plant where more than 1,000 demonstrators massed outside the barbed-wire barriers. A Springer delivery truck barreled into one of the protesters and badly injured him. In Frankfurt, 2,000 students clashed with mounted police officers. The troops beat the protesters with rubber truncheons. Police clubbed more demonstrators in Hanover. And in Munich, students staged a sit-down strike on the streets leading from the Springer plant. The revolutionary year of 1968 was still young, yet the tumult of April—the political shootings in Memphis and Berlin, the protests from Munich to Frankfurt, and the riots in Washington and Chicago—acted as a sign of things to come.[69]

Londoners, situated between Germany and the United States both geographically and politically, felt the impact of unrest in both countries. On April 15, anti-Springer demonstrations competed with memorials to Martin Luther King. The day's largest gathering was an antiwar protest organized by the Campaign for Nuclear Disarmament, which drew some 22,000 people. They marched through London with placards proclaiming, "WE DEMAND AMERICAN WITHDRAWAL FROM VIETNAM." While the larger peace protest remained nonviolent, four hundred demonstrators broke off from the march and headed to the West German embassy in Belgrave Square. They scuffled with the police and presented a petition expressing solidarity with German students. One thousand protesters also marched on London's *Daily Mirror* building, which housed Axel Springer's British offices. Police officers formed a cordon around the building as the students tried to force their way through, chanting "Axel Springer Out!" and "Rudi Dutschke!" In the late afternoon, the throng of nonviolent protesters streamed into Trafalgar Square for a final rally.[70]

A day that began in peaceful marching and transitioned to angry protests would end in somber reflection. As the sun set, many of the disarmament marchers continued to St. Paul's Cathedral, where Martin Luther King had preached less than four years prior. Thousands of Britons gathered on the steps of the church and spilled out onto the street to hear tributes to King. Speakers reflected on King's life and performers led the crowds in song. On that Easter Monday in London, all of the global crosscurrents converged: a large demonstration opposing the Vietnam War, a raging protest against Axel Springer, and an outpouring of grief for the worldwide leader of nonviolence, Martin Luther King.[71]

IN THE UNITED Kingdom, memories of King were fresh and vivid. He had traveled there just five months before his death. Eager to escape the mounting scorn of white Americans at home, King endured two days of international travel and spent all of eight waking hours in the comfort of Newcastle upon Tyne. On November 11, 1967, King embarked on his final trip across the Atlantic. He and Andrew Young flew from Chicago to London, stopped briefly at a hotel, then boarded an overnight train that rumbled from London to Newcastle. They arrived at six o'clock in the morning on November 13. King accepted an honorary degree at the University of Newcastle, returned to London that evening, and flew back to Atlanta the next day.[72]

King had warned his hosts in advance that he would not deliver a speech, but he was moved by the moment. He electrified the university audience with a brief address. King focused on three great problems the world faced: racism, poverty, and war. He elaborated on humanity's urgent challenge: "For all men of good will to work passionately and unrelentingly to get rid of racial injustice, whether it exists in the United States of America, whether it exists in England, or whether it exists in South Africa, wherever it is alive it must be defeated and . . . we have got to come to see that the destiny of white and colored persons is tied together." King told the rapt crowd that it supplied him with "renewed courage and vigor to carry on." The foreign setting reinvigorated him. In a plane up above the Atlantic Ocean, on a train that stopped at tiny English towns in the middle of the night, King was whisked far away from the United States—far from the media and politicians, from the skeptics and the haters and those who believed the world had passed him by. It was this fleeting feeling that he coveted: the freedom that comes with the overseas journey, the space to relieve oneself—if only for a couple of days—of the burdens of home.[73]

King later sent a thank-you letter to the University of Newcastle's vice-chancellor. It spelled out the connection between the hostile atmosphere in the United States and the satisfaction King derived from his trip to England. "In the course of constant criticism and malignment of one's best efforts," King wrote to Charles Bosanquet, "the recognition by an institution of higher learning of the historic significance of one's work in the ministry is a tremendous encouragement, far overshadowing the barbs and arrows from the daily press." He wrote the letter on January 30, 1968, at a moment when he was preoccupied with thoughts of his own death and keenly attuned to the "historic significance" of his life's work.[74]

He visited Britain at a time when it was gripped by debates over race, immigration, and civil rights. In the two decades after World War II, as Britain's empire unraveled, it witnessed an influx of 2 million immigrants, mostly from India, Pakistan, and the Caribbean. In 1962, the government passed a law that restricted immigration among Commonwealth citizens from Asia, Africa, and the Caribbean. At the same time, political leaders pledged to protect the rights and freedoms of those racial minorities who already resided in Britain. During King's 1964 trip to London, he met with black Britons who were beginning to organize against racial injustice. They formed the Campaign Against Racial Discrimination (CARD) and mobilized for civil rights laws. In 1965, the government passed the Race Relations Act, banning racial discrimination in many public places. The law was a small step forward.[75]

CARD immediately called for more robust legislation. In April 1967, two separate bodies released reports showing that discrimination was widespread in housing and employment—realms the law had not touched. Then in July 1967, shortly after riots tore through American cities like Detroit and Newark, the Labour government committed itself to an expanded Race Relations Act. The bill would include antidiscrimination ordinances that applied to housing, private employment, credit, and insurance.[76]

Conservatives opposed such a bill, while both sides cited the violence in America to bolster their own positions. Rev. John Muir of Newcastle strongly supported the new law. Muir wrote a letter to the *Newcastle Evening Chronicle* calling upon all members of the community to protect the rights of minorities. Failing such efforts, "the situation could very well become just as serious and violent as in the United States." Yet the opponents of the law noted that the United States had passed major civil rights legislation and its cities still exploded. Enoch

Powell, a leader in the Conservative Party who would soon become the single most important figure in Britain's racial politics, visited the United States in October 1967. Powell gazed up close at America's racial tensions. A horrified Powell concluded that attempts at racial integration could lead only to bloody eruptions. The combustible situation in urban America thus served as a warning to British leaders in both camps: it either demonstrated what would happen in the absence of tougher antidiscrimination laws, or it showed that any attempt to build a multiracial society was a quest born of folly.[77]

By 1968, racial minorities counted for only 2 percent of Britain's total population. Even in the cities, where most immigrants tended to live, they composed less than 10 percent of the population. In late 1967, people of Asian descent from Kenya—who held British passports—had begun to immigrate to Britain in greater numbers. Whites in Britain sounded the alarm. In response, the Labour government passed a restrictive immigration law in March 1968. It capped the number of Kenyan Asian immigrants and permitted only those with a relative who was already a resident. While the Labour government passed this severe immigration law, party leaders also increased their calls for an expanded Race Relations Act. Then came the shocking news from Memphis.[78]

In the days after King's death, the House of Commons passed a motion expressing outrage at the assassination. It also promised to "eliminate racial discrimination in this country." St. Paul's Cathedral planned a memorial service for April 10, and another tribute on Easter Monday. In Newcastle, the sting of King's death felt personal. University registrar Ernest Bettenson lowered the flag to half-staff. The Newcastle Journal lamented King's loss and noted the violence coursing through American cities. The editors asked, "Could it happen here?" That question haunted many Britons.[79]

On April 9, the Labour government finally introduced the Race Relations Act after almost a year of dawdling over the legislation. King's death helped to propel it toward passage. Home Secretary James Callaghan, a proponent of the bill, warned that if it proved ineffective, "there could be a racial explosion in 5 or 10 years' time." Other government officials hoped the new law would enable Britain to "avoid the American tragedy." As the *Christian Science Monitor* reported, "A few months ago no minister of Her Majesty's cabinet would even countenance talk of racial violence in Britain." But King's death, and the riots that followed, had reshaped the racial landscape on both sides of the Atlantic.[80]

Many supporters of the Race Relations Act referred to the violence in American cities. The *Times of London* remarked that the uprisings in the United States had "brought home to the British public, as perhaps never before, the dangers of failure in race relations." The editors advocated for the bill, though they worried that its medicine would be too mild. Lord Walston, chairman of the Institute of Race Relations, saw the events in America as "dreadful reminders of what can happen in a civilized and liberal country if the problems associated with race relations remain unsolved. . . . If effective action is not taken now we shall within ten years be suffering as is the United States today." Britain's luck could soon run out.[81]

In the Conservative Party, opposition to the law ran deep. On April 18, the Conservatives opposed a second reading of the Race Relations Act. Two days later, in a Birmingham hotel, the forces of nativism and prejudice found their champion.[82]

ENOCH POWELL'S SPEECH became one of the most influential in postwar Britain. It shocked the nation's political class, thrust a vicious racism to the surface of British life, and transformed the debate over the pending legislation.

Powell served as the defense minister in the Conservative Shadow Cabinet. He saw the spring of 1968 as a moment when chaos threatened the Western world. Powell was alarmed by the riots in American cities, the protests in Belfast, antiwar demonstrations in London, and the increase in non-white immigrants to British cities like his own Wolverhampton. Powell spoke for Britain's own silent majority: those

who longed for order in a time of tumult, who resented the political establishment, and who hoped they could return Britain to a white man's
country.[83]

On April 20, before an audience at the Midland Hotel in Birmingham, Powell gave himself fully to racial fears. He proposed to further
restrict immigration, compel mass repatriation, and defeat the Race
Relations Act. That last imperative had spurred Powell's speech. In the
wake of King's assassination, the Race Relations Act had gained trac-
tion in Parliament. Two weeks after King's death, Powell pushed back.[84]

He opened with a story of a middle-aged constituent who griped
that "in this country in 15 or 20 years' time the black man will have
the whip hand over the white man." By the year 2000, Powell claimed,
"whole areas . . . across England will be occupied" by immigrants. He
warned, "Those whom the Gods wish to destroy, they first make mad.
We must be mad, literally mad, as a nation to be permitting the annual
inflow of some 50,000 dependants. . . . It is like watching a nation busily
engaged in heaping up its own funeral pyre."[85]

Powell then charged that the Race Relations Act would disadvan-
tage white people and stir up hatred between the races. Such legislation
would "elevate" immigrants to "a privileged or special class," and the
upstanding white citizen would suffer. Antidiscrimination laws would
also encourage new immigrants to formulate bolder demands. To enact
such legislation "is to risk throwing a match on to gunpowder." Powell claimed that Commonwealth immigrants already enjoyed equality. They "entered instantly into the possession of the rights of every
citizen." Meanwhile, the flood of immigrants had reduced native-born
Britons to "strangers in their own country." Whites faced a doomsday
scenario, forced to fight for the social services that were their birth-
right. According to Powell, women were denied hospital beds for child-
birth and parents found themselves unable to enroll their children in
local schools. At the workplace, immigrants received special treatment.
The pending bill would establish a "one-way privilege." In this zero-
sum game, new immigrants enjoyed all of the government's largesse

while native-born Britons suffered. Whites had become "a persecuted minority," Powell insisted. And he exploited their sense of grievance.[86]

In his peroration, Powell looked back in time to ancient Rome, gazed across the Atlantic to the United States, and then peered toward Britain's own terrible tomorrow. "As I look ahead, I am filled with foreboding; like the Roman, I seem to see 'the River Tiber foaming with much blood.'" If the British did not stem the immigrant tide, their streets would become rivers of blood. "That tragic and intractable phenomenon which we watch with horror on the other side of the Atlantic . . . is coming upon us here by our own volition and our own neglect. Indeed, it has all but come." To avert an American-style race war, Britain needed to defeat the Race Relations Act and ship thousands of immigrants back across the seas.[87]

Many religious and political leaders recoiled in disgust at Powell's "Rivers of Blood" address. Francis Cocks, the minister at Powell's own church in Wolverhampton, wrote a letter to the *Times of London*. He wished to make clear that St. Peter's Collegiate Church did not stand with Powell. On April 21, the day after Powell's speech, St. Peter's held a memorial service for Martin Luther King. It attracted an interracial crowd and featured a eulogy by a reverend of Jamaican descent. CARD also held a memorial for King on that day. It mixed tributes to King with denunciations of Powell. Conservative Members of Parliament (MPs) criticized Powell as well. Nicholas Scott charged that Powell had assumed "the mantle of Governor [George] Wallace of Alabama." The kind of demagoguery that Britons associated with the American South had seemingly infected their nation. Humphry Berkeley, another Conservative MP, resigned from the party after Powell's speech. The head of the Conservative Party, Edward Heath, disavowed Powell's speech and promptly dismissed him from his post.[88]

While politicians rushed to condemn Powell, many white workers anointed him as their new hero. Powell received sacks of letters congratulating him on his speech. In letters to newspapers, whites openly expressed their racial hatred. "He's dead right about the darkies," wrote

J. Short to a Newcastle newspaper. Short thought it was "already too late to avoid completely the fate that is overtaking the United States," but perhaps government leaders could press immigrants to leave Britain. John Henderson, a resident of Westbury, wrote to the *Times of London*: "I have no doubt that Mr. Enoch Powell's views are held by 90 percent of the voters of this democracy." Judging by the massive outpouring of letters, Henderson's calculation did not seem far off. David Le Vay added his voice in a letter to the *Times*: "Mr. Powell's crime is to have said what every Englishman thinks."[89]

Whites backed Powell with their pens, their feet, and their fists. After Edward Heath removed Powell from the Shadow Cabinet, thousands of workers walked off their jobs in protest. On April 25, 3,000 dockworkers went on strike. One worker on London's West India Docks explained, "We think there are too many bloody coons coming into the country." There was nothing abstract about the rage that Powell stoked: it was racism, angry and unvarnished.[90]

His poisonous rhetoric reaped a whirlwind. From Birmingham to London, whites assaulted racial minorities. In Wolverhampton, a group of white youths attacked Wade Crooks, a fifty-one-year-old molder of West Indian descent, and his son Albert. The assailants chanted, "Powell, Powell!" and "Why don't you go back to your own country?!" Afterward, Wade Crooks noted that he had never before been the victim of racial violence during his thirteen years in Wolverhampton. "I am shattered," he said. Many Afro-Caribbeans in Britain experienced a new kind of hostility. Paul Boateng was a child in 1968 who would later become a Labour MP. Boateng recalled the climate of fear during the days following Powell's speech: "For the first time in the country of my birth . . . I was shouted at and spat at and abused in the street." Powell had inaugurated a new era. One migrant from Jamaica felt that race relations had recently been improving in Wolverhampton. But after the "Rivers of Blood" speech, the "sky fell in." Members of the West Midlands Caribbean Association found a way to mark the transformation.

They divided their history into two periods: BE and AE, Before Enoch and After Enoch.[91]

Though Powell had expressed horror at the rise of immigrant organizations, his own speech prompted racial minorities to further mobilize. In the Birmingham area, twelve Indian organizations formed a new body that would unite the community throughout the West Midlands. On April 28, twenty immigrant and Black Power organizations came together for their first national conference. They established the Black Peoples' Alliance and pledged to take "militant action" against racism. The event was "thanks to Powell," said Roy Sawh, the leader of one Black Power group. "I will give him a medal when I achieve power." Jagmohan Joshi, general secretary of the Indian Workers Association, was a driving force behind the meeting. Joshi hailed this event as "the first time in the history of race relations in this country that black people have come together against the onslaught of racialism." Enoch Powell inadvertently helped to spur that development.[92]

White students also mobilized against Powell. On April 28, 2,000 anti-Powell demonstrators marched from Hyde Park to Downing Street. Then on May Day, students assembled with trade unionists to participate in London's annual pro-worker rally. As they strode from Tower Hill toward Smith Square, the workers and students began to turn on each other. At the head of the march, a union leader chanted, "May Day is workers' day!" But the students had Powell on their minds. They roared, "Enoch, we want you—dead!" The students arrived at the House of Commons, chanting their slogans. Three hundred dockworkers had gathered nearby, waiting to lobby their MPs in favor of Powell. The dockworkers surged across the road toward the student protesters. A group of police officers prevented an attack, but the damage was done. Powell had charged the racial issue in a way that pitted white Britons against one another. White workers were the Labour Party's largest constituency, but most of them objected to the Race Relations Act. Although union officials stayed true to the Labour Party, many rank-and-file workers reconsidered their allegiances. Powell's speech also fractured the Conservatives, forcing political leaders to decide whether they would side with Edward Heath or with Powell and his open appeal to racism.[93]

Similar forces would roil American politics, helping to break apart the Democratic coalition. George Wallace whipped up white resentment during his third-party campaign for the presidency in 1968. He showed that by exploiting racial fear, politicians could peel white voters away from the Democratic Party. And Richard Nixon followed his lead. The riots after King's death lent an immediacy to the rhetoric about law and order, employed by both Nixon and Wallace, which accelerated the defections of white Democrats.[94]

The British Parliament debated the Race Relations Act into the early summer. It passed the new law in July, over the Conservatives' opposition. The law provided important safeguards against discrimination. But the nasty legacies of the "Rivers of Blood" address—open expressions of racial hatred, demonization of immigrants, and the politicization of racial fears—lived on.

The racial terrain in Britain had changed profoundly in the five months since Martin Luther King's visit to Newcastle. In November 1967, King had viewed Britain as a refuge. That transatlantic trip transported him away from the vitriol that engulfed him in America. By April 1968, racial hatred permeated Britain as well. For those seeking peace, fellowship, and interracial amity, the world offered fewer havens. King's death and its aftereffects helped give rise to an atmosphere that was uglier, more hostile, and more violent.

6

STOP THE SHOTS

O N CAPITOL HILL, King's death spurred an effort to rein in the
violence that seemed to envelop the United States.

Less than two hours before James Earl Ray aimed his rifle at the
balcony of the Lorraine Motel, the Senate Judiciary Committee was
debating proposals to regulate gun sales. The Johnson administration
had offered an amendment, attached to a larger crime bill, which would
outlaw the mail-order sale of firearms and would ban all interstate gun
sales. The Judiciary Committee rejected that proposal with a vote of
9–4. Senator Thomas Dodd then put forth a similar amendment, adding a clause that would allow states to opt out of the restrictions. The
committee defeated Dodd's version by a vote of 8–5. Dodd, a Democrat from Connecticut, had tried for five years to bring gun control
legislation to the Senate floor. But some of the leading advocates for
gun rights also sat on the Judiciary Committee. Roman Hruska, a Nebraska Republican, pushed to exempt rifles and shotguns from Dodd's
amendment. Dodd agreed verbally to this compromise. The committee put this proposal to a vote, but deadlocked at 6–6. It adjourned at
six o'clock eastern time. One hour later, James Earl Ray used a Remington Gamemaster deer rifle to murder Martin Luther King.[1]

King's assassination played a crucial role in the history of gun
control politics. Situating King's death within that history affords a
broader view of his life and career, and illuminates how his influence

extended well beyond the realms of civil rights and economic inequality. His legacy impacted not only the black freedom struggle, but also the nation's struggle with violence.

AFTER KING'S DEATH, Washington leaders promised to take action in his honor. But gun control was not foremost on their minds. They resolved to quickly pass the Civil Rights Act of 1968, which featured the Fair Housing Act. King had worked for open housing in his final years and hoped for the passage of federal legislation; historians have since characterized this law as "King's last victory."[2]

Johnson first proposed the housing bill in 1966. The House passed a weak version of it, but southern senators mounted a filibuster. Johnson reintroduced the bill in 1967, when senators again led a series of filibusters. In March 1968, Senate minority leader Everett Dirksen, a Republican from Illinois, facilitated a compromise to bring the bill up for a vote. The bill prohibited discrimination in the sale and rental of housing. It applied mostly to larger apartment buildings and to those property owners who received federal loans. Senate liberals then worked to strengthen the bill so that fair housing statutes would cover 80 percent of the nation's housing. The omnibus civil rights bill passed the Senate on March 11, 1968. Johnson called on the House to approve the legislation. Richard Nixon, the leading Republican presidential candidate, also expressed his support for the bill. But House minority leader Gerald Ford, a Republican from Michigan, resisted such entreaties. Ford wanted to maneuver the bill into a conference committee in an attempt to water it down. Then the shot rang out in Memphis.[3]

Many congressmen portrayed the housing bill as a monument to King. He "was a martyr to a cause," Speaker of the House John Mc-Cormack said on the night of April 4, "and that cause will be strengthened if the House concurs in the Senate civil rights bill." Twenty-one House Republicans had already drafted an appeal in support of the bill, which they planned to release on April 8. After King's death, they hurried to release the statement on April 5 and called for speedy passage of the legislation. On April 9, the day of King's funeral, legislators clamored for a vote. Representative Frank Annunzio of Illinois declared, "By [e]nsuring the prompt passage of this landmark legislation, we keep faith with Dr. King's dream of unity, nonviolence, and social justice." Some congressmen were compelled by that argument; others supported the bill as a response to the wave of urban violence. (The omnibus package also included an anti-riot bill, which imposed federal penalties on those who furnished firearms or explosives for the purpose of a riot.) On April 10, the House voted not to send the bill to a conference committee. Then came a vote on the measure itself, and the House passed the Civil Rights Act of 1968. The next day, Johnson signed it into law.[4]

The timing of events seems to suggest that King's death led directly to the bill's passage. Yet the legislation had already cleared the Senate, where it overcame a filibuster and gained the support of the powerful Everett Dirksen. At the most, King's death expedited the passage of the bill and prevented House conservatives from weakening it. The bill represented a landmark in that Congress finally took broad action against housing discrimination. But it had many flaws, including the lack of enforcement mechanisms and the failure to provide more affordable housing. It also failed to outlaw discrimination in several types of circumstances, from small boarding houses to home sales in which a broker was not used. From the perspective of many political leaders, the bill was significant primarily because it allowed them to boast that they had enacted a major civil rights law. They could argue that they had responded to King's death with meaningful legislation. Upon signing the bill, Johnson declared, "All America is outraged at the assassination of an outstanding Negro leader. . . . With this bill, the voice of justice speaks again."[5]

Some African Americans criticized the bill for its weaknesses and dismissed it as empty symbolism. Dorothy Ogle Graham, a Baltimore resident, had hoped for more forceful legislation. "This is only a token pledge that 'Whitey has at last gotten the message,'" Graham wrote in a letter to the *Baltimore Afro-American*. She hoped for legislative action on a more contentious front: "Let us now ask Congress for immediate passage . . . of the gun control bill."[6]

KING'S ASSASSINATION SET in motion a dynamic that ultimately led to the passage of the Gun Control Act later in 1968. This bill, despite its many flaws, represented a zenith in the nation's history of gun legislation. Most immediately, the assassination finally broke the stalemate in the Senate Judiciary Committee. On April 4, the Judiciary Committee had deadlocked on the compromise version of the gun amendment that would be added to the Safe Streets Act, which itself was part of an omnibus crime bill. Four senators had been absent from that meeting. Two days later, they registered their votes on the amendment. Three of the senators voted for the amendment, bringing the overall tally to 9–7 in favor and sending the bill to the Senate floor. The Senate had not considered a major piece of gun control legislation since 1938.[7]

For Thomas Dodd, that breakthrough was a long time coming. Dodd had served briefly in the FBI during the 1930s, and then as a prosecutor during the Nuremberg trials. He entered the US Senate in 1959 with a reputation as a law-and-order man. Dodd remained an ally of J. Edgar Hoover's and kept his commitment to crime fighting, but he devoted most of his energy to fighting communism. He was a staunch defender of Cold War policies and an outspoken supporter of the Vietnam War. Journalist Robert Sherrill described Dodd as a "full-fledged anti-Commie zealot." In 1965, Martin Luther King had voiced his first doubts about US policy in Vietnam. Dodd attacked King for his "arrogance," his "intrusion" into foreign affairs, his incompetence in that realm, and his "intemperate alignment with the forces of appeasement." After King's Riverside Church speech, Dodd grew more embittered in his critique. By that time, however, Dodd was the subject of a Senate investigation. In June 1967, the Senate voted to censure him for improper use of campaign funds. Dodd was embattled and embarrassed, his career sinking fast. The murder of Martin Luther King breathed into it a last bit of life.[8]

Dodd first started to explore the issue of gun control in 1961, when he served as chairman of the Juvenile Justice Subcommittee. Dodd saw it as a chance to become the public face of an important cause. Yet the politics of gun control were tricky. Dodd represented Connecticut, home to many leading gun manufacturers. He accepted donations from those companies even as he pledged to regulate their industry. Dodd tailored his initial gun control proposals so they would satisfy the Connecticut companies.[9]

After the murder of civil rights leader Medgar Evers in June 1963, President John F. Kennedy urged Dodd to bring his gun legislation to the Senate floor. Dodd worked with the National Rifle Association (NRA) and with gun manufacturers to craft a bill that they could support.* Dodd's bill required mail-order purchasers of handguns to secure affidavits that certified their age; it also restricted the importation of surplus military firearms from abroad. The ban on overseas weapons was crucial for New England manufacturers, because such imports ate into their profits. Dodd held hearings to highlight the issues, focusing on the perils of cheap mail-order handguns. The NRA backed his legislation.[10]

The assassination of President John F. Kennedy in November 1963 plunged the nation into collective agony. Many Americans were appalled when they learned how the assassin Lee Harvey Oswald had acquired his weapon. Oswald saw an ad for an Italian military rifle in the *American Rifleman*, the NRA's magazine. He ordered the rifle under a fake name, paid $21 to Klein's Sporting Goods in Chicago, and had the weapon delivered to him in Dallas. After those facts became public, popular opinion grew in favor of gun control. This spurred Dodd

---

* The federal government had been aiding the NRA for years, sending the US Army's surplus of firearms and ammunition to NRA members at bargain-basement prices.

toward further action, and also provided him with some independence from the gun lobby. He was freer to act in the name of the public good. Dodd amended his bill to include "long guns"—rifles and shotguns—in the mail-order restrictions. NRA leaders, recognizing the drift of popular sentiment in the wake of Kennedy's murder, agreed the bill should go forward. Furthermore, NRA leaders understood that if this legislation did not pass, stricter bans might soon be enacted instead. Dodd's inclusion of long guns nonetheless rankled the NRA. Its leaders privately applied pressure on senators to oppose the bill. Dodd's gun bill was routed through the Senate Commerce Committee, chaired by Senator Warren Magnuson of Washington, who represented many hunters. In August 1964, the bill died in the Commerce Committee.[11]

Dodd proposed a new bill in March 1965. Again, it was a weak piece of legislation focused mostly on mail-order handguns. President Johnson followed with a more comprehensive gun bill, of which Dodd became the chief sponsor. That bill failed to gain the approval of the NRA. Not only was Johnson's bill more wide-ranging in its regulations, but the NRA was becoming more extreme. While the NRA leadership remained in the hands of a relatively moderate old guard, the grassroots body of gun enthusiasts grew more radical, and they took direction from an increasing hyperbolic pro-gun press. The magazine *Guns & Ammo* opposed all controls on guns and stoked fears that any government action would lead ultimately to disarmament. The NRA's leadership moved in the direction of the rank and file, and by the end of 1965, there seemed no hope of compromise between the NRA and the proponents of gun control. Dodd's bill stalled in the Senate Judiciary Committee. In August 1966, a shooter murdered fifteen people at the University of Texas at Austin. Dodd urged Congress to take action on regulating firearms. He found it "tragic" that "those of us who call for stronger firearms control laws must rest our case on headlines such as these. How many times will we stand witness to such atrocities before we act?" By that point, Dodd himself had become a part of the problem. His Senate trial began in 1966, depriving him of any legitimacy. For him to sponsor a bill was to plant upon it a kiss of death. Ted Kennedy, also a member of the Senate Judiciary Committee, attempted to take the lead on gun control. But Dodd clung to the issue as his own.[12]

By 1967, the American public showed more widespread support for gun control. One of the prime reasons was racial fear. Whites feared blacks with guns, whether Black Panthers or urban rioters. In the spring of 1967, the California legislature proposed the Mulford Act. The bill would outlaw the open display of guns, and it was aimed directly at the Black Panther Party. (The NRA supported that legislation.) On May 2, 1967, the Black Panthers staged a dramatic protest against the bill: they traveled to the capitol in Sacramento, climbed the statehouse steps while clutching their guns, and entered the building. The Panthers found their way to the assembly chamber and stood in the back of the viewing area. They began to attract a horde of cameramen and soon gained the attention of the lawmakers. Finally, twenty-five Panthers were arrested for disturbing the peace. The legislature soon passed the Mulford Act, and Governor Ronald Reagan signed it into law.[13]

That summer, riots ripped through dozens of American cities. In some instances, snipers shot at policemen and firemen. These events convinced even more white Americans of the need for tighter gun regulation. And in April 1968, King's death—and just as critically, the violent uprisings in many cities—generated support for gun laws. In this atmosphere, the Senate Judiciary Committee finally voted to approve Dodd's compromise amendment.

LESS THAN FORTY-EIGHT hours after King's assassination, members of the NRA descended on Boston for their annual convention. Ted Kennedy was scheduled to address the convention on Palm Sunday. At the last minute, NRA leaders decided that Kennedy would deliver his speech to a private meeting of the national board rather than to the general membership. In the wake of King's death, NRA leaders appeared far less comfortable with hosting a speech by an advocate of gun control. Kennedy promptly canceled the address. Twenty thousand members gathered that week at the Sheraton Boston Hotel. In the exhibit hall, some vendors even hawked the Italian rifles known as "Kennedy specials"—distastefully named after their use in the assassination of President John F. Kennedy. NRA leaders railed against the pending Dodd amendment, notwithstanding the fact that the measure exempted rifles. On April 9, the association sent a letter to its 900,000 members, warning that Dodd's legislation could eventually end "the private ownership of all guns." The NRA urged members to make known their opposition. Many congressmen reported a deluge of mail that ran strongly against the Dodd bill.[14]

In response to the violence of early April, gun sales spiked. This trend had been growing steadily through the decade. Between 1963 and 1968, sales of handguns quadrupled in the United States, and sales of rifles and shotguns doubled. Particularly after the urban riots of 1967 and 1968, many more Americans purchased guns. For example, Detroit issued four times as many handgun permits in 1968 as it did in 1965. In the Virginia suburbs surrounding Washington, DC, handgun sales doubled during April 1968 alone. America was awash in guns.[15]

Despite the increase in gun sales and the NRA's lobbying campaign, King's assassination was beginning to change the larger political environment. Dodd linked King's murder with the broader epidemic of violence in America and with the need for gun control. "I hope that the folly of violence is now apparent to all Americans," Dodd said on the Senate floor. "I hope that this brutal, senseless killing will shock the Congress into backing me in this fight to take the guns from the hands of assassins and murderers." Other senators recognized the seriousness of America's gun problem. On April 8, Senator Daniel Brewster of Maryland declared that King's assassination "brutally dramatized the need for controls on the sale of weapons." He noted the "cruel irony" that the Senate Judiciary Committee had failed to approve such reforms on the very day of King's death. Many Americans became more public in their support for gun regulations. As *The Nation* editorialized on April 22, "The most practical memorial to Dr. King—and to

Kennedy—would be a tight gun-control bill, passed immediately." A Harris poll showed that 71 percent of Americans favored tighter restrictions on gun sales. Even in households with guns, which accounted for about half of all American homes, 65 percent expressed support for stricter gun regulations. The editors of the *Boston Globe* anticipated that on a terrain altered by King's death, the NRA would "get its first real comeuppance." In a letter to the *Boston Globe* on April 12, Jewish leader Julius Bernstein asked what other citizens were wondering: "How many assassinations must we have before the Congress will pass gun control legislation?"[16]

James Eastland, a Democrat from Mississippi and the chairman of the Senate Judiciary Committee, tried to thwart such legislation. Eastland was also an NRA supporter. He called a surprise meeting of the committee for the morning of April 24, when he informed the senators that he had not yet reported the Dodd amendment to the floor. That was because Roman Hruska had expressed some confusion about the committee's April 4 meeting. Hruska maintained that the written text of the amendment did not match the verbal description Dodd had offered during the meeting. Dodd first learned of this new controversy on April 17. He then agreed to meet with Hruska on April 23; Senator Joseph Tydings of Maryland, another advocate of gun control, also attended. Dodd and Tydings explained that the written text was in fact the same as the verbal compromise, and that all of the other committee members understood the terms of the original vote. But Hruska remained unconvinced. He advised Eastland to schedule a committee meeting for April 24, presumably to hold a new vote. Dodd and his allies were livid. Dodd worried that perhaps the gun rights forces had convinced a member of the committee to switch his vote. "I know what is going on," Dodd said. "The man from the rifle association has mounted a massive lobbying campaign against this bill."[17]

The NRA had another fierce ally on the Senate Judiciary Committee: Strom Thurmond of South Carolina. At the April 24 meeting, Thurmond suggested that the committee should simply vote on the

Safe Streets Act without any gun amendment attached. Dodd replied that a crime bill without any gun regulations was no crime bill at all. "You can't talk about a safe streets bill ... and leave out any provision with respect to guns. We have had two major assassinations in this country. It is ironic that we [were] sitting here within the hour of the assassination of King. And we had the assassination of President Kennedy. And the American people, as you told me, are overwhelmingly in favor of it." Yet Roman Hruska would not budge. He proposed a substitute gun bill that was weaker than Dodd's compromise amendment. Dodd saw an opening. If Hruska and Eastland wanted to consider new legislation, then he too would offer a new amendment. Now that the nation had absorbed the effects of King's assassination, Dodd realized he could strengthen the legislation. "May I say, Senator Hruska, that at the time I agreed to that I would have agreed to anything in order to give the Senate an opportunity to work its will ... I think the situation has changed, and more and more people are coming to recognize that this is right. And I don't intend to retreat from it." Hruska considered this suggestion and then finally gave in. At the end of a contentious meeting, the Senate Judiciary Committee voted to report the Dodd amendment to the Senate floor—eighteen days after it had voted to do exactly the same thing.[18]

On May 16, the bill came up for debate in the Senate. The Dodd amendment banned mail-order sales of handguns as well as interstate sales of handguns, and it prohibited the sale of handguns to minors or criminals. It also outlawed the importation of surplus military firearms, except sporting weapons. Gun control supporters attempted to strengthen the regulations. Ted Kennedy proposed an amendment to include rifles and shotguns in the mail-order restrictions. Kennedy had a profound personal stake in the matter of mail-order rifles. But that did not impress a majority of senators. Kennedy's amendment failed by a vote of 53–29. Dodd offered another amendment, slightly weaker, which was defeated by a similar margin. As a last-ditch effort, Senator Jacob Javits of New York proposed an amendment that prohibited mail-order long guns, but with a significant qualifier. It would allow long gun sales if the purchasers filed sworn affidavits; Roman Hruska had previously offered this type of formula for the sale of handguns. Dodd spoke in favor of Javits's amendment. "There is absolutely no justification for excluding from the federal law the weapons which have been used in this the age of snipers to gun down a President, to sustain rioting in our cities and to take the life of Dr. Martin Luther King." But Javits's amendment fared no better than Kennedy's or Dodd's. In the end, the original Dodd amendment remained attached to the Safe Streets Act. "We hoped to do better, but I'm glad we got this much," Dodd said afterward. "At least we've approved the first gun control statute in 30 years."[19]

One voice was conspicuously absent from the day's debate: that of New York's junior senator, Robert Kennedy. He was on the campaign trail at the time, mounting a spirited bid for the Democratic presidential nomination. King's death had shaken Kennedy and shaped his last political crusade. Subsequently, Robert Kennedy's own assassination would help to spur the passage of even more expansive gun control legislation.

IN THE FIRST week of March, after months of vacillation, Kennedy decided to run for president. Then on March 12, Senator Eugene McCarthy won a stunning 42 percent of the votes in the New Hampshire primary—a devastating result for President Lyndon Johnson. Four days later, Kennedy officially announced his candidacy. He threw himself into the campaign with abandon and visited sixteen states during the last two weeks of March. He needed to make up significant ground. Many of the antiwar voters were already committed to Eugene McCarthy; young canvassers cut their hair and shaved to make themselves "Clean for Gene." Johnson kept the backing of party leaders and working-class whites, many of whom would eventually transfer their support to various establishment stand-in candidates after Johnson announced, on March 31, that he would not run for reelection.

As Kennedy began his campaign, he found his most devoted groups of voters among the party's racial minorities: Latinos and African Americans.[20]

Black voters' allegiance to Kennedy stemmed in large part from their affection for his brother. Although President John F. Kennedy was slow to embrace the civil rights movement, embrace it he finally did. Many African Americans perceived him as a fighter for the cause of black freedom, and Robert Kennedy benefitted from his brother's reputation. Benjamin Bell, treasurer of the Radical Action Program in Indianapolis, noted in 1968 that his group was generally unimpressed with the Democratic Party. But "we dig Kennedy. His brother's image still lingers with us." Robert Kennedy was one of the only white politicians who enjoyed a degree of legitimacy among African Americans.[21]

John Lewis was drawn to the promise of Kennedy's candidacy. Lewis, a former head of the Student Nonviolent Coordinating Committee who still favored nonviolence, felt that by 1968 the more militant black freedom struggle had little place for him. He was compelled by Kennedy's promises to oppose the Vietnam War, to devise policies to help the poor, and to unite blacks and whites. Lewis volunteered to work for Kennedy and found himself dispatched quickly to the campaign trail. The battle would be joined in Indiana, which held its primary on May 7.[22]

Lewis arrived in Indianapolis late in March, working with the campaign staff and forging connections with local African Americans. He helped to organize a rally in the heart of the city's black neighborhood, scheduled for the night of April 4. More than 1,000 people, about three-quarters of them African Americans, gathered on a basketball court outside the Broadway Christian Center. They stood in the cold and the wind, waiting for Kennedy. One hour before the candidate was due to arrive, Kennedy aide Walter Sheridan rushed up to John Lewis and told him that King had been shot in Memphis. "At that moment I had no feeling," Lewis remembered. "I was obliterated, blown beyond any sensations whatsoever . . . I just stood there, not moving, not thinking."

Sheridan hustled through the crowd, looking for the local black leaders who would be sharing the stage with Kennedy. Sheridan ushered them into a nearby school and informed them of the shooting. They all agreed that the rally should go on as planned. Lewis and the other campaign workers concurred. "Kennedy has to speak," said Lewis, "for his own sake and for the sake of these people." They could not just turn the crowd loose into that awful night.[23]

It was Kennedy's first full day of campaigning in Indiana. He spoke at Ball State University in Muncie in the early evening. At the Delaware County Airport he received the news that King had been shot; when Kennedy's plane landed in Indianapolis, he learned King was dead. Kennedy "seemed to shrink back," recalled *Newsweek* reporter John Lindsay, "as though struck physically." Kennedy put his hands to his face and uttered, "Oh, God. When is this violence going to stop?" Even before King's shooting, Indianapolis Mayor Richard Lugar wanted the Kennedy campaign to cancel the event out of fear that it would attract a violent black crowd. Now, Indianapolis's chief of police advised Kennedy to stay away from the rally site. But John Lewis, Walter Sheridan, and other staffers at the Broadway Christian Center held firm in their belief that Kennedy needed to address the crowd. Of all the responses to Martin Luther King's assassination, none is more legendary than the speech Kennedy delivered.[24]

Adam Walinsky, a Kennedy speechwriter, pulled up to the rally site several minutes before Kennedy arrived. He beheld a "phantasmagoric scene." A flatbed truck had been purposed as a speakers' platform. A couple of floodlights illuminated the stage, while the throng of people milled in the darkness. Kennedy arrived and climbed aboard the truck, a black overcoat his only defense against the elements.[25]

According to the popular tale, Kennedy informed the audience of King's death. That is partially true. On the periphery of the crowd, several groups of people had gathered around transistor radios to track the reports from Memphis. Some had walked over to the Broadway Christian Center *after* they heard the reports of King's death. The Ten

Percenters, a local group of militants, roamed through the neighborhood in an effort to find violent recruits. But many in the crowd, particularly those who stood near the speakers' platform, had not yet heard the news. Kennedy asked people to put down their signs and banners and told the audience he would be brief. "I have some very sad news for all of you, and, I think, sad news for all of our fellow citizens, and people who love peace all over the world, and that is that Martin Luther King was shot and killed tonight in Memphis, Tennessee." The crowd let out an anguished moan. Kennedy spoke without notes for six minutes. At such a terrible hour, he ventured, "it's perhaps well to ask what kind of a nation we are and what direction we want to move in." He understood that African Americans might be moved toward revenge. But there was a better way. "We can make an effort, as Martin Luther King did, to understand, and to comprehend, and replace that violence, that stain of bloodshed that has spread across our land, with an effort to understand, compassion and love."[26]

For the first time in public, Kennedy reflected on his brother's death. Speaking directly to African Americans who felt tempted by hatred and violence, he confided, "I would only say that I can also feel in my own heart the same kind of feeling. I had a member of my family killed, but he was killed by a white man." He urged the audience to "go beyond these rather difficult times." From memory he quoted Aeschylus: "'Even in our sleep, pain which cannot forget / falls drop by drop upon the heart / until in our own despair, against our will / comes wisdom through the awful grace of God.'" John Lewis understood what he had just witnessed. Kennedy "never talked about the murder of his brother," Lewis noted. "To do it that night was an incredibly powerful and connective and emotionally honest gesture. He stripped himself down. He made it personal. He made it real." One black man in the audience recalled that Kennedy "had tears in his eyes, I saw it, he felt it man, he cried." Kennedy showed his wound to the crowd, and shared his intimate knowledge of what it was like to persist in the world amid such pain.[27]

Senator Robert F. Kennedy addressed a crowd in Indianapolis on the night of Martin Luther King's assassination. Before a largely African American audience, Kennedy spoke about the need for peace and racial healing in America—and asked the crowd to "say a prayer for the country." Indianapolis was one of the few major cities that did not erupt in violence that night.

Indianapolis Recorder Collection, Indiana Historical Society

He delivered a final appeal for peace and compassion. "What we need in the United States is not hatred . . . is not violence or lawlessness, but is love and wisdom and compassion toward one another." As members of the crowd exhibited grief, rage, and disbelief, he offered guidance. "So I ask you tonight to return home, to say a prayer for the family of Martin Luther King—yeah, it's true—but more importantly to say a prayer for our own country." He reached back again to ancient Greece for some last pieces of wisdom. "And let's dedicate ourselves to what the Greeks wrote so many years ago: to tame the savageness of man and to make gentle the life of this world. Let us dedicate ourselves to that, and say a prayer for our country and for our people." As Kennedy came down from the flatbed truck, people stretched out their hands to touch him. Mary Evans, a white member of the crowd, felt as if Kennedy had "laid his hands upon the audience." Kennedy soothed their anger. Said one member of the Ten Percenters, "We went there for trouble." But "after he spoke we couldn't get nowhere." There was no violence in Indianapolis that night.[28]

Kennedy returned to his hotel, flopped on the bed, and cried. Then he called Coretta Scott King to express his condolences and to offer his help. He advised Coretta that she would need additional phone lines at her home, and he promised to have them installed. He also offered to charter a jet to take her to Memphis. Kennedy knew what a grieving family might need.[29]

Walinsky and Jeff Greenfield worked late into the night to craft his next speech. He would deliver it the following day in Cleveland. Kennedy was scheduled to stop first at the city's Public Square, where 10,000 people—equal numbers of blacks and whites among them—had gathered for a memorial to King. He decided to skip the large outdoor event for safety reasons, and he headed to his next venue, the City Club, where a crowd of 2,000 waited.[30]

Kennedy's speech was a meditation on violence in America. He asked, "What has violence ever accomplished? What has it ever created? No martyr's cause has ever been stilled by his assassin's bullet.

No wrongs have ever been righted by riots and civil disorders." Kennedy not only condemned the assassins; he also criticized those who fomented "civil disorders." Yet Kennedy realized the urban riots had their roots in a scourge of poverty that policy makers had failed to effectively confront. He spoke of "the violence of institutions; indifference and inaction and slow decay. This is the violence that afflicts the poor, that poisons relations between men because their skin is different colors. This is a slow destruction of a child by hunger, and schools without books and homes without heat in the winter." Kennedy went on to indict America's jingoistic foreign policy and faulted a populace that "calmly accepted" news reports of civilian slaughter in distant lands. He lamented a culture that glorified violence on television and movie screens. And he bemoaned the lack of any significant regulations on firearms. "We make it easy for men of all shades of sanity to acquire whatever weapons and ammunition they desire." Kennedy ended on an uplifting note, however, emphasizing the common bonds that linked humanity. "Surely we can begin to work a little harder to bind up the wounds among us and to become in our own hearts brothers and countrymen once again." Kennedy offered himself as the one who would begin to heal the nation and make it whole. The Cleveland audience rose to its feet in a standing ovation, as tears flowed freely.[31]

In this speech, Kennedy articulated the themes on which he would focus over the next two months. He would continue to rail against violence, not only in the guise of assassins with easy access to guns, but also among urban rioters. He also continued to speak eloquently of the injuries of poverty, the persistence of racial injustice, and the urgent need for the races to come together.

King's assassination created a climate in which Kennedy's message would resonate more deeply. Before King's death, many liberal Democrats were torn between McCarthy and Kennedy. Daniel Patrick Moynihan, a Harvard professor who had previously served in the Johnson administration, was one who supported Eugene McCarthy at first. But after King's death, his thoughts shifted. Moynihan confessed that Kennedy "has a far better chance of building the bridge between white and black that will have to be built if the nation is not indeed to become two nations." After King's assassination, Kennedy's claim to the Democratic nomination became "irresistibly strong."[32]

King's death further drove Kennedy and African Americans into one another's arms. Kennedy was already the candidate of the ghettos and the barrios. After King's death, he embraced that political identity more fully. King's murder "enabled Kennedy to glimpse the deeper roots of America's internal disease," thought journalist Jack Newfield, "and to imagine himself as the possible healer of that disease." Kennedy stopped talking quite so much about Vietnam, and he began to speak more forcefully about poverty, racial inequality, and violence. Kennedy came to see that his career "also belonged to the dispossessed who cheered him with such hopes and voted for him in such numbers." To Newfield, "it was only King's passing that crystallized this feeling in the ghettoes, that Kennedy was now their last friend left." Many of those who had placed their hopes in King would transfer those hopes onto the shoulders of Robert Kennedy. On a flatbed truck in Indianapolis, Kennedy began to bear that burden.[33]

Kennedy attended King's funeral in Atlanta, then returned to Indiana on April 10. He spoke to a crowd that morning at Fort Wayne's Scottish Rite Temple. He called King's death "one of those huge events that signals a turning point in our country's history." Amid a wave of urban riots, America confronted "the most terrible and urgent domestic crisis to face this nation since the Civil War." Americans had reached a crossroads. They needed either to work together for racial understanding, or face worsening tensions and perpetual unrest. "The choice is up to us," Kennedy said, whether King's death will act as "a summons to battle or to the meeting of reconciliation and peace." Whites needed to honor the "simple claims" of African Americans for equality of opportunity. The white majority had to make it known by its attitudes, and leaders needed to inscribe in the nation's policies, that African Americans "are part of this country." Otherwise, the nation would break in two.[34]

Kennedy continued to Terre Haute later in the day, where journalist David Halberstam started to travel with the campaign. Halberstam also believed King's death marked a turning point for the country, but for Halberstam the change was much more ominous. He glimpsed not a grieving nation but a nasty one. Whites in Terre Haute had shifted their hatred, rather than their hopes, from King to Kennedy. Protesters lined the streets from the airport; several people yelled, "Coon-catcher, coon-catcher." Such bitterness, on the day after King's funeral, unsettled Halberstam. "White America, by and large, was not mourning Dr. King, rather it was frightened by the violence which took place in the wake of the assassination, and it felt that the politicians were too permissive." In the aftermath of King's killing, African Americans were enraged and heartbroken. They were sick of white America's promises and repelled by its entrenched racism. In turn, white Americans seethed at black radicalism and cowered before images of black violence. Halberstam saw evidence of a country that had grown more vicious in the days since King's death. "What I remember about that day and the ones to follow was how exposed the raw nerve of the society had become, how anxious people had become, alternately angry and impassioned." King's death thrust that anger to the surface.[35]

Many white Americans long perceived Kennedy as cold-hearted, conniving, and "ruthless." He had been viewed as John F. Kennedy's hatchet man. James Reston of the *New York Times* characterized the opposition to Kennedy as "irrational" and "almost chemical." On the campaign trail in 1968, Kennedy absorbed a vitriol made ever more intense by King's killing and the urban riots that followed.[36]

He confronted scornful crowds throughout the Hoosier State. At the Indiana University Medical Center on April 26, Jack Newfield described the audience of medical students as "rows of satisfied WASP crew cuts." Kennedy spoke about expanding Social Security and improving health facilities in poor urban areas. An audience member demanded, "Where are we going to get the money to pay for all these new programs?" Kennedy replied, "From you!" Undeterred by the hostile crowd, even energized by it, Kennedy spoke passionately about the conditions in black neighborhoods and on Native American reservations. "You sit here as white medical students," he charged, "while black people carry the burden of the fighting in Vietnam." He would continue to talk about the poor and the disempowered at future campaign stops, and refused to pander to his audiences.[37]

Except when it came to law and order. Kennedy reminded white voters of his many years in law enforcement, and he decried the urban riots. Yet he always paired his criticism of rioters with calls for racial justice. While this did not seem to compel a groundswell of support among whites, neither did it turn off his base of black voters. It is a central part of Kennedy's mystique that he forged a coalition of working-class whites with African Americans. Indeed, he seemed to be the only leader who could bridge that divide. To judge by the election returns in the Indiana primary, he was just beginning to stitch together that coalition.[38]

Indiana Democrats went to the polls on May 7 and delivered a victory to Kennedy. He finished with 42 percent of the vote, compared with 31 percent for Indiana governor Roger Branigin (the stand-in for the party establishment), and 27 percent for Eugene McCarthy. Ronald Steel, a Kennedy critic, later described Kennedy's constituency as a mix of "blacks, Hispanics, some blue-collar ethnics, and Camelot sentimentalists." Kennedy won 83 percent of the votes among African Americans in Indiana. Among whites, he won an estimated 37 percent of the votes, a respectable figure in a three-way race. Kennedy demonstrated that one month after King's assassination, in a time of racial violence and smoldering tensions in the cities, a white candidate could win the hearts, minds, and votes of African Americans. And perhaps he could win over racial minorities without entirely forfeiting white support. He said to his campaign director Larry O'Brien, "I've proved I can really be a leader of a broad spectrum. I can be a bridge between blacks and whites without stepping back from my positions." One state primary was not enough to "prove" Kennedy's claim, but it was sufficient to raise the prospect. That is why his candidacy stood out as unique at the time, why so many Americans still hold the memory of his campaign so dear, and why the hopes it raised were so enchanting.[39]

The battle for the Democratic nomination moved westward. Kennedy won in Nebraska before the candidates headed to Oregon, which was a suburban and rural state with a small number of racial minorities. There, Kennedy's speeches about urban poverty and racial justice would ring hollow.

On May 23, five days before Oregon's primary, the United States Senate voted to pass the omnibus crime bill. It included the Safe Streets Act, with Dodd's amendment on gun control.[40]

Kennedy had grown accustomed to speaking his mind before hostile crowds, and he brought that spirit with him to Roseburg, Oregon, on May 27. One of his staffers handed him a fact sheet about the area. It was a lumber town of 15,000 people where the most important issues were log exports, dams, and gun control. The sheet read, "LOCAL SHERIFF CAUTIONS THERE MAY BE AN AIRPORT DEMONSTRATION BY OPPONENTS OF GUN CONTROL LEGISLATION." In the gun-loving terrain of the West, Kennedy boldly waded into the debate.[41]

He proceeded to the steps of the Douglas County Courthouse, where he spoke before a crowd of 1,500. Some hoisted signs that read, "PROTECT YOUR RIGHT TO KEEP AND BEAR ARMS." Kennedy stepped to the microphone and confronted the issue. "I see signs about the guns. I'm wondering if any of you would like to come and explain." After a period of silence, a Sutherlin resident named Bud Schoon came forward. Schoon was a Republican candidate for local office and director of the Association to Preserve Our Right to Keep and Bear Arms. "The signs refer to the Senate bill," Schoon explained, "and we think it's a backdoor bill for the registration of guns and it would let the Supreme Court make the final decision." Kennedy understood that the gun legislation was unpopular in Oregon, that the John Birch Society had spread lies about it, and local radio stations had railed against the gun laws. "If we are going to talk about this legislation, let's talk about it honestly and not say that it does something that it does not do," Kennedy reasoned. "All this legislation does is keep guns from criminals and the demented and those too young. With all the violence and murder and killings we've had in the United States, I think you will agree that we must keep firearms from people who have no business with guns or rifles." The jeering crowd certainly did not agree. One man shouted, "They'll get them [guns] anyway." Another yelled, "Nazi Germany began with the registration of guns." Kennedy pleaded with the crowd, explaining that the bill said nothing about the registration of guns. He tried to reassure the audience. "So protect your right to keep and bear arms. The legislation doesn't stop you unless you're a criminal."* The gun owners of Roseburg were unmoved.[42]

While Kennedy expressed his support for gun control, McCarthy studiously avoided the issue. McCarthy would skip all of the 1968 votes on gun control. In June 1968, McCarthy claimed he favored the regulation of "heavy arms," but that gun control legislation should not be passed "under panic conditions." Gun control was one factor that helped to lift McCarthy to victory in the Oregon primary. He defeated Kennedy by a margin of 45 percent to 39 percent.[43]

The big prize of the primary season loomed—and California seemed more like Kennedy country. Kennedy stood with Latino farm workers in the Central Valley and met with African Americans in Watts. Antonio Orendain, a cofounder of the United Farm Workers union, called Kennedy "a beacon of hope for the farm worker." James Thomas Jackson recalled Kennedy's visit to the Watts Writers' Workshop Los Angeles Underground. "I told him he was a 'boss cat,'" said Jackson, "and that we dug his brother, also." On May 29, the day after the Oregon primary, Kennedy's motorcade rolled through Los Angeles as he stopped to glad-hand with citizens black, white, and Latino. He campaigned everywhere from strawberry festivals in Orange County

---

* In 2015, Roseburg, Oregon, would appear in national headlines again when a gunman murdered nine people at a community college.

to the streets of San Francisco's Chinatown. On June 4, California voters went to the polls. Some majority-black and majority-Latino districts set records for voter turnout. Kennedy's supporters gathered at the Ambassador Hotel to wait for the results. Word of a Kennedy victory thrilled the late-night crowd. The final results would show that Kennedy defeated McCarthy by a margin of 46 percent to 42 percent. At eleven thirty, the crowd began to chant, "We Want Kennedy!" (And "We Want [Cesar] Chavez!") Kennedy appeared in the hotel ballroom and delivered a jubilant victory speech. Then, minutes after midnight, another shot rang out.[44]

Kennedy became the latest martyr in a decade haunted by them. His assassination traumatized the entire nation in a way Martin Luther King's had not. Many white Americans felt an emotional connection with Kennedy that was lacking in their feelings toward King. And Kennedy's death hit with such shattering force because it followed so closely after King's. In the days between April 4 and June 5, the divisions in the country widened and the mood grew even angrier. After the shooting of Kennedy, a deep melancholy enveloped the country.

Americans woke to a dreadful dawn. Many thought immediately of the carnage in Memphis, and flashed back five years to John F. Kennedy's assassination. There was "the Kennedy before," said one woman in Harlem, "the King in between, and the Kennedy after." In the memories of so many Americans, the assassinations of King and Robert Kennedy often blended together, constituting one terrible moment. To black Americans, the killings had a clear racial component. As one man on 125th Street in Harlem put it, "It seems like every time a man speaks up for black people they knock him off." For Andrew Young, the assassinations of King and Kennedy represented the death of the Second Reconstruction—and the possible beginning of a sort of Second Redemption. He feared that racism would grip the country in the 1970s as it had in the 1870s. "A country can't afford to lose, you know, three men like Robert Kennedy and John F. Kennedy and Martin King. It takes too long to build people like that."[45]

In many minds, Kennedy had represented the last best hope for an interracial America. That light no longer flickered. In the space King had long inhabited, and then Kennedy, there was only darkness.

KENNEDY'S DEATH GENERATED added momentum for gun control laws. President Johnson addressed the nation on the night of June 5 to grieve for Robert Kennedy. He also announced that he would appoint a panel to study the problem of violence in America, and would order the Secret Service to provide protection for all major presidential candidates. Johnson demanded further action on gun control: "Let the Congress pass laws to bring the insane traffic in guns to a halt." The following day, the House of Representatives passed the omnibus crime bill.[46]

Some leading liberals denounced that legislation. The editors of the *New York Times* called it "a monstrous bill" and urged Johnson to veto the legislation. The Omnibus Crime Control and Safe Streets Act included several provisions to expand police powers, increase the government's wiretapping authority, and restrict the rights of the accused. Johnson also made clear that its gun regulations were far too weak. "This halfway measure is not enough," said Johnson. The bill included "watered-down" gun restrictions. "Weapons of destruction can be purchased by mail as easily as baskets of fruit or cartons of cigarettes." Johnson beseeched Congress to include long guns in the prohibitions on gun sales. He promised to propose a series of specific amendments by the following week. "Let us now spell out our grief in collective action."[47]

The movements for gun control and gun rights grew in tandem—both of them feeding off of the violent 1960s, the string of political assassinations, the rebellions in city streets—with each movement responding to the other. Harold Glassen, the president of the NRA, insisted that additional gun controls were unnecessary. But public opinion polls showed that the vast majority of Americans favored stronger gun restrictions. Many white Americans had undergone a three-stage evolution in the span of two months. The murder of King further opened their eyes to the problem of gun violence. The urban riots put them on edge. And the assassination of Robert Kennedy wrenched their collective heart, finally moving some of them to action.[48]

The forces for gun control began to mobilize more powerfully than before. Nearly every major newspaper and church organization called for more gun regulations, as did most big-city mayors and police chiefs, the American Bar Association, and J. Edgar Hoover's FBI. After Robert Kennedy's murder, ordinary Americans also expressed more passionately their views on gun control. Letters poured in to newspapers. "The only practical solution is a total ban on firearms for all but law enforcement officers," wrote Alexander Markovich of Ardsley, New York. "Deadly weapons have no useful function in a truly civilized society." James Lincoln, a student at Kent State, agreed. He wrote to the *New York Times*, "The shooting of Senator Robert F. Kennedy following so closely after the murder of Dr. Martin Luther King Jr. . . . must force the realization upon the United States that individual citizens must not be allowed to bear firearms indiscriminately." Indeed, that realization was dawning on many Americans. A group of citizens formed the first major organization dedicated to gun control: the National Council for a Responsible Firearms Policy.[49]

One week after Kennedy's assassination, Johnson offered a bill that would prohibit mail-order and interstate sales of long guns, outlaw the sale of long guns to minors, and restrict interstate sales of ammunition. Dodd introduced the bill to the Senate. "Only in this way," Dodd said in a lengthy speech on June 11, "can we move to disarm the many hundreds of thousands, and perhaps millions of irresponsible elements who have been able to obtain arms for themselves under the weak gun controls that have heretofore existed." Dodd also offered a bill of his own that called for the registration of all firearms, a measure that was seen before (and since) as politically impossible. Senator Joseph Tydings of Maryland attempted to outdo both Dodd and Johnson.

Tydings proposed a bill that not only mandated the registration of all guns, but also required a license for the purchase of firearms and ammunition. Of course, this was all too much for the NRA. Dodd himself had uttered the dreaded word: "disarm." In response, Harold Glassen unfurled his most apocalyptic language. He beheld "a strange and masochistic spectacle" in which "tens of thousands of normally proud and level-headed Americans" suddenly found themselves "begging the Federal Government to take from them by force one of their basic civil rights." In apparent seriousness, he even compared the proponents of gun control to the leaders of Nazi Germany.[50]

President Johnson hoped that the shock of Kennedy's assassination would push Congress to support stronger gun laws. But Senator Tydings knew it would take more than that. "Nothing is going to move the Congress . . . except a most tremendous outpouring of demands from this country." Tydings added, "We are not going to get a bill through the Senate unless the people themselves get on the telephone and get a hold of their senators and say 'we demand action.'" Many individuals did precisely that.[51]

On Friday, June 7, Senate majority leader Mike Mansfield had expressed doubt that the Kennedy assassination would change the political calculus on gun control. He believed the Senate would continue to oppose any further gun regulations. Then came the deluge of mail. No legislator was immune. Senator Charles Percy of Illinois reported that between the assassinations of King and Kennedy, he received some 3,500 letters regarding gun control, a vast majority of them opposed to stronger gun legislation. But on June 10 alone, his office received 1,300 letters that favored stronger regulations. In the week after Kennedy's death, Senator Harrison Williams of New Jersey received 6,000 letters advocating stronger gun laws—the most mail he received on any matter, in such a short period of time, during his nine years in the Senate. Joseph Tydings received 5,000 letters in five days, almost all of them supporting stronger controls. Tydings was an obvious magnet for such letters, as he had offered a forceful gun control bill. It was clear enough how Tydings would vote. But the fate of any such bill rested in the hands of others: western senators who represented the nation's hotbeds of hunting.[52]

Those legislators also received a blitz of mail in support of gun control. Nevada senator Alan Bible's mail had previously opposed gun control by a margin of about 9–1. After Kennedy's assassination, his mail ran 3–1 in favor of gun regulations. Some Democratic senators from hunting states had compiled liberal voting records on virtually every issue except gun control. This list included George McGovern of South Dakota, Gaylord Nelson and William Proxmire of Wisconsin, Warren Magnuson of Washington, and majority leader Mike Mansfield himself, who represented Montana. Proxmire reported that his mail ran 12–1 in favor of tighter controls. Nelson called it "a real avalanche" in support of gun control. McGovern, for the first time in his Senate career, called for stronger gun regulations. By June 12, Mansfield guessed that the Johnson administration's suggested restrictions on long guns had the votes to pass the Senate. Everett Dirksen's shifting positions illuminated the chamber's transformation. On June 10, Dirksen stated, "There is enough gun legislation on the books now." Three days later Dirksen said, "If they want long guns covered, I have no objection." Warren Magnuson went further. On June 14, he told the Senate he was prepared to accept not only a mail-order ban on long guns but also provisions for the registration and licensing of all firearms. In a matter of days, the climate on Capitol Hill had changed completely.[53]

Retailers also responded to the pressure of a newly energized public. Some of them decided voluntarily to halt their sales of guns and ammunition. Sears, Roebuck & Company, the largest merchandiser in the country and the leading retailer of guns, had taken such steps in May—before Kennedy's assassination—and effectively ended all mail-order sales. Montgomery Ward followed suit. Two weeks after Kennedy's death, Jordan Marsh, New England's largest department store, announced it would no longer carry guns or ammunition. In Columbus, Ohio, the Schottenstein department stores informed patrons that they would sell guns and ammunition only in the month before hunting season. Kaufman's Surplus in midtown Manhattan removed all firearms from its shelves. Modell's required a police department permit for all gun sales. Even the nation's leading gun manufacturers began to support stricter regulations on the sale of firearms. The three top producers of guns and ammunition—Remington, Winchester, and Savage—all advised Congress to restrict mail-order sales of long guns. They calculated that passage of a mail-order ban at that moment might forestall a stronger law in the future.[54]

Lyndon Johnson delayed action on the Omnibus Crime Control and Safe Streets Act for as long as he could. He finally signed the bill into law on June 19, hours before the deadline. After his own "searching examination," Johnson concluded that the bill held "more good than bad." Five days later, Johnson gave a major address on guns. He noted that the United States stood "alone among the modern nations of the world" in its lax gun laws. Johnson then called for the registration of all firearms as well as federal licensing of every citizen who wished to own a gun. Whereas the Tydings proposal allowed states to register firearms, Johnson insisted on a federal registry. He noted that Americans dutifully registered possessions like cars, boats, and dogs, and obtained licenses for fishing, hunting, and driving. Lethal weapons needed to be regulated at least as well as vehicles or canines.[55]

The summer of gun control began to repair Thomas Dodd's reputation. He appeared regularly on network television, introduced the administration's bills in the Senate, and delivered crusading speeches. "I guess the gun-control business has done me some good," Dodd conceded. Dodd promised to stand for reelection in 1970. The deaths of Kennedy and King seemed to have resurrected his career.[56]

As the summer wore on and the assassinations began to fade into memory, gun rights groups found their footing. In Washington and at home, gun rights activists confronted Dodd. The Connecticut legislature was considering a strict gun registration law. On July 16, the Judiciary Committee of the Connecticut General Assembly held a public hearing. Gun rights supporters dominated both the morning and afternoon sessions. They testified about the dangers of gun registration, invoking examples from Nazi Germany and the Soviet Union. William Wallace, an executive at Winchester Repeating Arms, argued against the registration law and likened it to Prohibition. The crowd whipped itself into a frenzy before Thomas Dodd entered the legislative chamber to a chorus of boos. The audience interrupted Dodd throughout his presentation. He assured the hecklers, "Nobody is going to take your guns away from you." Audience members shouted, "That's just the first step!" Dodd finally lashed out in frustration. "Eighty or 90 percent of the decent people in America want this law, and your bad manners can't prevent it. You are the gun nuts." The hostility in Hartford reflected the fact that pro-gun organizations had regrouped and launched a counteroffensive.[57]

NRA members showered their congressmen with mail. That effort emboldened the gun lobby's allies on Capitol Hill. Strom Thurmond, James Eastland, and Roman Hruska worked to stall Johnson's proposed gun legislation in the Senate Judiciary Committee. Thurmond targeted the sections of the bill that dealt with gun registration. But Tydings refused to allow the bill out of the committee without those sections. The back-and-forth continued through the summer.[58]

A gun bill eventually made it to the Senate floor, but without any provisions that pertained to the registration of guns or the licensing of gun owners. Congress finally passed a multipronged bill called the Gun Control Act. It banned interstate mail-order sales of all firearms and ammunition. (It superseded the regulations in the Safe Streets Act.) It also prohibited the sale of firearms to certain classes of citizens, including felons, drug addicts, and minors. In addition, it required dealers to keep a record of the names and addresses of those to whom they sold ammunition.* It charged the Bureau of Alcohol, Tobacco, and

---

* This provision was doomed from the start. The federal government quickly backed away from requiring dealers to report such information.

Firearms with enforcing the new regulations. Johnson signed the legislation on October 22. This was the most expansive gun control legislation in the nation's history. Yet Johnson knew it fell far short. "We have
made much progress" on gun control, said Johnson, "but not nearly
enough." The federal committee on violence, appointed by Johnson,
pointed out that the Gun Control Act failed on the two most important
scores: it neither curbed secondhand sales nor decreased the nation's
overall arsenal of guns. Journalist Robert Sherrill savaged the law as
a "wretched" piece of legislation, "one of the grand jokes of our time."
To its critics, the Gun Control Act was a weak bill masquerading as a
legislative landmark.[59]

In the end, the leaders of the gun control forces—Dodd and Tydings and even Lyndon Johnson, the legislative master himself—overestimated the effect of the assassinations upon members of Congress.
Johnson thought the country's grief and shock could be converted into
political will. In June, thousands of citizens had mailed letters to their
congressmen, which did indeed help to generate momentum for the
blanket ban on mail-order firearms that ended up in the Gun Control
Act. And opinion polls continued to show broad swaths of the public
in favor of stricter gun regulations. Yet few were moved to protest, to
march, or to otherwise rise up in support of a national firearms registry
or a licensure law. No mass movement emerged to try to stop the shots.

The violence of the 1960s also energized pro-gun groups. The urban
riots sparked an increase in gun sales and ultimately helped organizations like the NRA. The NRA began to shape itself into a radically
conservative force. NRA leaders came to oppose all attempts to regulate guns. As the country tilted toward the right in the 1970s and 1980s,
the NRA composed a major part of the conservative coalition. In the
mid-1970s, NRA president Woodson Scott called for a complete repeal
of the Gun Control Act. President Ronald Reagan signed the Firearm
Owners' Protection Act in 1986, which weakened many of the provisions of the Gun Control Act.[60]

The Gun Control Act was hobbled from the beginning and enfeebled in the end. But in the larger context of American history, the summer of 1968 still represented a rare moment in which legislators successfully enacted federal gun control legislation. The King and Kennedy assassinations, together with the urban riots, established gun control as an issue of broad public concern—one on which Congress needed to act.

7

FROM OUTLAW
TO SAINT

D AYS BEFORE THE nation celebrated the first Martin Luther
King Day in 1986, Andrew Young reflected on Americans'
veneration of his old comrade: "We want to celebrate Martin Luther
King, but we don't want to celebrate all of him." Most African Americans, along with a segment of liberal whites, were eager to celebrate
the whole King—including the man who decried foreign wars and
who died for the poor. But many others preferred to remember just
one King: the one frozen on the Washington Mall, who longed for the
day when his children would "not be judged by the color of their skin
but by the content of their character." They molded King into a gentle
champion of colorblindness. A bland invention of the popular imagination, this King could appeal to Americans of all ideologies, races,
and creeds.[1]

Americans were able to so admire King because they picked and
chose which parts of his career they wanted to embrace. They scrubbed
his message and blunted his meaning. Eventually, the historical
King—a courageous dissident who unsettled the powerful—would be
replaced by a mythical one. Many white Americans concentrated on
that single line from King's "I Have a Dream" speech and effectively

reduced his life to one quotation. They began to appropriate King's legacy and wield it in their own causes.

Immediately after King's death, groups of African Americans journeyed to the Lorraine Motel and laid wreaths upon the balcony. As Memphis schoolteacher William Comstock said, "To us that spot, by that door, is the Liberty Bell, the Washington Monument, Canterbury and Mecca—it is the soul of our people." It had become their shrine. These pilgrims were eager to recall all of King: the interracial dreamer and the antiwar radical, the politic conciliator and the crusader for the poor, the man who consorted with kings and conservatives and even communists. Yet in order for white America to hail King as a national hero, his message would need to be shaped into something simpler and less threatening. That process began in the days after King's assassination, and it continued through the decades.[2]

CONGRESSMAN JOHN CONYERS proceeded to work for a federal King holiday, but he failed to gain sufficient support on Capitol Hill. Some states started to enact King holidays of their own. By 1971, nine states had declared his birthday, January 15, as Martin Luther King Day. In 1973, Illinois became the first state to make it a paid holiday for state workers. Massachusetts and Connecticut enacted official holidays in 1974. Momentum was building, state by state. The United Auto Workers and the American Federation of State, County, and Municipal Employees both instituted a paid holiday for King as a regular demand in their contract negotiations. Some activists saw King's birthday as a time to enlist his memory in their ongoing struggles for social justice. On King's birthday in 1976, 15,000 people marched in Atlanta. In Louisville, 2,500 marched not only in honor of King but also to support school busing in that city. They hoped to resurrect King's crusading spirit.[3]

King's legacy remained bitterly contested. Governor Meldrim Thomson of New Hampshire was a particularly fierce critic. Thomson was perhaps best known for forcing all of his state's drivers to travel with the words "LIVE FREE OR DIE" on their license plates. As head of the National Conservative Caucus in 1977, he led a campaign to discredit Andrew Young. Young was serving as the US ambassador to the United Nations, the first African American to hold the post. Thomson appeared most concerned with Young's ties to King, and King's supposed links with communists. Thomson sent a letter to fellow conservatives in July 1977, seeking to generate support for Young's ouster. He cited "Andrew Young's outrageous record of pro-Marxist agitation." The letter came with "Andrew Young must go action kits," including an image of a severely burned white child who was the supposed victim of "black power" movements. That same summer, Young was organizing a dinner in New York City to honor Martin Luther King Sr. In August, Young mailed dinner invitations to virtually every governor, Thomson included. Thomson sent a caustic reply, slandering Young as well as Martin Luther King Jr. "I heartily agree with the appraisal of Dr. Martin Luther King by the late J. Edgar Hoover and believe that King did a great harm to the American Way of Life through his association with communist inspired organizations." When reporters pressed Thomson on his views about King, he elaborated: "I am one who has never subscribed to what I consider the personality myth" about King. Thomson chose to align himself with J. Edgar Hoover rather than Martin Luther King.[4]

In January 1979, when King would have celebrated his fiftieth birthday, President Jimmy Carter spoke in favor of a federal King holiday from the pulpit of Ebenezer Baptist Church.* Congressional Republicans started to see that such a tribute to King made political sense, and the holiday legislation soon gained more than ninety sponsors. But some conservatives continued to resist. Congressman John Ashbrook, an Ohio Republican, became a leading opponent of the holiday. Ashbrook cautioned that Americans would be "misled into believing

---

* When Carter was Georgia's governor, he had declined to support a state holiday for King.

that King was a great man." King sought "not to work through the law but around it, with contempt and violence." Ashbrook was an exception. Many opponents of the holiday conceded King's greatness—or, at least, his usefulness as a champion for racial harmony. They objected on the grounds that a holiday would be too expensive, or that other great Americans did not have federal holidays in their name. On November 13, 1979, the House voted in favor of a King holiday with a tally of 255–133. But the sponsors of the bill had wanted to speed it through Congress, and they needed a two-thirds majority for the accelerated procedure. They fell four votes short. Republican Robin Beard of Tennessee then offered a hostile amendment that would place the holiday on a Sunday and make it unpaid, essentially creating a non-holiday. It passed by a slim margin. The sponsors of the original bill moved to pull the legislation from the floor.[5]

While the holiday legislation flagged, King's critics aired their grievances. James Kilpatrick, a syndicated columnist and onetime defender of segregation in Virginia, argued against the holiday. King was the "father of civil disobedience," Kilpatrick wrote in January 1980. Kilpatrick gave King high marks for personal courage, but his "political perception was pathetic." King was "naïve" and "sophomoric" in his estimate of communism. Thirteen years after King's antiwar speech at Riverside Church, Kilpatrick still regarded it as unforgivable—a "wildly intemperate" address. Kilpatrick spoke for the many Americans who thought King undeserving of a national holiday. On January 14, 1980, one day before his birthday, King's tomb in Atlanta was vandalized. On his birthday, Coretta Scott King laid a wreath upon the grave.[6]

Stevie Wonder lent his voice to the holiday movement. During the 1970s, Wonder had experimented with a song about King. He released a new album in the fall of 1980; "Happy Birthday" was the feature track. He sang of King as a loving and unappreciated hero: "I just never understood / How a man who died for good / Could not have a day that would / Be set aside for his recognition." On Halloween, Wonder launched a national tour. It arrived in Washington, DC, on January 15,

1981, as the city braced for Ronald Reagan's inauguration. More than 50,000 people gathered to see Wonder in a massive rally for the King holiday. A junior high school student read his prize-winning essay on why King should have a federal holiday, and the audience joined with Wonder as he sang "Happy Birthday."[7]

Seventeen states observed a King holiday by 1982. And for African Americans throughout the country, King's birthday was already a day of celebration. "In the black community, it is a holiday," said Danny Bakewell, head of the Brotherhood Crusade in Los Angeles. "We're not waiting for the white folks to declare it such; we celebrate it." During the Reagan years, African Americans would hold out even less hope for "the white folks." Kevin Sample, an aide to John Conyers, lamented that the struggle to enact the federal holiday now seemed more difficult: "I think that also symbolizes a return to the precivil rights period in some people's attitudes." He noted the Reagan administration's action to restore tax-exempt status to private schools that practiced discrimination. In addition, Reagan slashed funding for food stamps and welfare programs, and relaxed the enforcement of existing civil rights laws.* Said Charles Stith, pastor of the Union United Methodist Church in Boston, "There's an out and out assault against what Martin accomplished." When the Voting Rights Act came up for an extension in 1982, Reagan initially took no position on the matter before trying to weaken the bill. Congress ultimately passed the extension, and Reagan signed it. Reagan would go on to veto the Civil Rights Restoration Act, and to cripple the Equal Employment Opportunity Commission. He was turning back the clock on racial progress. Hodding Carter III, a liberal white journalist from Mississippi, observed, "To watch this administration do its work is to watch the deliberate destruction of all that the dream proclaims." Reagan added insult to injury in January

---

*Neither did African Americans forget that during the 1980 presidential campaign, Reagan had delivered a speech in Neshoba County, Mississippi, where he uttered paeans to "states' rights."

1983, when he stated his opposition to a federal holiday for Martin Luther King.[8]

Despite Reagan's position, many Republicans on Capitol Hill moved to support the King holiday. Endorsing the holiday seemed like a painless way to burnish the Republican Party's civil rights bona fides. Such a stand would do little to address black poverty, rebuild inner cities, or strike at segregation in schools and housing. Republicans did not have to support increased government spending for the poor. They could simply embrace the holiday, lionize King, make speeches about freedom for all Americans, quote from "I Have a Dream," and hope that would revamp their reputation.

Senate majority leader Howard Baker attempted to convince his Republican colleagues to back the holiday legislation.* In the House, Jack Kemp of New York—a longtime opponent of the holiday—had come around. Kemp appealed to his fellow Republicans to make good on the GOP's heritage as the party of Lincoln. Other conservatives joined Baker and Kemp as the holiday bill came to the House floor on July 26, 1983. At first, many congressmen saw it as a vote without consequences. They assumed that even if the legislation passed the House and the Senate, Reagan would exercise the veto. On August 2, the Democratic-controlled House passed the legislation by a wide margin: 338–90. A majority of Republicans supported the measure, including Wyoming's Dick Cheney and Georgia's Newt Gingrich. So did Illinois's Robert Michel, who had criticized King mere hours before his death in 1968. Trent Lott of Mississippi voted against the holiday, as did Ron Paul of Texas and John McCain of Arizona. Four days after the House vote, Reagan's aides noted that the president planned to shift his position.[9]

---

* In March 1968, Baker had criticized King's Poor People's Campaign. King's proposed march in Washington would be "like striking a match to look in your gas tank to see if you're out of gas" (Hampton Sides, *Hellhound on His Trail: The Stalking of Martin Luther King Jr. and the International Hunt for His Assassin* [New York: Doubleday, 2010], 113).

The debate in the Senate did the Republican Party no favors. The sponsors of the holiday legislation beat back a series of hostile amendments before Republican Jesse Helms of North Carolina staged a filibuster. Helms was a longtime critic of what he termed "the so-called civil rights movement" and of Martin Luther King. In January 1968, when Helms was a television journalist, he claimed to hear in King's voice only "the crackle of anarchy and the threat of violence." That April, Helms had denounced the Duke vigil and referred to those protesters as "the clutter on the lawn." He later asserted that King "may have participated in the creation of an atmosphere of terrible tension in Memphis," leading to his assassination. Surprisingly, Helms held his tongue during King holiday hearings in 1975, 1979, 1982, and early in 1983. But when the legislation came back to the Senate floor on October 3, 1983, Helms launched an attack. Martin Luther King "appears to have welcomed collaboration with communists," Helms claimed. He recounted how President John F. Kennedy had warned of King's subversive activities. Helms charged, "Dr. King's action-oriented Marxism . . . is not compatible with the concepts of this country." King's legacy "was really division, not love . . . Dr. King's political views were those of a radical political minority that had little to do with racial minorities." Helms insisted that the Senate should conduct full hearings to investigate King's background, and scrutinize all FBI files that pertained to his communist affiliations. He distributed a three-hundred-page packet detailing King's supposed treachery. Helms then asserted to a television reporter, "He attacked this country in the most vicious way." But Helms found few like-minded colleagues. Ted Kennedy denounced Helms's "Red smear" tactics. Democrat Daniel Patrick Moynihan dismissed Helms's document as a "packet of filth." Republican Bob Dole spoke in favor of the holiday legislation while other Republicans distanced themselves from Helms. Helms finally agreed to end his filibuster. Reagan suggested he would sign the legislation if it passed the Senate.[10]

On October 19, the Senate passed the holiday legislation by a wide margin: 78 to 22. Eighteen Republicans voted against the holiday, among them Barry Goldwater of Arizona, Charles Grassley of Iowa, and Orrin Hatch of Utah. The bill moved to the Oval Office.[11]

Even as many Republicans in Congress voted for the holiday, Reagan felt pressure from right-wing opponents. The Conservative Caucus collected 43,000 signatures on a petition urging him to veto the holiday. Reagan had always been suspicious of King, and he still wondered whether King was a communist. Meldrim Thomson had written a letter to Reagan on September 30, urging him to veto the holiday bill if it reached his desk. Thomson called King "a man of immoral character whose frequent association with leading agents of communism is well established." Reagan wrote back to Thomson on October 3 and admitted, "I have the same reservations you have." Reagan observed that the public's veneration of King was "based on an image, not reality." He continued, "We hope some modifications might still be made in Congress." That exchange became public on the day following the Senate vote, as Reagan was trying to extinguish another fire of his own making. Reagan had held a news conference just after the Senate vote. A reporter asked Reagan whether he believed Jesse Helms's charges about King's communist sympathies. Referring to the fact that the FBI files on King would not be opened until 2027, Reagan responded, "Well, we'll know in about 35 years, won't we?" Reagan added that he did not "fault Senator Helms's sincerity." He explained that he would have preferred something analogous to Lincoln's birthday, which was not an official federal holiday. Reagan's remarks about the FBI files generated an outcry. He phoned Coretta Scott King to apologize. Then he left for a weekend at the Augusta National Golf Club, which had no African American members. Yet Reagan eventually yielded to the holiday supporters. Reagan said, "They seemed bent on making it a national holiday." On November 2, he signed the King holiday bill into law.[12]

While Jesse Helms continued to spew racist invective in the US Senate, Martin Luther King rose to the status of a national hero. "The tragedy of which Helms is unaware," wrote Gilbert Caldwell in the *Washington Post*, "is that in the year 2027 the citizens will recognize that Martin Luther King Jr. was one of the greatest patriots this country has ever produced, and Helms . . . was not the patriot he pretended to be or thought he was." Helms's screed was too vicious even for Strom Thurmond, the man who had denounced King on the very night of his assassination. Thurmond ultimately voted for the holiday. Ronald Reagan underwent a similar change. Reagan, like Thurmond, had opposed the 1964 Civil Rights Act as well as the 1965 Voting Rights Act—and had stood among the outspoken King skeptics. Yet Reagan finally gave his blessing to Martin Luther King Day and signed it into law. He eventually became the holiday's celebrator-in-chief.[13]

KING WAS NOT only glorified with an official holiday, but also immortalized in the realm of popular culture. In 1984, U2 released an album called *The Unforgettable Fire*, featuring two songs about King. "MLK" was an ode to King, repetitive but gentle and moving. *Billboard* described it as "a warm ambient hum"; lead singer Bono called it "a great lullaby." The band offered a more stirring tribute in "Pride (In the Name of Love)." Bono sang of King as a man who came "in the name of love." Most of the lyrics were general enough to apply to any nonviolent, loving hero. "Pride" was inspiring, triumphant, and addictive, though it suffered from historical inaccuracy. "Early morning, April four," sang Bono, "shot rings out in the Memphis sky / Free at last, they took your life / But they could not take your pride." In fact, the shot rang out in the evening, not the early morning. Bono later acknowledged the error. In a version of the song that appeared on *Rattle and Hum*, Bono also praised Archbishop Desmond Tutu, a South African who won the Nobel Peace Prize in 1984. *The Unforgettable Fire* climbed to number twelve on the *Billboard* chart. It signified a larger cultural shift: King was becoming an icon.[14]

That represented a monumental change since King's last years, when he had been particularly despised by white Americans. When

Gallup asked about King in 1966, only 33 percent of Americans thought favorably of him; 63 percent regarded him unfavorably. Among white Americans, fully 72 percent held unfavorable views of King. Gallup also asked respondents to place King on a numerical spectrum from plus-five—for an individual that the respondent liked very much—to minus-five, for someone they disliked very much. In 1966, fully 41 percent of white Americans placed King at the lowest point on the spectrum. In the history of Gallup's "scalometer" ratings, only one public figure had received scores as negative: Richard Nixon at the time of his resignation.[15]

Yet King's reputation would be restored in the decades after his death. By the middle of the 1980s, he had become a hero to whites and conservatives as well as African Americans and liberals. In 1987, 76 percent of whites rated King favorably. They did not all celebrate the same King, and few of them celebrated the whole King. But they didn't need to. In death, more completely than in life, King appealed to many constituencies at once. Coretta Scott King had testified at the congressional hearings on the King holiday in 1979. She noted that other African Americans certainly deserved holidays. But many of those individuals addressed issues that "concern blacks exclusively." Martin Luther King "spoke to us all."[16]

During his life, King had acted as a bridge between black militants and moderate civil rights leaders, between poor sharecroppers in the South and the most powerful men in Washington. He commanded audiences in the cotton fields of Mississippi and the pool halls of Chicago, on university campuses across the country and in churches throughout the world. He spoke in languages white Americans could understand: the languages of the Bible and the Constitution. For many whites, he made the black freedom struggle comprehensible and even noble. Furthermore, different international constituencies embraced him. Europeans on both sides of the Cold War regarded him as a hero. He inspired African American soldiers in Vietnam as well as freedom fighters who battled western imperialism. After his death, all of these various groups (and more) wished to claim King for their own cause.

Black workers felt he had died for them. Black Power advocates may have disagreed with King's tactics, but they saw his killing as a personal affront and a call to arms. White liberals held up King as a model for social activism: he knew how to work within the system in order to change it, how to criticize America while still believing in its ideals. Distinct groups also drew upon King's example in order to defend very different policy prescriptions. Conservatives viewed King as a champion of colorblindness and argued that he would have opposed race-specific policies. Progressives asserted that to honor King's legacy was to increase government spending for the poor, strengthen voting rights laws, expand affirmative action, and work for peace rather than war.

Yet King was no shape-shifter. He was clear and consistent. He believed in nonviolence, at home and abroad. He believed in civil disobedience and in the power of mass protest. It was the right and the obligation of citizens to wage such demonstrations in the face of injustice. He believed that societies had a duty to root out poverty and to redistribute riches. Governments needed not to build more weapons, but to feed, shelter, and clothe the poor and the weak. He believed that humanity's responsibilities were universal, not confined to the borders of nations and states. His beliefs did not translate to all political ideologies. And still, he tapped into a yearning that resided deep within many Americans—a hope that whites and blacks could find a way to live together as equals, that their society could be truly just and free.

RONALD REAGAN PRESIDED over the nation's first Martin Luther King Day, in January 1986. In the week leading up to the holiday, Reagan delivered tributes to King and met with Coretta Scott King. He depicted King as an all-American hero, an emblem of the American Dream more than a crusader against injustice. On January 13, Reagan declared, "Dr. King believed in the great promise of America and an America in which all of us can progress as fast and as far as our own ability, our vision, and our heart will take us." Reagan shaped King into a rugged individualist and asserted that he was carrying on King's

legacy. "That is the very promise that I came to Washington to restore."
While many African Americans were encouraged by the country's official recognition of King, Reagan's words left them unsettled.[17]

The discomfort resulted from the dissonance between Reagan's
respectful homilies and his retrograde policies. "Two American men
who lived in the same century could hardly have agreed on less," wrote
Roger Wilkins about King and Reagan. As Wilkins saw it, one man
devoted his life to the poor, the oppressed, and the alienated. The
other used his power to expand the coffers of the rich. "King's profound concern for the poor and the powerless is matched by Reagan's
concern—as indicated by his tax, domestic and budgetary policies—
for the wealthy and the powerful." Reagan also gutted civil rights laws
while claiming to follow in King's footsteps. Reagan was "pretending
to adhere to ideals that his policies clearly indicate he opposes." From
Wilkins's perspective, to be black in Reagan's America was a humiliating and maddening experience. "We feel, in short, that we are having our pockets picked—with our knowledge—without the slightest
power to prevent the crime." In the mid-1980s, observed the editors of
the *New York Times*, "the nation seems utterly uninterested in minority
rights." Because the first Martin Luther King Day arrived at the zenith
of the Reagan era, it tasted bittersweet.[18]

Yet the optics of that first holiday were stunning: a conservative
president led a majority-white nation, founded in slavery and still rife
with segregation, in honoring a black man who had been a fierce critic
of the country. On January 20, the third Monday of the month, an enormous crowd marched through the streets of Atlanta. Police estimated
the procession at half a million people, more than double the size of
King's funeral march. A smaller crowd gathered in Memphis and held
a vigil in the parking lot of the Lorraine Motel. Many cities closed
municipal offices and canceled school. In those assorted places where
schools remained open—for example, Plaquemines Parish, Louisiana,
and Tulsa, Oklahoma—large numbers of black students stayed home
to pay homage.[19]

Coretta Scott King hoped the spirit of the holiday would radiate beyond America's borders. She reminded the world that King had toiled not only for the civil and economic rights of African Americans, but for human rights across the globe. Indeed, Martin Luther King was celebrated across many continents. The city of Calcutta, India, recognized the first King Day by renaming a street in King's honor. By that time, there was already a forest in Israel named after King, a public-housing development in Panama, plazas in Sweden and India, and a sculpture in Debrecen, Hungary. In Havana, Cuba, Rev. Raul Suarez founded the Centro Memorial Martin Luther King Jr. to provide training in King's philosophy of nonviolence. Coretta called for a day of world peace on January 20, urging a suspension of all hostilities.[20]

The Reagan administration certainly did not practice a King-style philosophy in its foreign affairs. That became most apparent in Reagan's stance toward South Africa. Reagan pursued a policy of "constructive engagement" with the South African government that maintained military and economic ties. Meanwhile, thousands of Americans joined the anti-apartheid movement, particularly on college campuses. Protesters demanded that universities divest from South Africa and urged the federal government to impose economic sanctions on the apartheid regime. In March 1985, the South African police had killed nineteen protesters at a march commemorating the Sharpeville massacre. Reagan suggested that some of the "rioters," who were in fact peaceful, had provoked the violence. His comments incited further outrage at home. On April 4, 1985, the seventeenth anniversary of King's death, anti-apartheid activists organized a national day of protest. Four thousand people marched on the South African embassy. The United States Congress was eventually moved to action. In 1986, Congress passed the Comprehensive Anti-Apartheid Act. It banned all new American loans and investments in South Africa, prohibited the importation of South African goods, and denied landing rights to South African Airways. President Reagan vetoed the legislation. But the Congress overrode his veto. After the United States imposed these sanctions, many European nations and Japan followed suit. This eventually led to a recession in South Africa and helped to hasten the demise of apartheid. Reagan also intensified his covert war against the Sandinistas in Nicaragua and secretly offered aid to a group of anticommunist insurgents in Angola. King would have stood aghast not only at Reagan's accommodation with the apartheid regime, but also at the astronomical military spending and the ethos of jingoistic nationalism that were the hallmarks of the Reagan presidency.[21]

Reagan's supporters never claimed that King would have condoned the administration's militarism. But they invoked King's name in order to advance some of Reagan's domestic policies. On January 15, 1986, Attorney General Edwin Meese offered a proposal to eliminate minority hiring goals for federal contractors. It would reverse an executive order from 1965, and it would bar the Department of Labor from using guidelines that encouraged contractors to hire more racial minorities and women. This was an open assault on affirmative action. Meese quoted from "I Have a Dream" and claimed he was only "trying to carry out the original intent of the civil rights movement." King "foresaw a colorblind society," Meese maintained, "and this is what we're very much dedicated to." Furthermore, Meese asserted that his aim—"that there should be no discrimination"—matched that of the original 1965 executive order. Meese contended that his proposal was "very consistent with what Dr. King had in mind."[22]

In his own writings, King made it clear where he stood on the issue of affirmative action. "The Negro must have 'his due,'" he wrote in *Where Do We Go from Here?* And "giving a man his due may often mean giving him special treatment." King explained, "A society that has done something special *against* the Negro for hundreds of years must now do something special *for* him, in order to equip him to compete on a just and equal basis." He recognized that such "special treatment" would make many white Americans uncomfortable. But justice demanded it. King had also addressed the issue in *Why We Can't Wait*, published in 1964. He advised the federal government to offer "some compensatory compensation" to African Americans for centuries of unpaid labor.

"The payment should be in the form of special, compensatory measures. . . . Such measures would certainly be less expensive than any
computation based on two centuries of unpaid wages and accumulated
interest." King had in mind something like the GI Bill, in which the
federal government had assisted veterans with employment, housing,
and college tuition. He suggested a Bill of Rights for the Disadvan-
taged, which would enact similar policies on behalf of black Americans. King thus urged the federal government to do something *special*
for African Americans, not to treat them exactly the same as whites.
By the 1980s, aggrieved whites would call this kind of idea "reverse
discrimination." Whether one labeled it "reverse racism," "affirmative
action," or "special treatment" for black Americans, King supported
precisely such a policy.[23]

The battle over affirmative action would grow most heated in the
1990s, when every opponent of race-specific policies seemed to have a
King citation at the ready. In January 1996, Louisiana's governor signed
an executive order to halt affirmative action programs. "King sort of
believed like I do," said Republican Mike Foster. "I can't find anywhere
in his writings that he wanted reverse discrimination." That same year,
California voters approved a ballot referendum, Proposition 209, that
eliminated affirmative action policies throughout the state. Ward Connerly, an African American businessman who led the effort for the referendum, declared, "We're going to fight to get the nation back on the
journey that Dr. King laid out." In reality, Connerly and his ilk had
defeated the very kinds of programs that King proposed.[24]

FROM THE 1970S through the 1990s, even after the federal King holiday was created, state legislatures debated King holiday proposals as
cities battled over whether to name streets after King. While the arguments about state holidays attracted more national publicity, the
struggles over street names inflamed the passions of local residents.
To rename streets for King was to weave his legacy into the fabric of
everyday life. Today, most King streets wind through black neighborhoods. That is because many whites actively opposed King streets in

their own neighborhoods. These whites feared their property values would decline, or their businesses would suffer, if they lived or worked on or around a Martin Luther King Boulevard. At the same time, King streets that ran through black communities served as reminders of the enduring connection between King and ordinary African Americans. The streets often acted as hubs for black businesses and centers of African American life. The majority of streets were in the South, with the most in King's native Georgia. By 2000, there were at least 650 King streets scattered across the country. Martin Luther King Boulevard in Galveston, Texas, runs right to the shore of the Gulf of Mexico; Atlanta's Martin Luther King Drive ends at Oakland Cemetery, the resting place for five Confederate generals and author Margaret Mitchell. Even Salt Lake City, Utah, renamed part of a downtown street for Martin Luther King, affording drivers a view of the Wasatch Mountains. As Annie Williams, a resident of Belle Glade, Florida, remarked, "Every town got a Martin Luther King." And for each town with a King Way, there was a story of strain and strife and spatial segregation.[25]

Austin, Texas, eventually extended its Martin Luther King Boulevard out of an African American neighborhood and into the university area, but only after an acrimonious struggle. In March 1975, a group of African American citizens, including State representative Wilhelmina Delco, asked the Austin City Council to rename Nineteenth Street after Martin Luther King. The proposal sparked controversy, but ultimately passed by a vote of 4–2. Workers began to put up new street signs, but only on the part of the street that ran east of Interstate 35, which was home to many of Austin's African Americans. Whites who lived west of the interstate had opposed the name change, and city officials deferred to them. Black leaders called on the city to change all of Nineteenth Street to Martin Luther King Boulevard, and the city council held a meeting on May 1. White citizens in attendance hoisted signs that said "PRESERVE 19TH STREET!" J. J. Seabrook, president emeritus of Huston-Tillotson University and an elder statesman in the black community, spoke in favor of a King street that would run through all of Nineteenth Street. Midway into his passionate speech, Seabrook collapsed from a heart attack. The opponents of Martin Luther King Boulevard were undeterred.[26]

White citizens formed the West 19th Street Association, whose stated "sole purpose" was to "oppose changing the name of any existing street in Austin without the consent of the property owners concerned." One white citizen asserted, "We, the property owners, own 19th Street." Over the coming years, white residents in many other cities would voice similar cries. When elected officials attempted to name streets in white neighborhoods after Martin Luther King, white citizens suddenly invoked their supposed right to approve any name change. The Austin Black Assembly, a group led by Representative Delco, noted that the city council had during the previous decade adopted fifty-eight different resolutions to change street names without any great outcry. But the West 19th Street Association employed a variety of delaying tactics, filing lawsuits and circulating petitions for a ballot referendum. They were unsuccessful. In a victory for black leaders, city officials finally did name all of Nineteenth Street after Martin Luther King. Austin's Martin Luther King Boulevard began in predominantly black East Austin, spanned a bridge over the interstate, then reached into the whiter university area and out toward West Austin. In 2010, residents from both east and west of the interstate came together to rename the King Boulevard bridge after J. J. Seabrook.[27]

SAN DIEGO'S MARTIN Luther King Way suffered a sorrier fate. In January 1986, while the nation prepared to observe the first Martin Luther King Day, Michel Anderson asked the city council to name a street after King. Anderson had worked for San Diego's former mayor and served on California's King holiday commission. On January 13, the city council approved the idea of naming a street after King. Officials held a public meeting in the southeast area of the city, the heart of the black community, seeking feedback on different proposals. Residents expressed support for a plan to rename a five-mile segment of Euclid

Avenue and Fifty-Fourth Street in honor of King. Local black leaders explained that the route cut through neighborhoods of different ethnic and income groups, a fitting tribute to King. City manager Sylvester Murray, an African American, backed that proposal. The white residents of Mid-City were furious.[28]

Homeowners and businessmen in the Oak Park area argued that a name change would be inconvenient and expensive. Ed Vires, a resident of Fifty-Fourth Street, expressed additional concerns: "I just feel that the colored people were pursuing a cause that . . . I do not accept . . . and I think there are many white people that don't accept that cause, even though [King's birthday] was established as a national holiday." Vires organized a petition drive to oppose the King street, collecting nine hundred signatures. City manager Murray reported that he had received more than five hundred negative responses, with only around fifteen letters in support of the plan. Uvaldo Martinez and William Jones, the two racial minorities on the city council, received a barrage of "disgusting" phone calls. The surge of anger forced the council to rethink its proposal.[29]

City councilors revisited another option they had considered at the first meeting: to rename Market Street after Martin Luther King. Market Street began at San Diego Bay and ran through the downtown and east for six miles to the city limits. Historically, the street provided a home to the black community, with thriving jazz clubs and black-owned businesses. By 1986, African Americans composed 9 percent of San Diego's overall population; they made up 41 percent of the residents who lived in census tracts adjacent to Market Street. These areas included some of the city's poorest neighborhoods, along with old rental housing, churches, liquor stores, and taco stands as well as successful downtown businesses. Thomas McPhatter, an African American minister and former navy chaplain, urged the city council to rename Market Street after King. "Market has a cross-section of people living on it," he wrote in a letter to the *Los Angeles Times*. "It is also a beautiful street. On a clear day, Coronado Island can be seen from Mount

Hope." Market Street, so named in 1915, had once been a site of vice and prostitution. There was nothing honorable about the name "Market Street," McPhatter asserted. By contrast, the name Martin Luther King Way "will bring redemptive honor to the street, the businesses, the residents, our city, and our nation." On April 21, 1986, the city council shelved the Euclid/Fifty-Fourth Street proposal and instead voted on a resolution to rename Market Street after Martin Luther King. It passed by a vote of 6–1. But the controversy was far from over.[30]

Over the next two years, the white businessmen of Market Street waged a bitter struggle against the name change. Merchants posted placards in their shop windows: "KEEP MARKET STREET." They complained it would prove costly to reprint stationery with the new address. Some claimed the name change would be an insult to King, as drug dealers and prostitutes frequented certain stretches of Market Street. The angry storeowners insisted it was "not a racial situation." Less than a week after the council's vote, businessmen presented a petition signed by three hundred people who opposed the change to King Way. The council took another vote at the end of April and declined to undo its decision. Despite the ongoing protests, the city changed the name of Market Street to Martin Luther King Way.[31]

The storeowners demanded the city place the issue on the ballot in November 1986 and allow voters to choose between Market Street and King Way. The group commissioned a survey, which found that 64 percent of voters disagreed with the city council's action and 86 percent believed a referendum ought to appear on the ballot. Their opposition begged the question: If Euclid Avenue and Fifty-Fourth Street could not be Martin Luther King Way, and if Market Street also could not be King Way, then what street could? The Market Street merchants suggested Imperial Avenue, which ran through the center of the black neighborhood—and had just as many storeowners who would need to order new stationery. The merchants also noted that it was not their job to come up with an alternative. They only knew that they wanted King Way far from their own businesses.[32]

In July 1986, the council voted not to place the issue on the November ballot. Business owners redoubled their efforts and launched a petition drive to place a referendum on the ballot in the following year. They needed to collect 50,000 signatures by March 1987. San Diego's black leaders bristled at the idea of a referendum. They feared what might become of King's legacy if it were subject to the whims of the city's white majority. And they knew what would happen to Martin Luther King Way: it would either be situated in a segregated black neighborhood, or nowhere.[33]

The storeowners gathered more than 79,000 signatures. G. T. Frost Jr., the vice president of the Keep Market Street Initiative Committee, claimed that the merchants fully supported a King street in San Diego—just not on Market Street. That reasoning persuaded few African Americans. Willie Morrow, the owner of a business on the eastern end of what had already become Martin Luther King Way, knew the petition was racially charged. "Basically, it comes down to a simple matter of black and white," Morrow explained. "They can sugar-coat it any way they want to, but that's what it is. What they are saying is, 'Dr. King was a great person who should be honored as long as it's not in my neighborhood.' No one on our end of the street is complaining. It's only the people downtown." Rev. George Walker Smith, pastor of the Christ United Presbyterian Church and a former member of the board of education, was even blunter. The ballot initiative showed the "negative attitude that white folks here have toward King and other things. There's no secret a lot of people who are behind this are red-necked racists." Other black leaders agreed. "I can't believe it is anything but racially induced," said Gloria Vinson, general manager of a black newspaper called the *Voice and Viewpoint*. The ballot initiative was "an embarrassment for San Diego."[34]

Once the signatures on the merchants' petition were certified, the matter came before the city council. Councilors could either decide to change the name of Martin Luther King Way back to Market Street immediately, or face a referendum to do so on the November ballot.

In April 1987, the council voted 6–1 to keep King Way. Mayor Maureen O'Connor announced her support for King Way, as did the local Chamber of Commerce. Martin Luther King Way would remain, at least until the voters weighed in.[35]

The opponents of King Way tried to contort themselves into keepers of King's legacy. City councilwoman Abbe Wolfsheimer, who had cast the lone vote in favor of changing the name back to Market Street, said the renaming had proved "costly in terms of human relations. And it's going to get worse, I'm afraid." She invoked King as a way of validating her position. "That was not Dr. Martin Luther King's way. His way was to avoid controversy, and all we've had is controversy." The comment betrayed a total misunderstanding of King's career. Controversy had followed King from the jails of the Deep South and the streets of Chicago to the pulpit of New York City's Riverside Church. He welcomed controversy as a way of bringing injustice to light. Yet white leaders in San Diego ignored that dimension of King's life. Tod Firotto, the owner of a restaurant supply firm on King Way, charged that the city council had infringed on his own rights. "I feel my civil rights were violated," Firotto said, "and I'm only doing what Dr. King would want me to do." Firotto claimed that the merchants meant King no disrespect. "The initiative doesn't have anything to do with Dr. King. We don't want the name of George Washington out here, either." More outlandishly, he added, "Dr. Martin Luther King is my hero, too." He did not explain why he objected to conducting business on a street named after his hero. The San Diego businessmen thus warped King's teachings and then claimed that King himself would have supported their cause. King had become such an elastic figure that his legacy could even be mobilized by those who opposed Martin Luther King Way.[36]

San Diego's African Americans viewed the ballot initiative, known as Proposition F, as an indignity. If the initiative passed, said Urban League president Herb Cawthorne, "the effect on the black community here would be one of anger, insult and rejection. It would be a wound that would continue to bleed for a long, long time." The ballot initiative "is racism," charged Rev. W. E. Manley. "We can't avoid that." To pass Proposition F would be to inflict the most visible of insults, as city workers would be forced to take down the street signs that had been standing since the spring of 1986. King had fought for many years to see southern cities bury different kinds of signs: those that said "WHITES ONLY." Now, in 1987, the Market Street merchants hoped to see the King Way signs—which stood as so many monuments to the man— come tumbling down.[37]

On November 3, nearly 60 percent of San Diego voters approved Proposition F. It directed that "the street now named as Dr. Martin Luther King Way irrevocably be renamed Market Street." Jennifer Bollard, a white San Diego resident, delighted in the result. She reported that San Diego's "social conscience" was "firmly intact." She added that the supporters of Proposition F were not racists. And she claimed the name "Market Street" held great value for local residents: "The historical equivalent would be to rename Rome or something." While the majority of voters sided with Bollard, some San Diego residents expressed outrage and chagrin. Caroline Moran doubted the merchants' repeated claims that their stance had nothing to do with race. "Shame on them," Moran wrote in a letter to the *Los Angeles Times*. "They should have been proud to have had their businesses on Martin Luther King Way." Moran hoped a different downtown street, perhaps Broadway, would be named after King. "In this way no one can ever call San Diego a racist city." San Diegan Douglas Kemp opined, "Racism did indeed play a role in the final tally." He noted that some whites still considered King to be a troublemaker. San Diego voters "said his life was not worth the asphalt that carried his name."[38]

Some citizens clamored for San Diego to find another street to rename for King. But African American leaders, scarred and sobered, urged the city to proceed with caution. They were exhausted from the two-year battle, and angered at the open white resistance. The city formed a twenty-one-member commission that would hold hearings for six months in 1988. Market Street businessman G. T. Frost Jr.

insisted, "There are going to be some wonderful things done in this city in memory of Dr. King." That proved an empty promise. In 1989, San Diego renamed a chunk of Highway 94 after King. The city council also approved a proposal to name the new convention center after King. But the Port of San Diego, which retained formal authority over that land, chose to name it simply the San Diego Convention Center. African Americans boycotted the convention center for five years, to no avail. San Diego finally found a small stretch of downtown parkland to name the Martin Luther King Jr. Promenade. Said George Stevens, a former member of the city council, "That was a little dab of something." Years of struggle had produced little fruit.[39]

San Diego's experience was not unique. The city of Harrisburg, Pennsylvania, named a street after King in 1986, and the voters rejected it the following year. Harrisburg eventually renamed a smaller street in honor of King. Voters in Portland, Oregon, attempted to place a referendum on the ballot in 1990 to rename their own Martin Luther King Boulevard. Polls suggested that a majority of voters would oppose the King street name, but the local courts intervened and canceled the vote. In 1993, Americus, Georgia, was convulsed by a yearlong debate over a King street. That saga featured arguments, threats, and a suggestion from the deputy fire chief that half the street be named for King and the other half for James Earl Ray. Whites continued to resist King streets in their own neighborhoods, which produced an ironic result. While King streets honored the country's champion of integration, they showed that American cities remained deeply segregated.[40]

SAN DIEGO'S ORDEAL began in January 1986, as the nation celebrated the first King holiday. By the end of that year, forty states had enacted King holidays of their own. Only ten holdouts remained. The governor-elect of Arizona, Republican Evan Mecham, vowed to remove his state from the ranks of the celebrants and to join the holdouts. Early in 1986, Arizona's legislature had defeated (by a single vote) a bill to establish a King holiday. Democrat Bruce Babbitt, the lame-duck governor, nevertheless signed an executive order to create a statewide

Martin Luther King Day. Then Mecham won the November election. On January 12, 1987, just after taking office, Mecham rescinded Babbitt's executive order. He claimed that Babbitt lacked the authority to declare such a holiday, and that the state lacked the funds to absorb the expense. Mecham added that King was undeserving of a holiday. Arizona became both a laggard and a trailblazer, the first state to revoke its King holiday.[41]

One week after Mecham reversed the state holiday, a high school student from Tucson penned him a letter. "With all due respect, you are a bigot," wrote Steve Frost, a junior at Amphitheater High School. "Martin Luther King has won hundreds of awards including a Nobel Peace Prize. What have you done for humanity?" Though Mecham attracted national scorn for his executive order, many whites in Arizona remained apathetic about the King holiday. Cities like Phoenix and Tucson soon enacted municipal King holidays, but Mecham dug in his heels.[42]

Musicians and entertainers started to cancel events in Arizona. Civil rights groups called for a boycott of Arizona, costing the state $18 million in convention and hotel bookings during 1987 alone. On January 15, 1988, some 20,000 holiday supporters marched in Phoenix. One month later, Mecham was impeached for making illegal loans to his car dealership. Secretary of State Rose Mofford, a Democrat, succeeded him. Mofford announced she would sign a King holiday bill if the legislature passed it. By the time of King's sixtieth birthday in January 1989, only six states still declined to observe a King holiday: Arizona, Idaho, Montana, New Hampshire, South Dakota, and Wyoming. All of those states had small African American populations; in Arizona, it was 3 percent. But the political calculus in Arizona had begun to change due to the financial pressure applied by the boycott. In September 1989, after more than two years as a national pariah, Arizona's legislature passed the King holiday bill by one vote. Mofford signed it into law.[43]

A conservative organization filed a ballot measure to challenge the holiday. The 1990 ballot ultimately contained two different propositions regarding a paid state holiday in honor of King. The voters defeated both proposals. Proposition 301 would have substituted Martin Luther King Day for Columbus Day. Three-quarters of the voters rejected that proposal. Proposition 302 asked more generally whether to make Martin Luther King Day a paid state holiday. That proposal lost by a margin of 50 percent to 49 percent. A poll taken afterward suggested that roughly 60 percent of voters had supported at least one of the propositions. The presence of two different ballot questions had muddled the issue. But the upshot was clear: the voters defeated the King holiday. Arizona earned a reputation as a racist backwater all over again.[44]

This was not just a story of governors and legislators. Rev. Warren Stewart, pastor of the First Institutional Baptist Church in Phoenix, led a grassroots effort in support of the King holiday. It became his fate to push that rock back up the hill time and again. Stewart had formed an organization called Arizonans for a Martin Luther King Jr. State Holiday. In October 1987, he wrote to Governor Mecham to propose a measure that would establish a Martin Luther King/Civil Rights Day in January, and a George Washington/Abraham Lincoln Day in February. It would cost the state nothing extra. But Mecham was unconvinced. Stewart lamented that Mecham "saw Martin Luther King as a black hero and also as an agitator." Stewart was ecstatic when Rose Mofford signed the holiday into law in 1989. But the voters' rejection of the holiday one year later left him reeling. Stewart felt he had exhausted all options at that point.[45]

Then the National Football League trained a bright spotlight on the state's resistance and transformed the contours of the holiday debate. In March 1990, the NFL chose Sun Devil Stadium in Tempe, Arizona, as its location for the 1993 Super Bowl. That was after Mofford had signed the holiday bill, but while its challengers were gaining support for a ballot referendum. On the Sunday before the November referendum, sportscaster Greg Gumbel reported on CBS's *The NFL Today* that Arizona would lose the Super Bowl if the voters defeated the King holiday. Arizonans proceeded to reject the holiday, and the NFL kept its promise. Early in 1991, the NFL announced it would move the 1993 Super Bowl to Pasadena, California, and that Tempe would provisionally host the big game in 1996. The NFL was giving Arizona five years to enact a state holiday for Martin Luther King.[46]

The NFL's owners did not display any particular interest in King or in civil rights. But Arizona was bad for business. The state had rescinded the holiday not once but twice. Arizona was living up to its nickname as "the Mississippi of the West."[47]

To Chuck D, the lead singer of Public Enemy, Arizona's revocation of the holiday "was so much of a smack in the face." He said to himself, "This needs to be addressed." In November 1991, Public Enemy released an album with a song entitled, "By the Time I Get to Arizona." It was an indictment of the state and its voters. "Seein' people smile wild in the heat / 120 degree / 'Cause I want to be free," Chuck D rapped. He asked, "What's a smiling face when the whole state's racist?" Public Enemy focused much of its anger on Mecham. "The cracker over there / He try to keep it yesteryear / The good ol' days / The same ol' ways / That kept us dyin'." An incendiary music video aired on MTV in January 1992. It opened with a Mecham-like character who claimed he was not a racist, yet vowed that there would be no King holiday in Arizona. It then pictured Chuck D with a group of armed African Americans, dressed in fatigues and plotting violent retaliation. The video interspersed scenes from the 1960s. In black-and-white dramatizations, civil rights marchers confronted attack dogs and fire hoses, and white officials stopped African Americans from registering to vote. A Martin Luther King–like character staged a sit-in at a diner and endured humiliating treatment. At the video's climax, it alternated between different assassinations. It re-created a scene of King on the motel balcony, recoiling from a rifle shot. Then it skipped ahead to the Arizona capitol, where a state senator died from a poisoned box of chocolates. In the final scene, Chuck D detonated a car bomb that killed the governor. MTV did not air the video again.[48]

Public Enemy became the pariah. Politicians, civil rights activists, and journalists all condemned the video's wanton violence. Chuck D explained the video as "a revenge fantasy." Harry Allen, Public Enemy's spokesman, went a step further. "We like to think that this video finishes the work that Martin Luther King Jr. started." No amount of mental gymnastics could sustain the assertion that more political assassinations would have finished King's work. Allen was twisting King's dream as badly as had the opponents of affirmative action. Indeed, Rev. Warren Stewart thought Public Enemy's video trampled on King's legacy. The video suggested that "if someone disagrees with you on a racial issue, assassinate him." Stewart added, "That's an insult to the memory of Dr. King and a *terrible* message for our young people." Chuck D insisted on his right to artistic license. The video was "a trip into the fantasy world of Public Enemy. You know, the big payback." Chuck D appeared on *Nightline* on Martin Luther King Day in January 1992, along with *Chicago Tribune* columnist Clarence Page. While Chuck D defended the video, Page argued that it conveyed "the exact opposite of the message that Dr. King died for." Chuck D explained himself more fully in an interview with *Spin*, twenty years later. "Dr. King died a violent death and I was answering that," he said. "As a child, I was pissed off that they killed Dr. King and I was answering that. Regardless of what Dr. King believed, the act of his life being taken was not a passive thing." The song and the video were emotional responses to King's brutal death, and to the indignity Arizona's voters had heaped upon him.[49]

On Martin Luther King Day in 1992, Warren Stewart launched another campaign for a King holiday in Arizona. He would no longer wage a lonely crusade. This time around, leading businessmen and religious groups joined with him. In 1990, Stewart had chosen not to work too closely with business leaders. He believed that they wanted a King holiday only for selfish economic reasons and had little interest in actually honoring King. But by 1992, Stewart realized that a united front— and funding from the businesses—could help bring the holiday back to life. At the same time, business groups had all the more incentive to support Stewart's cause. The state had lost an estimated $250 million in tourist dollars because of the holiday controversy. Twenty-one cities in Arizona had already enacted municipal King holidays. And the new governor, Republican Fife Symington, advertised his support for a state holiday. Holiday advocates placed a referendum on the ballot for November 1992. By that time, forty-eight states had established either a Martin Luther King Day or a paid holiday on King's birthday (or both). Only two recalcitrants remained: Arizona and New Hampshire.[50]

Stewart formed a new organization called Victory Together, focused on registering voters and educating citizens about the proposed holiday. In some parts of the state, "they thought I was a Communist because I wanted Martin Luther King Day," Stewart said. "But we educated people that Martin Luther King Day represented the American promise that all people are created equal, and his nonviolent revolution bettered America. It was an American holiday, not a black holiday." He was pragmatic, depicting King as a devotee of the ideals espoused in the Constitution and the Declaration of Independence. In Stewart's hands, King became a saintly hero palatable to all. The holiday "represents a basic American principle that all persons are created equal by God. We believe that when people are alerted to that principle, that it's not a black holiday, but one honoring those principles that he embodied, we think that they will vote for it." This was a King for all seasons, one who could withstand even the sunbaked conservatism of Arizona.[51]

Victory Together registered 75,000 new voters, and Stewart's campaign bore fruit. He drove home his message: "Martin King helped this nation fulfill the basic tenets of the Constitution, the Preamble, the Pledge of Allegiance." And the white voters "finally got it." In November 1992, the electorate supported the holiday ballot measure by a wide margin. Arizona thus became the only state to enact a King holiday by popular vote. Arizona observed the holiday in January 1993. Rosa Parks and Stevie Wonder led a crowd of 19,000 in celebration.[52]

That left New Hampshire the only state without a King holiday. Many New Hampshire residents clung to their reputation as political iconoclasts and rock-ribbed worshippers of individual liberty. It was a nearly all-white state whose leading newspaper, the *Manchester Union Leader,* had for decades printed anticommunist diatribes. The state's voters had also elected Meldrim Thomson, the arch-conservative who had savaged King (as well as Andrew Young), as their governor three times. Thomson left office in 1979. That same year, Portsmouth Democrat James Splaine introduced a King holiday bill in the state legislature for the first time. Legislators defeated that bill, and subsequent ones to create a King holiday in 1981, 1985, 1987, and 1989. Portsmouth-area residents then formed the Seacoast Martin Luther King Jr. Coalition to build public support for a holiday. In 1991, lawmakers approved a measure to observe Civil Rights Day on the third Monday in January. That legislation made no reference to King, nor was it a paid holiday. Two years later, the *Union Leader* finally voiced its support for a King holiday, yet the legislature defeated another King holiday bill. Representative Vivian Clark claimed, "Naming the day after one hero adds to the divisiveness." To JerriAnne Boggis, director of the Portsmouth Black Heritage Trail, legislators saw the holiday as "divisive" only because King was black. "The real reason was that we really didn't want to honor a man of color." Throughout the 1990s, New Hampshire's governors issued proclamations each January to rename Civil Rights Day as Martin Luther King Day. Each time, the state's House of Representatives refused to permanently approve the change. Legislators could tolerate a vague celebration of "civil rights," but they declined to honor King himself. The irony was that no individual had more genuinely embodied New Hampshire's motto: "Live Free or Die."[53]

The legislature's resistance became a source of increasing embarrassment. On Martin Luther King Day in 1996, a Mississippi-based white supremacist group paraded outside the New Hampshire statehouse. Indeed, New Hampshire seemed in danger of anointing itself as the "Mississippi of the North." Democrat Jeanne Shaheen became governor in 1997 and immediately dedicated herself to the King holiday. But the house defeated another holiday proposal, albeit by a single vote. In response, a diverse coalition of groups mobilized in support of the holiday: the AFL-CIO as well as the New Hampshire Business and Industry Association, the Christian Coalition along with the Citizens Alliance for Gay and Lesbian Rights. New Hampshire citizens organized marches and petition drives. Shaheen used her second inaugural address in 1999 to proclaim, "We cannot end this century without making Martin Luther King Day a part of the heritage we leave to our children." The legislature finally yielded. After two hours of spirited debate, the house voted for a King holiday, by a margin of 212–148. (The state senate had already approved a similar bill.) Legislators broke into applause and rallied on the steps of the statehouse. Shaheen signed the holiday bill into law.[54]

By the year 2000, all fifty states had enacted paid holidays in honor of Martin Luther King. In 2000, Utah renamed Human Rights Day— which had been a paid state holiday—as Martin Luther King Day. South Carolina, which had previously observed Martin Luther King Day only as an unpaid holiday, made it a paid state holiday. Through the end of the twentieth century, Virginia had celebrated Martin Luther King Day together with Robert E. Lee Day. Virginia ended that practice in 2000, but it prevailed in other southern states. Today, fifty years after King's death, Arkansas, Alabama, and Mississippi still pair Martin Luther King Day with Robert E. Lee Day. These states cannot bear to celebrate King by himself; they must simultaneously honor the slave-owning Confederate general.[55]

At the beginning of the twenty-first century, every state had an official King holiday and hundreds of cities boasted King boulevards. A 1999 Gallup poll found that to Americans, King was the second-most-admired individual of the twentieth century, just behind Mother Theresa and ahead of John F. Kennedy. King assumed his place in the pantheon of heroes because Americans could shape his legacy as they pleased. "Once a leader becomes a martyr, myth naturally follows," wrote William Manchester in his book on the death of John F. Kennedy. "The hero must be clothed in raiments which he would have found strange, but which please the public eye. . . . What the folk hero was and what he believed are submerged by the demands of those who follow him." After the leader is buried, "he becomes what they want him to have been." And so Ronald Reagan wanted King to stand for the ideals of colorblindness and rugged individualism. The white voters of Arizona wanted him to utter paeans to the Constitution. Merchants in San Diego wanted him to protect the "right" of citizens to select their own street name. To democratic socialists, King was the man who waged the Poor People's Campaign and demanded a guaranteed annual income for all Americans. To pacifists, King was the brave resister who denounced bombs and bullets and barbarism. He had become everything to everybody. Yet that state of affairs could exist only because King no longer spoke for himself. He could not clarify his positions on affirmative action and Obamacare, on the wars of the twenty-first century, on immigration and mass incarceration, on border walls and Muslim bans, on Trayvon Martin and Tamir Rice. If King could have somehow offered his own thoughts on the issues of the day, then Americans could no longer sustain the fiction central to his canonization: that he belonged to everyone and to every cause.[56]

Conclusion
KING IN
OUR TIME

K ING CAME BACK in the fall of 2000. Or so he did in the alternate
reality spun by *The Boondocks*, Aaron McGruder's animated television series based on his comic strip. An episode entitled "Return of
the King" aired on King's birthday in 2006.

The episode begins with a re-creation of the shooting at the Lorraine Motel. King survives, but he falls into a coma. He awakens in
October 2000, in the midst of the presidential campaign. King shows
up at a polling place on Election Day, but he is barred from voting. He
capitalizes on his fame and signs a lucrative book deal for his autobiography, to be titled *Dream Deferred*. He options the movie rights for a
biopic starring Cuba Gooding Jr. King is riding high.[1]

The tragedy of September 11, 2001, changes everything. After the
terrorist attacks, King pleads for nonviolence. On the television show
Politically Incorrect, King is asked how the United States should respond to the attacks. He reflects, "As a Christian, we are taught that
you should love thy enemy, and if attacked, you should turn the other
cheek." Other pundits denounce King as a lover of al-Qaeda. The anti-
King rhetoric in *The Boondocks* mirrors the criticism King received in
1967 for his antiwar activities. In the months after 9/11, many Americans treated all dissent as treachery. And in *The Boondocks*, news tickers

on cable channels read: "KING HATES AMERICA." One commentator snaps, "Go take another 30-year nap, Commie bastard!" CNN names King one of the most unpatriotic Americans. King's house is vandalized. His publisher cancels his book deal. King renames his autobiography *Dream Deferred*, and a small press publishes it. Nobody shows up to his book signings. Americans cannot accept King in the flesh because they cannot muzzle him. He is no longer safely dead, but dangerously alive.[2]

King bemoans the state of black life in the twenty-first century. He is disheartened by African Americans' quest for "bling" and their hesitance to protest against injustice. He flips through the television channels, disgusted by vulgar hip-hop lyrics and offensive music videos. King then joins the "first all-black political party" and organizes a meeting. Radio stations and media outlets help to generate a large turnout for the event. But that turns the affair into a dance party rather than a political gathering. There are bouncers and alcohol, scuffles and general mayhem. King delivers a speech, and laces into his audience. He demands, "Will you ignorant niggers please shut the hell up?!" Martin Luther King has silenced the crowd with the ugliest of epithets. He continues in that vein, chiding the "trifling" African Americans before him. He asks, "This is it? This is what I got all those ass-whoopings for?" He tells his audience that he has seen the future, and it offers more of the same complacency. "No, I won't get there with you," he announces. "I'm going to Canada." So King moves north of the border.[3]

King's speech is replayed on television the following day, with shocking effect. African Americans begin to both lift themselves up and to mobilize against injustice. Dropout rates decline. Every African American basketball player refuses to suit up for games until the government withdraws its military troops from foreign lands. African Americans besiege their representatives with letters and phone calls. Thousands gather outside the White House, demanding justice. As the narrator puts it, "The revolution finally came." An epilogue explains that King would pass away in Vancouver in 2020, at the age of ninety-one. Later that year, Oprah Winfrey would be elected president. The episode ends with the words: "It's fun to dream."[4]

THAT MOST FANCIFUL dream became a reality in 2008, with the election of Barack Obama. King's struggle paved the way for America's first black president. Yet King's slaughter also presaged the other racial dynamic that shapes the United States in the early twenty-first century. It helped to usher in a world of racial hatred and political division. We as a society have yet to recover from that blow.

The kind of hostility that bubbled to the surface in 1968 seems to have reappeared fifty years later, often in even nastier forms. After King's death, African Americans took to the streets, some in violent revolt and others in peaceful and interracial marches. Many whites were fearful of African Americans and appalled by the protests in the streets more than they were outraged at King's assassination. In 1968, they responded to a presidential candidate who promised to restore law and order. That candidate, Republican Richard Nixon, divided the nation so that he could conquer it. George Wallace's third-party candidacy had whipped up whites' racial anger. And Nixon played on that rage to win the presidency. (In the United Kingdom, Enoch Powell exploited similar racial fears.) Writing from the vantage point of 2018, that narrative seems hauntingly familiar. Unarmed black men have been gunned down in our streets, yet many white Americans remain unmoved by those acts of racial violence. Instead, they see a profound threat in a mass movement led by African Americans. Their response has not been to mourn the loss of black lives or to call for racial justice, but to embrace a white identity politics all over again.

King's heroic life and his brutal death thus anticipated the central irony of race in our time. If he tried to bring the races together during his life and pointed our country toward a multiracial tomorrow, then his death illuminated the depths of white racism, quickened the pace of black radicalism, and helped to break the races further apart. We now stand in the wake of a vicious backlash against our first black president and navigate a world in which black lives remain uniquely threatened. It is five decades since King's murder, but our nation still seems to tear along the same lines of racial hatred. Our social fabric has not yet been mended.

KING FIGURED PROMINENTLY in Obama's political ascent and in his presidential campaign. For Obama, the stories of the civil rights movement had long loomed as a touchstone. As Obama struggled to make sense of his own racial identity and then committed himself to community organizing in the 1980s, the romantic images from the civil rights years acted as inspiration: "Such images became a form of prayer for me, bolstering my spirits, channeling my emotions in a way that words never could." Obama was in law school when he read *Parting the Waters*, Taylor Branch's history of "America in the King years." Obama came to see his own life through the lens of that history. It was his story—the story of racial struggle, of forcing America to live up to its ideals. And as Obama pursued electoral politics, he continued to refer back to King. Obama ran for the United States Senate in 2003, launching his campaign with a speech that revolved around the refrain, "What would Dr. Martin Luther King, Jr., say?" Obama not only connected with King in a personal sense; he also knew it was good politics to associate his plight with King's.[5]

Obama burst onto the national scene in the summer of 2004 with his speech at the Democratic National Convention. By that time, Martin Luther King's fame was never greater. In 2004 and 2005, two scholars conducted a survey among high school students across the country. They asked the students to name the five most famous Americans, excepting presidents. Two-thirds of the students listed King, far and away the most of any individual. King had become a transcendent figure, one who soared above racial and ideological divides. And when Obama announced his bid for the presidency, he promised to bridge those same divides.[6]

On March 4, 2007, Obama spoke at the Brown Chapel AME Church in Selma, Alabama. He paid tribute to members of the "Moses generation," like Rosa Parks, John Lewis, and King. Obama remarked that his own generation of African American leaders stood "on the shoulders of giants." He acknowledged his debt to them and positioned himself as their heir. He would fill the void that had stood empty since the late 1960s. "Ever since the assassination of King ... and of Robert Kennedy," wrote David Remnick in his biography of Obama, American liberals "had been waiting for a savior figure." Barack Obama offered himself as that leader. As Obama inched nearer to the presidency, civil rights veterans began to accept the narrative he was offering. Said former SCLC leader C. T. Vivian, "Martin Luther King was our prophet—in Biblical terms, the prophet of our age. The politician of our age, who comes along to follow that prophet, is Barack Obama." Obama triumphed in 2008, forever changing the color of American political history. And he cemented his place in the larger civil rights story. On Martin Luther King Day in January 2009, which fell one day before Obama's inauguration, John Lewis declared, "Barack Obama is what comes at the end of that bridge in Selma." Obama had managed to situate himself alongside King, who had finally become the most hallowed of American heroes.[7]

King's popularity only grew as he passed from memory into history. In an August 2011 Gallup poll, 94 percent of Americans expressed a favorable view of King; just 4 percent held an unfavorable view. The poll also found 51 percent of Americans judged that King's dream had been realized. Fully 54 percent of black Americans believed the nation had achieved King's dream of racial equality, compared with 49 percent of whites. At the time of the poll, Obama had only been in office for two and a half years. African Americans could still bask in the glow of his victory. He had brought the nation back from the financial abyss, rescued the auto industry, captured Osama bin Laden, and signed the Affordable Care Act, which provided health insurance for 20 million uninsured Americans. Yet as Barack Obama's presidency unfolded, many white Americans flung at him the same kind of abuse whites had hurled at King. They seethed at the sight of a black man in a position of such authority, and cursed the fact that an African American family inhabited the White House. Through Obama's second term, African Americans' optimism faded. That was largely because the nation's first black president appeared powerless against the continued assault on black bodies.[8]

Their names have become rallying cries: Michael Brown, Eric Garner, Tamir Rice, Freddie Gray, and many others. They were black people killed by the police; most of the incidents were captured on cellphone videos and beamed to the rest of the world. The killings helped to fuel the Black Lives Matter movement. Its slogan was simple: a stark reminder that America, through the centuries, had failed to value the lives of African Americans. To simply exist as a black person was to court danger. By the end of Obama's presidency in 2016, African Americans still remained especially vulnerable to state-sponsored violence. This reality reinforced the fact that no individual—not Obama, not King—could compel white America to truly value black lives.

As a violent racism surged to the center of American life yet again, African Americans found it necessary to assert their own humanity. They waged that struggle through the Black Lives Matter movement. But many whites would have none of it. Counterdemonstrators appeared at Black Lives Matter protests, shouting, "All Lives Matter!" Leading conservatives rushed to denounce Black Lives Matter. And to make their case, they often quoted from one line of King's "I Have a Dream" speech—the line in which King envisioned a day when his children would be judged by the content of their character. The selective appropriation of Martin Luther King—a black leader murdered because he was a *black* leader—continued apace. Such observers vilified the Black Lives Matter movement in the same way that King's critics had denounced him. Bill O'Reilly of Fox News charged that Black Lives Matter "encourages violence through irresponsible rhetoric." He claimed,

"Dr. King would not participate in a Black Lives Matter protest." Mike Huckabee, the former governor of Arkansas, appeared on CNN and explained, "When I hear people scream, 'black lives matter,' I think, 'Of course they do.' But all lives matter. It's not that any life matters more than another. That's the whole message that Dr. King tried to present, and I think he'd be appalled by the notion that we're elevating some lives above others." On the radio program *Breitbart News Sunday,* former vice presidential candidate Sarah Palin alleged that the Black Lives Matter movement was "the antithesis of Martin Luther King's message." Every opponent of Black Lives Matter claimed to stand with King.[9]

Richard Land, president of the Southern Evangelical Seminary, proceeded in the same vein. He declared, "I, for one, refuse to give up on Dr. Martin Luther King Jr.'s dream of a nation where Americans are not 'judged by the color of their skin but by the content of their character.'" That was the only quotation from King that he offered. He then condemned Black Lives Matter for "engaging in counter-productive rhetoric, which divides rather than unites." Land savaged Black Lives Matter for its "inflammatory rhetoric." He concluded, "Dr. King faced down far greater bigotry and lethal violence than we face today. Let us draw inspiration and dedication from his courage and vision and join hands and resolve to finish the work to which he so eloquently called us." Land disfigured King's career in an attempt to assert that King would have opposed the black protesters.[10]

King's own critics had castigated him for "provoking violence," engaging in "inflammatory rhetoric," and endangering law and order. Strom Thurmond, Robert Byrd, Lionel Lokos, and many others accused King of inciting tensions and dividing Americans against one another. The Black Lives Matter movement endured similar opprobrium, as protesters were often denounced as disruptive and dangerous. When the opponents of Black Lives Matter referenced King, they conveniently ignored the massive disruptions that King organized throughout the nation. He did so week after week, year after year. For that he was scorned and reviled. In King's most famous writing, the

"Letter from Birmingham City Jail," he criticized those white moderates who were "more devoted to 'order' than to justice." He pointed out that true peace could only exist alongside the presence of justice. There could be no "order" until justice reigned. He also expressed grave worries about the devaluing of black lives. He had written to SCLC donors just before his death: "In the halls of Congress, Negro lives are too cheap to justify resolute measures." King called on Americans to take such forthright action in their battle against injustice.[11]

In the fall of 2016, Clemson football coach Dabo Swinney delivered an attack on Colin Kaepernick, the quarterback of the San Francisco 49ers who knelt during the national anthem to protest the killing of black men. Swinney claimed that Kaepernick's actions were divisive and offered protesters like him a word of advice. If "everything is so bad and this world's falling apart . . . some of these people need to move to another country." Swinney recommended that Black Lives Matter protesters should heed King's shining example: "I think the answer to our problems is exactly what they were for Martin Luther King when he changed the world. Love, peace, education, tolerance of others, Jesus." Missing from Dabo Swinney's portrait of King was the man who criticized his country and paralyzed American cities with street protests.[12]

Those who cite King as an example so often ignore his manifest commitment to civil disobedience. Their distortions reflect the fact that many Americans still have not reckoned with the actual King. Even those who brandish his legacy have little understanding of the causes for which he sacrificed.

We the living are left with a duty to King: to make clear the substance of his actual teachings and actions. Our challenge is to keep alive the memory of a man who died for striking sanitation workers, who deplored American barbarism overseas, who spoke to black militants as well as mainstream civil rights leaders, who clung to nonviolence yet empathized with the cries of urban rioters, who beseeched his government to protect the vulnerable and employ the poor. As he looked out from the motel balcony in April 1968, he was still evolving as a leader—adjusting his voice to the realities of the late 1960s, modulating his tone to keep in tune with society's most alienated, still ready to strap on his marching shoes, to log long nights in jail, and to make the ultimate sacrifice for his cause. He was all of thirty-nine years old. It seemed that a lifetime stood before him.

ACKNOWLEDGMENTS

I first visited Memphis in 1998. It was the summer before my senior year of college, and I traveled there to work on an honors thesis about the 1968 sanitation strike. When not in the archive, I explored the city. I walked along Beale Street and went to the Civil Rights Museum; I ate biscuits and barbecue of a kind you couldn't get in my native Massachusetts. I played basketball at the YMCA with my friend Steve Manthe, and we later took a bus from East Memphis to Graceland. Ever since that trip, I have wanted to study in more depth the events of early 1968 that rocked Memphis and the nation.

Given the existence of so many excellent biographies of Martin Luther King, and Michael Honey's masterful book on the Memphis strike, I thought a lot about how I might contribute something new on King's life and death. If I have succeeded at all, it is due to the many wonderful people who have helped me along the way: friends and family who supported me, colleagues who engaged my ideas, archivists who patiently and painstakingly helped me to explore this tragic part of our country's past.

I am grateful to those archivists who assisted me both during my research trips and with my requests from afar. I thank the Special Collections staff at the University of Memphis, especially Christopher Ratliff and James Cushing. Thanks also to Randall Burkett and the staff at the Rose Library at Emory University. Allen Fisher at the Lyndon B. Johnson Library was extremely helpful. Amy McDonald at Duke

University's Rubinstein Rare Book & Manuscript Library also offered invaluable assistance. Thanks to Lisa Francisco Abitz at the University of Memphis Art Museum. In addition, I thank the staffs at the University of Connecticut's Thomas Dodd Research Center, the Wisconsin Historical Society, and the Scholars Room at the Paley Center for Media.

I extend my heartfelt thanks to those who have read chapters and given feedback. Steve Estes read the entire manuscript with great care and offered many crucial suggestions. His comments have improved the book immeasurably. Neal Allen read a chapter and also generously shared much of his own research. Ted Segal gave valuable comments regarding the Duke vigil, and William Chafe pointed me toward additional resources. Brian Ward offered suggestions on my analysis of events in Britain. Thomas Jackson offered early encouragement and shared some very helpful research material with me. I thank Harvard Sitkoff for discussing King with me, and Brian Purnell for our ongoing conversations about civil rights.

I am proud to be part of the University of New Hampshire's History Department, and privileged to work in a department that is at once so collegial and filled with such impressive scholars. I would particularly like to thank those who attended a faculty workshop and offered their feedback on one of my chapters: Jeff Bolster, Kurk Dorsey, Molly Girard-Dorsey, Cathy Frierson, Jan Golinski, Nicky Gullace, Mike Leese, Jessica Lepler, Julia Rodriguez, and Lucy Salyer. I also thank Jan Golinski and Lige Gould, who served as the department chairs while I worked on this book. In addition, I thank Ellen Fitzpatrick for her support of the project. I am also grateful to Bill Harris for the opportunity to present some of my material in his class.

Many others helped me during the course of this project. Susannah Deily-Swearingen offered research assistance and put her sterling command of German to work on behalf of *The Heavens Might Crack*. Giles Edwards helped me locate an interview with King in the

BBC's archives. Mark Rudd was generous with his time and responded thoughtfully to my questions. Dolph Smith graciously granted an interview, and also allowed me to reproduce an image of his artwork.

Several institutions and organizations have given crucial assistance for this project. The UNH College of Liberal Arts has provided great support, under the leadership of both Dean Heidi Bostic and Dean Ken Fuld. Funds from the Arthur K. Whitcomb Professorship enabled me to devote two summers to research and writing.

It was a great honor to receive a Public Scholar fellowship from the National Endowment for the Humanities. (Of course, the views expressed in this book do not necessarily reflect those of the NEH.) I simply could not have completed this book without the year off from teaching that the NEH fellowship afforded me.

The Hutchins Center at Harvard University continues to provide me with an additional intellectual home. I thank Henry Louis Gates Jr., Abby Wolf, and Krishna Lewis.

My own teachers still inspire me. Gary Kornblith not only advised my original thesis on the Memphis sanitation strike; he has also remained a close friend and colleague. At the University of California, Berkeley, Leon Litwack and Waldo Martin were the greatest mentors one can ask for. They are engaged historians and passionate teachers, and they continue to serve as my models.

I feel fortunate to have worked with Basic Books. I thank my agent, Brettne Bloom, for pairing me with Basic and for her eager support of this book from the day that we first discussed the idea. I thank Lara Heimert for taking on the project, and for her insightful suggestions about how to revise the manuscript. Thanks to Leah Stecher for editing each line with great care and for offering further ideas about how to improve the book. Alia Massoud helped to shepherd the book through the various phases of editing and production. I would also like to thank my production editor, Stephanie Summerhays, as well as copy editor Bill Warhop.

Thanks to my friends in Newburyport, including everyone at Middle Street Foods, whose food and camaraderie have sustained me through many afternoons of writing and editing.

Most of all, I thank my family. My parents, Fred and Betsy Sokol, have seen me through it all—they have offered advice, support, laughter, and love. My brother, Scott Sokol, helps me to occasionally take my mind off of history so that I can obsess about other important things: the Mets, March Madness, fantasy baseball.

Throughout the process of research and writing, Nina Morrison has reassured me in times of doubt, joined in arcane discussions of grammar and word choice, endured my neuroses, and encouraged me to savor the small triumphs. I do need to offer her an apology for the poor timing of this book. I was not anywhere close to completing the book when we learned that our first child would be coming into the world. Our first semester back to teaching (when Arlo was eleven weeks old) would have been hard enough even if I had not been trying to revise the entire manuscript at that time. It was difficult, very difficult, but in retrospect I wouldn't have done it any differently. (So I guess my apology is characteristically half-hearted.) It is the joy of my life to raise a child with Nina, and I delight in each moment with her. If this book is any better because of the happiness that I felt while working on it, that is because of Nina. Of course, the subject matter of the book is often extremely painful. But while I was exploring the impact of King's death, Nina and Arlo helped me to discover an even greater zest for life. They do that every day.

NOTES

INTRODUCTION: SHOT RINGS OUT

1. Fred Crawford, Roy Norman, and Leah Dabbs, *A Report of Certain Reactions by the Atlanta Public to the Death of the Reverend Doctor Martin Luther King Jr.* (Atlanta, GA: Center for Research in Social Change, Emory University, 1969), 15; Rebecca Burns, "The Remarkable Behind-the-Scenes Story of King's Funeral," *Atlanta*, April 2008, 99.

2. James Baldwin, "On Martin Luther King," 1978, reprinted in Jennifer Schuessler, "James Baldwin's Archive, Long Hidden, Comes (Mostly) into View," *New York Times*, April 12, 2017, https://www.nytimes.com/2017/04/12 /arts/james-baldwins-archive-long-hidden-comes-mostly-into-view.html ?_r=0; James Baldwin, "Malcolm and Martin," *Esquire*, April 1972.

3. Harry Golden, *The Nation*, April 29, 1968, 572.

4. Dorothy Newby, Hamilton High Essays, Folder 51, Container 8, Sanitation Strike Collection, Special Collections, McWhorter Library, University of Memphis; Frankie Gross, Hamilton High Essays; Joan Turner Beifuss, *At the River I Stand: Memphis, the 1968 Strike, and Martin Luther King* (Brooklyn, NY: Carlson Publishing, 1989), 402.

5. Michael Honey, *Black Workers Remember: An Oral History of Segregation, Unionism, and the Freedom Struggle* (Berkeley: University of California Press, 1999), 312–313; Michael Honey, *Going Down Jericho Road: The Memphis Strike, Martin Luther King's Last Campaign* (New York: W.W. Norton, 2007), 447.

6. Martin Luther King, "I Have a Dream," August 28, 1963, in *A Testament of Hope: The Essential Writings of Martin Luther King Jr.*, ed. James Washington (San Francisco: Harper & Row, 1986), 217; Martin Luther King, "The Birth of a New Nation," April 7, 1957, http://kingencyclopedia.stanford.edu /primarydocuments/Vol4/7-Apr-1957_BirthOfANewNation.pdf.

7. King, "I Have a Dream," 217.

8. Joshua Bloom and Waldo Martin, *Black Against Empire: The History and Politics of the Black Panther Party* (Berkeley: University of California Press, 2013), 116, 122.

9. *Miami Negroes: A Study in Depth* (Miami, FL: *Miami Herald*, 1968), 51; Marshall Frady, *Martin Luther King Jr.* (New York: Viking, 2002), 182–183.

10. "Europe Dismayed by Slaying and Fearful over U.S. Stability," *New York Times*, April 6, 1968.

11. David Caute, *The Year of the Barricades: A Journey Through 1968* (New York: Harper & Row, 1988), 241, 402–403, 391–392; Jeremi Suri, *The Global Revolutions of 1968* (New York: W.W. Norton, 2007).

12. "Dr. King Told B.B.C. Thoughts on Death," *New York Times*, April 5, 1968; "Doubts and Certainties," Martin Luther King Talks to Gerald Priestland, British Broadcasting Company, April 4, 1968.

13. Murray Schumach, "Martin Luther King Jr.: Leader of Millions in Nonviolent Drive for Racial Justice," *New York Times*, April 5, 1968; Beverly Gage, "What an Uncensored Letter to M.L.K. Reveals," *New York Times Magazine*, November 11, 2014.

14. Martin Luther King, "The Drum Major Instinct," in Washington, ed., *Testament of Hope*, 266–267.

15. Rachel Lapp, "Vincent Harding: King for the 21st Century Calls Us to Walk with Jesus," Goshen College Press Archive, January 21, 2005, www.goshen.edu/news/pressarchive/01–21–05-MLK-Harding-folo.html.

CHAPTER 1: LOSING KING

1. Lerone Bennett Jr. wrote that King was engaged "in a struggle for his very existence as a national leader." Lerone Bennett Jr., "The Martyrdom of Martin Luther King Jr.," *Ebony*, May 1968, 176; David Levering Lewis, *King: A Biography*, 2nd ed. (Urbana: University of Illinois Press, 1978), 363.

2. David Halberstam, "The Second Coming of Martin Luther King," *Harper's*, August 1967, 48.

3. Michael Honey, *Going Down Jericho Road: The Memphis Strike, Martin Luther King's Last Campaign* (New York: W.W. Norton, 2007), 295–296.

4. Garry Wills, "Martin Luther King Is *Still on the Case!*," *Esquire*, August 1968, 129.

5. Taylor Branch, *At Canaan's Edge: America in the King Years, 1965–68* (New York: Simon & Schuster, 2006), 764; Interview with Andrew Young, by Paul Steckler, October 27, 1988, Eyes on the Prize II Interviews, Henry Hampton Collection, Film and Media Archive, Washington University

Libraries, http://digital.wustl.edu/cgi/t/text/textidx?c=eop;cc=eop;rgn
=main;view=text;idno=you5427.0112.179.

6. Joan Turner Beifuss, *At the River I Stand: Memphis, the 1968 Strike, and
Martin Luther King* (Brooklyn, NY: Carlson Publishing, 1989), 363–364;
Interview with James Lawson, Number 141, Sanitation Strike Collection,
University of Memphis, 58; *At the River I Stand* (San Francisco: California
Newsreel, 1993), DVD; Martin Luther King, "I See the Promised Land," in
James Washington, ed., *A Testament of Hope: The Essential Writings of Martin
Luther King Jr.* (San Francisco: Harper & Row, 1986), 286.

7. Coretta Scott King, *My Life with Martin Luther King, Jr.* (New York:
Holt, Rinehart and Winston, 1969), 303; Bernard Lafayette, oral history, in
Rebecca Burns, "The Remarkable Behind-the-Scenes Story of King's Fu-
neral," *Atlanta*, April 2008, 101; Bennett, "The Martyrdom of Martin Luther
King Jr.," 180.

8. Interview with Andrew Young, Eyes on the Prize II Interviews; *At the
River I Stand*, California Newsreel.

9. Interview with Andrew Young, Eyes on the Prize II Interviews; *At the
River I Stand*, California Newsreel; Interview with Gwen Kyles, by Jerry
Viar, Joan Beifuss, and Carol Lynn Yellin, May 28, 1968, Sanitation Strike
Collection, University of Memphis, 12, 14–15.

10. Interview with Andrew Young, Eyes on the Prize II Interviews; *At
the River I Stand*, California Newsreel; "'That Song, Precious Lord, Sing it
Real Pretty,' was the Last Request of Slain Civil Rights Leader," *Commer-
cial Appeal*, April 5, 1968; Robert Samsot, "King's Assassination Etched in
Witnesses' Eyes, Ears," *Commercial Appeal*, April 5, 1968; Hampton Sides,
*Hellhound on His Trail: The Stalking of Martin Luther King Jr. and the Interna-
tional Hunt for His Assassin* (New York: Doubleday, 2010), 163–166; "Dr. King
Slain in Memphis," *Nashville Tennessean*, April 5, 1968.

11. Wills, "Martin Luther King Is *Still on the Case!*," 99; Beifuss, *At the
River I Stand*, 389–390.

12. King, *My Life with Martin Luther King*, 317–319.

13. Ivan Allen Jr., with Paul Hemphill, *Mayor: Notes on the Sixties* (New
York: Simon & Schuster, 1971), 196–201; King, *My Life with Martin Luther
King*, 319–320.

14. Kathryn Johnson, oral history, in Burns, "Remarkable Behind-the-
Scenes Story of King's Funeral," 99; Re: Mrs. King, April 10, 1968, Box 34,
Folder 17, *Newsweek* Collection, Manuscript, Archives, and Rare Book Li-
brary, Emory University.

15. Wills, "Martin Luther King Is *Still on the Case!*," 99; Gregory Jaynes and Charles Thornton, "Tears and Vows Mingle in Poignant Flood," *Commercial Appeal*, April 6, 1968; Beifuss, *At the River I Stand*, 413; Rebecca Burns, *Burial for a King: Martin Luther King Jr.'s Funeral and the Week That Transformed Atlanta and Rocked the Nation* (New York: Scribner, 2011), 67.

16. Beifuss, *At the River I Stand*, 414; Jaynes and Thornton, "Tears and Vows Mingle in Poignant Flood"; Burns, *Burial for a King*, 68.

17. Wills, "Martin Luther King Is *Still on the Case!*," 100–101.

18. J. Anthony Lukas, "Memphis Approves a Memorial Parade," *New York Times*, April 6, 1968.

19. Walter Rugaber, "Dr. King's Funeral to Be Held Tuesday in Church Where He Was Co-Pastor," *New York Times*, April 6, 1968; Burns, *Burial for a King*, 74, 90; Philip Gailey, "All Night, They File Silently In," *Atlanta Constitution*, April 6, 1968; "He Never Hated—Never Despaired," *Commercial Appeal*, April 7, 1968; King, *My Life with Martin Luther King*, 327; Stephen Oates, *Let the Trumpet Sound: The Life of Martin Luther King Jr.* (New York: Harper & Row, 1982), 495; Burns, "Remarkable Behind-the-Scenes Story of King's Funeral," 134; Coretta Scott King, *My Life, My Love, My Legacy* (New York: Henry Holt, 2017), 165.

20. Ben W. Gilbert and the Staff of the *Washington Post, Ten Blocks from the White House: Anatomy of the Washington Riots of 1968* (New York: Praeger, 1968), 221; Thomas Jackson, *From Civil Rights to Human Rights: Martin Luther King, Jr., and the Struggle for Economic Justice* (Philadelphia: University of Pennsylvania Press, 2007), 341.

21. *At the River I Stand*, California Newsreel; Mary Mayhue, Students' Responses to Assassination: Porter Junior High School, Folder 54, Sanitation Strike Collection, University of Memphis; Sherry Echols, Hamilton High Essays, Folder 51, Container 8, Sanitation Strike Collection, Special Collections, McWhorter Library, University of Memphis; Interview with James Lawson, Number 142, Sanitation Strike Collection, University of Memphis, 20.

22. To: Nation, Iselin, From: Jaffe, Sheraton Peabody, Memphis, Re: Nonviolence on the Line in Memphis, Box 34, Folder 17, *Newsweek* Collection; John Means, "Somber Throng of 19,000 Marchers Is Urged to Let King's Spirit Live," *Commercial Appeal*, April 9, 1968; Honey, *Going Down Jericho Road*, 478.

23. To: Nation, Iselin, From: Jaffe, Sheraton Peabody, Memphis, Re: Nonviolence on the Line in Memphis, *Newsweek* Collection; Edwin Stanfield,

"In Memphis: Mirror to America?," Second Supplement to Special Report of March 22, 1968 (Atlanta, GA: Southern Regional Council, April 28, 1968), 8; "CBS News Special Report: The Memphis March, April 8, 1968," Paley Center for Media; Beifuss, *At the River I Stand*, 444–445; Honey, *Going Down Jericho Road*, 477.

24. Means, "Somber Throng"; Beifuss, *At the River I Stand*, 446; "CBS News Special Report: The Memphis March," Paley Center for Media.

25. "CBS News Special Report: The Memphis March," Paley Center for Media.

26. Ibid.

27. Ibid.; Re: Mrs. King, April 10, 1968, *Newsweek* Collection.

28. "CBS News Special Report: The Memphis March," Paley Center for Media; *At the River I Stand*, California Newsreel.

29. To: Nation, Iselin, From: Jaffe, Sheraton Peabody, Memphis, Re: Nonviolence on the Line in Memphis, *Newsweek* Collection.

30. "Quiet March, Loud Talk," *Commercial Appeal*, April 9, 1968.

31. Stanfield, "In Memphis: Mirror to America?," 9–10.

32. Joseph Smith Jr., Hamilton High Essays; Frankie Gross, Hamilton High Essays.

33. Barbara Chandler, Hamilton High Essays.

34. Wills, "Martin Luther King Is *Still on the Case!*," 98, 100; Interview with Garry Wills, by Cal Fussman, Evanston, IL, July 2015, http://classic.esquire.com/martin-luther-king-is-still-on-the-case/.

35. Wills, "Martin Luther King Is *Still on the Case!*," 100–101.

36. Ibid., 104.

37. Ibid., 104, 126.

38. Burns, *Burial for a King*, 158; "City Pauses Today for King Funeral," *New York Times*, April 9, 1968; James Baldwin, "Malcolm and Martin," *Esquire*, April 1972; Sides, *Hellhound on His Trail*, 277.

39. Maria Saporta, oral history, in Burns, "Remarkable Behind-the-Scenes Story of King's Funeral," 135; Diane Stepp, "Mourners Come Hundreds of Miles to Stand in Lines," *Atlanta Constitution*, April 9, 1968; Lubenow/Atlanta, Nation (Kosner): Riot Wrapup, April 11, 1968, Box 34, Folder 17, *Newsweek* Collection.

40. Baldwin, "Malcolm and Martin"; Gary Pomerantz, *Where Peachtree Meets Sweet Auburn: The Saga of Two Families and the Making of Atlanta* (New York: Scribner, 1996), 360; Burns, *Burial for a King*, 147.

41. Baldwin, "Malcolm and Martin."

42. King, *My Life with Martin Luther King*, 330; Jethro English, oral history, in Burns, "Remarkable Behind-the-Scenes Story of King's Funeral," 140–141; Burns, *Burial for a King*, 150; Bennett, "The Martyrdom of Martin Luther King Jr."; Nation–Goldman, From: Lubenow, Atlanta, Re: Funeral, April 11, 1968, Box 34, Folder 17, *Newsweek* Collection; Baldwin, "Malcolm and Martin."

43. Bernard Lafayette, oral history, in Burns, "Remarkable Behind-the-Scenes Story of King's Funeral," 134.

44. Elizabeth Omilami, oral history, in Burns, "Remarkable Behind-the-Scenes Story of King's Funeral," 134; Burns, *Burial for a King*, 87, 133, 135–136, 153.

45. Alex Coffin, "Leader Is Laid to Rest," *Atlanta Constitution*, April 10, 1968; Sam Williams, oral history, in Burns, "Remarkable Behind-the-Scenes Story of King's Funeral," 143; Nation–Goldman, From: Lubenow, Atlanta, Re: Funeral, April 11, 1968, *Newsweek* Collection; Homer Bigart, "Leaders at Rites," *New York Times*, April 10, 1968.

46. Pomerantz, *Where Peachtree Meets Sweet Auburn*, 362; Anthony Ripley, "Funeral Is Ignored by Whites but Some Atlanta Stores Close," *New York Times*, April 10, 1968.

47. Larry Williams, "Memorial to Fallen Leader Is Lost in a Network Maze," *Commercial Appeal*, April 9, 1968; Fred Crawford, Roy Norman, and Leah Dabbs, *A Report of Certain Reactions by the Atlanta Public to the Death of the Reverend Doctor Martin Luther King Jr.* (Atlanta, GA: Center for Research in Social Change, Emory University, 1969), 15, 17.

48. Coffin, "Leader Is Laid to Rest"; Honey, *Going Down Jericho Road*, 482; Arthur Schlesinger Jr., *Robert Kennedy and His Times* (New York: Ballantine Books, 1978), 943.

49. Stepp, "Mourners Come Hundreds of Miles"; Laurence Smith Jr., to Ralph McGill, April 10, 1968, Box 18, Folder 8 (Series II: Correspondence, 1968 April 8–10), Ralph McGill Papers, Manuscript, Archives, and Rare Book Library, Emory University.

50. Cathy Aldridge, "Black, White Came to Bury Martin Luther King Jr.," *Amsterdam News*, April 13, 1968; Lewis, *King*, 391; Nation–Goldman, From: Lubenow, Atlanta, Re: Funeral, April 11, 1968, *Newsweek* Collection; King, *My Life with Martin Luther King*, 332.

51. Nation–Goldman, From: Lubenow, Atlanta, Re: Funeral, April 11, 1968, *Newsweek* Collection; Means, "Somber Throng."

52. Pomerantz, *Where Peachtree Meets Sweet Auburn*, 363; Pat Watters, "Beale Street and Points North," *The Nation*, April 22, 1968.

53. Jesse Jackson, oral history, in Burns, "Remarkable Behind-the-Scenes Story of King's Funeral," 142; Lewis, *King*, 391.

54. Ralph McGill, "Until Minds Are Changed," *Atlanta Constitution*, April 10, 1968.

55. Robert Dallek, *Flawed Giant: Lyndon Johnson and His Times, 1961–1973* (New York: Oxford University Press, 1998), 533; "Statements in the Capital," *New York Times*, April 5, 1968.

56. "Troops Build Up," *Commercial Appeal*, April 7, 1968; "CBS News Special Report: The Memphis March," Paley Center for Media; Lyndon Johnson, *The Vantage Point: Perspectives of the Presidency, 1963–1969* (New York: Holt, Rinehart and Winston, 1971), 176. In the many biographies of Johnson, and in memoirs written by his staffers, Johnson's decision merits passing mention. See Dallek, *Flawed Giant*, 533–534; Joseph Califano, *The Triumph and Tragedy of Lyndon Johnson: The White House Years* (College Station: Texas A&M University Press, 2000), 282; Irving Bernstein, *Guns or Butter: The Presidency of Lyndon Johnson* (New York: Oxford University Press, 1996), 496.

57. Memo to Marvin Watson, Re: Don Kendall, April 5, 1968, White House Central Files (WHCF), Box 5, Folder Ex FE 3-1/King, Lyndon B. Johnson Library (LBJL); Memo from Charles Maguire to Tom Johnson, April 8, 1968, WHCF, Box 5, Folder Ex FE 3-1/King, LBJL; Memo from Charles Maguire to Jim Jones, April 8, 1968, WHCF, Box 5, Folder Ex FE 3-1/King, LBJL; Memo from Stu Eizenstat to Jim Jones, April 8, 1968, WHCF, Box 5, Folder Ex FE 3-1/King, LBJL; Memo from Jim Jones, Re: Jack Valenti, April 5, 1968, WHCF, Box 5, Folder Ex FE 3-1/King, LBJL.

58. Memo from Mike Manatos to Lyndon Johnson, Re: Bill Helis, April 8, 1968, WHCF, Box 5, Folder Ex FE 3-1/King, LBJL; Memo from Marvin Watson to Lyndon Johnson, Re: Phil Landrum, April 8, 1968, WHCF, Box 5, Folder Ex FE 3-1/King, LBJL; Memo from Barefoot Sanders to Jim Jones, April 8, 1968, WHCF, Box 5, Folder Ex FE 3-1/King, LBJL; Memo from Marvin Watson to Lyndon Johnson, Re: Buford Ellington, April 8, 1968, WHCF, Box 5, Folder Ex FE 3-1/King, LBJL; Memo from Joe Califano to Lyndon Johnson, April 8, 1968, WHCF, Box 5, Folder Ex FE 3-1/King, LBJL.

59. Memo from James Rowley to Lyndon Johnson, April 8, 1968, Document #8b, WHCF, Box 14, Folder FE 3-1 Deaths & Funerals, LBJL; Cable

from FBI Atlanta 157-3094 to Director, Attn: Mr. DeLoach, April 8, 1968, Document #8d, WHCF, Box 14, Folder FE 3-1 Deaths & Funerals, LBJL.

60. Sides, *Hellhound on His Trail*, 278; Clay Risen, *A Nation on Fire: America in the Wake of the King Assassination* (Hoboken, NJ: Wiley, 2009), 207; Roger Wilkins, *A Man's Life: An Autobiography* (New York: Simon & Schuster, 1982), 215; Jean Stein, *American Journey: The Times of Robert Kennedy* (New York: Harcourt Brace Jovanovich, 1970), 259.

61. Baldwin, "Malcolm and Martin."

62. Ibid.

CHAPTER 2: THE LAST PRINCE OF NONVIOLENCE

1. Ben W. Gilbert and the Staff of the *Washington Post*, *Ten Blocks from the White House: Anatomy of the Washington Riots of 1968* (New York: Praeger, 1968), 98; Clay Risen, *A Nation on Fire: America in the Wake of the King Assassination* (Hoboken, NJ: Wiley, 2009), 4; "New Violence Erupts in Riot-Torn Kansas City," *Commercial Appeal*, April 12, 1968.

2. Aaron Dixon, *My People Are Rising: Memoir of a Black Panther Party Captain* (Chicago: Haymarket Books, 2012), 111; Interview with Aaron Dixon, by James Johnson, July 11, 1970, Seattle Black Panther Party History and Memory Project, University of Washington, http://depts.washington.edu/civilr/aaron_dixon.htm.

3. Dixon, *My People Are Rising*, 71–74; "Franklin Sit-In Protests School Suspensions," *Seattle Post-Intelligencer*, March 30, 1968, Seattle Civil Rights and Labor History Project, University of Washington, http://www.civilrights.washington.edu; Interview with Larry Gossett, Seattle Civil Rights and Labor History Project.

4. Andrew Kopkind, "Soul Power," *New York Review of Books*, August 24, 1967. One poll found that shortly before King's death, 57 percent of blacks considered him to be irrelevant. Tavis Smiley, *Death of a King: The Real Story of Dr. Martin Luther King's Final Year* (New York: Little, Brown, 2014), 243.

5. "McKissick Says Nonviolence Has Become Dead Philosophy," *New York Times*, April 5, 1968; Lawrence Van Gelder, "Dismay in Nation," *New York Times*, April 5, 1968.

6. "President's Plea," *New York Times*, April 5, 1968; "CBS News Special Report: The Death of Rev. Dr. Martin Luther King Jr.," April 4, 1968, Paley Center for Media; Risen, *A Nation on Fire*, 92.

7. Interview with Charles Cabbage, by James Mosby, 1968, 22, Ralph J. Bunche Oral History Collection, Moorland-Spingarn Research Center,

Howard University; Interview with an Anonymous Participant in the Riot in Washington, D.C., April 4–8, 1968 (Anonymous A), by James Mosby, April 26, 1968, 5, Ralph J. Bunche Collection.

8. Interview with Cornelia Crenshaw, by James Mosby, July 1968, Ralph J. Bunche Collection; Michael Honey, *Going Down Jericho Road: The Memphis Strike, Martin Luther King's Last Campaign* (New York: W.W. Norton, 2007), 114; "CBS News Special Report: The Death of Rev. Dr. Martin Luther King Jr.," Paley Center for Media.

9. Peniel Joseph, *Stokely: A Life* (New York: Basic Civitas, 2014), 253–255; Risen, *A Nation on Fire*, 55–56.

10. Joseph, *Stokely*, 255; Ben Franklin, "Army Troops in Capital as Negroes Riot," *New York Times*, April 6, 1968.

11. Joseph, *Stokely*, 257–258; Risen, *A Nation on Fire*, 92; Gilbert et al., *Ten Blocks from the White House*, 60–61; Franklin, "Army Troops in Capital as Negroes Riot."

12. Joseph, *Stokely*, 258; Tom Wicker, "Thousands Leave Washington as Bands of Negroes Loot Stores," *New York Times*, April 6, 1968; Gilbert et al., *Ten Blocks from the White House*, 145.

13. Interview with Anonymous A, 2, 6, 9, Ralph J. Bunche Collection.

14. Ibid., 6, 8–9, 11, 13, 18; Gilbert et al., *Ten Blocks from the White House*, 224.

15. Interview with Anonymous A, 16, 23, Ralph J. Bunche Collection; Interview with Anonymous B, a Participant in the Race Riot in Washington, April 4–6, 1968, by James Mosby, April 24, 1968, 15–16, Ralph J. Bunche Collection. Another black rioter (who did not participate in the Howard interviews) echoed these thoughts. "The death of Martin Luther King had nothing to do with what happened," said this young Washingtonian. He stressed a long-term dissatisfaction. "It was an excuse to be destructive. . . . Ever since the Watts riot, this has been picking up. Deep in your mind you have been preparing yourself for it." Gilbert et al., *Ten Blocks from the White House*, 50.

16. Interview with Anonymous A, 19–21, Ralph J. Bunche Collection.

17. Interview with Anonymous B, 42, 8–9, 18, Ralph J. Bunche Collection.

18. Ibid., 2–5, 9, 11.

19. Ibid., 15–16.

20. Interview with an Anonymous Participant in the Riot That Occurred in Washington, D.C., April 4–6, 1968 (Anonymous C), by James Mosby, May 16, 1968, 4–5, Ralph J. Bunche Collection.

21. Ibid., 5–6, 31–32, 10.

22. Ibid., 32–33, 42.

23. Gilbert et al., *Ten Blocks from the White House*, 158–159.

24. Ibid., 163–164.

25. Ibid., 143, 178, 181, 187–188.

26. Adam Cohen and Elizabeth Taylor, *American Pharaoh: Mayor Richard J. Daley—His Battle for Chicago and the Nation* (Boston: Little, Brown, 2000), 454–455; Risen, *A Nation on Fire*, 166, 179.

27. "Looters in Hartford," *New York Times*, April 5, 1968; "San Francisco Looting," *New York Times*, April 6, 1968; Maurice Carroll, "Philadelphia Bars Closed," *New York Times*, April 6, 1968; "Angry Negroes Spill into Streets in Some Cities Across the Country," *Atlanta Constitution*, April 5, 1968; "Mississippi Guard Alerted," *New York Times*, April 6, 1968; Jan Skutch and Jenel Few, "The Dream Revisited," *SavannahNOW*, April 3, 2003, http://savannahnow.com/features/mlk35/; "Three Hurt in Savannah," *New York Times*, April 6, 1968; "New Violence Put Down," *Tuscaloosa News*, April 8, 1968; John Morganthaler, "Looting and Fires Flare Up," *Atlanta Constitution*, April 8, 1968; Risen, *A Nation on Fire*, 166, 178.

28. Thomas A. Johnson, "12 Are Arrested Here," *New York Times*, April 5, 1968.

29. "Voice of New York: The King Assassination," *New York*, April 11, 1988; Johnson, "12 Are Arrested Here"; Gloria Steinem and Lloyd Weaver, "Special Report: The City on the Eve of Destruction," *New York*, April 22, 1968.

30. Thomas A. Johnson, "Negroes Strive to Ease Tensions," *New York Times*, April 6, 1968; Sylvan Fox, "Outbreaks Here Relatively Mild," *New York Times*, April 6, 1968; Martin Gansberg, "Damage Here Since Slaying of Dr. King Is Near '64 Riot Level," *New York Times*, April 10, 1968; Richard Reeves, "Mayor, Quoting King, Urges Racial Peace Here," *New York Times*, April 6, 1968.

31. Fox, "Outbreaks Here Relatively Mild"; Reeves, "Mayor, Quoting King, Urges Racial Peace Here."

32. Risen, *A Nation on Fire*, 62, 59.

33. Vincent Cannato, *The Ungovernable City: John Lindsay and His Struggle to Save New York* (New York: Basic Books, 2001), 212–213; Gansberg, "Damage Here Since Slaying of Dr. King"; Martin Gansberg, "More Blazes Set in Brownsville," *New York Times*, April 11, 1968; Martin Gansberg, "Negroes Protest Looting Losses," *New York Times*, April 16, 1968; George

Barner, "Merchants Seek Help, 68 Closed," *Amsterdam News*, April 20, 1968; Editorial, "Mutt and Jeff," *Amsterdam News*, April 27, 1968.

34. Bennett Kremen, "Night Walk in Harlem," *The Nation*, April 22, 1968, 531.

35. *The Night James Brown Saved Boston* (Los Angeles: FremantleMedia, Shout! Factory, 2008), DVD.

36. J. Anthony Lukas, *Common Ground: A Turbulent Decade in the Lives of Three American Families* (New York: Alfred A. Knopf, 1985), 29–30. Thomas Morgan, who became John Lindsay's press secretary in 1969, had used this phrase to describe New York. The city "tensed but did not snap," Morgan recalled. Thomas Morgan, "Lindsay and the King Assassination," *New York*, April 19, 1993, 112.

37. Lukas, *Common Ground*, 32–33; *The Night James Brown Saved Boston*.

38. Lukas, *Common Ground*, 33; *The Night James Brown Saved Boston*.

39. Risen, *A Nation on Fire*, 171.

40. George Favre, "Newark 'Contains' New Outbreak," *Christian Science Monitor*, April 12, 1968.

41. Martin Luther King Jr., Dear Friend Letter, April 1968, Records of Presidents Office, Papers of the Southern Christian Leadership Conference (hereafter SCLC Papers), Part 1, Reel 2.

42. Ibid. King's supporters had heard some of this language before. He used many of these same lines in a fund-raising letter mailed in February. Martin Luther King Jr., Dear SCLC Supporter, February 15, 1968, Records of Presidents Office, SCLC Papers, Part 1, Reel 2. And he would use some of these lines again in an article for *Look* magazine. The issue went on sale on April 2, though it was dated April 16. Martin Luther King Jr., "Showdown for Nonviolence," *Look*, April 16, 1968; "Dr. King Sees Peril in Negroes' Rioting," *New York Times*, April 1, 1968.

43. See Kenneth Jackson, *Crabgrass Frontier: The Suburbanization of the United States* (New York: Oxford University Press, 1985).

44. King, Dear Friend Letter, SCLC Papers; Martin Luther King, "The Other America," Grosse Pointe, MI, March 14, 1968, www.gphistorical.org /mlk/mlkspeech/.

45. Senator Wayne Morse received his copy of the letter on April 8. 114 Cong. Rec. S9196 (April 8, 1968).

46. Ronald Spector, *After Tet: The Bloodiest Year in Vietnam* (New York: Free Press, 1993), 244; "Democracy in the Foxhole," *Time*, May 26, 1967;

Thomas Borstelmann, *The Cold War and the Color Line: American Race Relations in the Global Arena* (Cambridge, MA: Harvard University Press, 2001), 215.

47. Christian Appy, *Patriots: The Vietnam War Remembered from All Sides* (New York: Penguin, 2003), 308.

48. Wallace Terry, *Bloods: An Oral History of the Vietnam War by Black Veterans* (New York: Random House, 1984), 167; Dennis McIntosh, Letter to the Editor, *Ebony*, August 1, 1968, 17, 20.

49. Morocco Coleman, Letter to the Editor, *Ebony*, August 1, 1968, 17; James Westheider, *Fighting on Two Fronts: African Americans and the Vietnam War* (New York: New York University Press, 1997), 98; Spector, *After Tet*, 249; Bernard Weinraub, "Rioting Disquiets G.I.'s in Vietnam," *New York Times*, April 8, 1968.

50. Joshua Bloom and Waldo Martin, *Black Against Empire: The History and Politics of the Black Panther Party* (Berkeley: University of California Press, 2013), 159.

51. Interview with Huey Newton, by Louis Massiah, May 23, 1989, Eyes on the Prize II Interviews, http://digital.wustl.edu/e/eii/eiiweb/new5427.0458 .119hueypnewton.html; David Hilliard and Lewis Cole, *This Side of Glory: The Autobiography of David Hilliard and the Story of the Black Panther Party* (Boston: Little, Brown, 1993), 183.

52. Hilliard and Cole, *This Side of Glory*, 183; Henry Hampton and Steve Fayer, eds., *Voices of Freedom: An Oral History of the Civil Rights Movement from the 1950s Through the 1980s* (New York: Bantam Books, 1990), 514–515.

53. Hampton and Fayer, *Voices of Freedom*, 515; Bloom and Martin, *Black Against Empire*, 183. Bloom and Martin note that Hilliard was "under duress" while following Cleaver.

54. Robert Scheer, Introduction, in Eldridge Cleaver, *Post-Prison Writings and Speeches* (New York: Random House, 1969), xviii; Eldridge Cleaver, "The Death of Martin Luther King: Requiem for Nonviolence," in Cleaver, *Post-Prison Writings and Speeches*, 73–75.

55. Cleaver, "The Death of Martin Luther King," 76–80.

56. Eldridge Cleaver, "Affidavit #2: Shoot-out in Oakland," in Cleaver, *Post-Prison Writings and Speeches*, 84, 86, 89; Hampton and Fayer, *Voices of Freedom*, 515–517; Bloom and Martin, *Black Against Empire*, 118–119, 425; Hugh Pearson, *The Shadow of the Panther: Huey Newton and the Price of Black Power in America* (Reading, MA: Addison-Wesley, 1994), 155; Risen, *A Nation on Fire*, 166; Donna Murch, *Living for the City: Migration, Education,*

and the Rise of the Black Panther Party in Oakland, California (Chapel Hill: University of North Carolina Press, 2010), 163–166.

57. Dixon, *My People Are Rising*, 73–74.

58. Ibid., 74–75; Bill Sheverling and Forrest Williams, "Four Men in Franklin High Case Released Without Bail," *Seattle Post-Intelligencer*, April 6, 1968, Seattle Civil Rights and Labor History Project; Mike Wyne, "'Harassment Fires' but No Riots Occur Here," *Seattle Times*, April 6, 1968, Seattle Civil Rights and Labor History Project.

59. Bloom and Martin, *Black Against Empire*, 119, 321; Interview with Bobby Seale, November 4, 1988, Eyes on the Prize II Interviews, http://digital.wustl.edu/cgi/t/text/text-idx?c=eop;cc=eop;rgn=main;view=text;idno=sea5427.0172.147; Interview with Huey Newton, Eyes on the Prize II Interviews.

60. Hampton and Fayer, *Voices of Freedom*, 514–515; *The Black Panthers: Vanguard of the Revolution* (New York: Firelight Films, 2015); Bloom and Martin, *Black Against Empire*, 150, 145.

61. Rickey Vincent, *Party Music: The Inside Story of the Black Panthers' Band and How Black Power Transformed Soul Music* (Chicago, IL: Lawrence Hill Books, 2013), 22; *The Black Panthers: Vanguard of the Revolution*; Bryan Shih and Yohuru Williams, eds., *The Black Panthers: Portraits from an Unfinished Revolution* (New York: Nation Books, 2016), 157, 216.

62. Bloom and Martin, *Black Against Empire*, 119–120; Pearson, *Shadow of the Panther*, 156. Bloom and Martin estimate that 2,000 mourners attended Hutton's funeral, while the *New York Times* reported that the number was "perhaps 800." Lawrence Davies, "Black Panthers Denounce Policemen," *New York Times*, April 13, 1968; Interview with Elmer Dixon, Seattle Black Panther Party History and Memory Project, University of Washington.

63. Hampton and Fayer, *Voices of Freedom*, 517; Bloom and Martin, *Black Against Empire*, 119–120; Pearson, *Shadow of the Panther*, 156.

64. Interview with Elmer Dixon, Seattle Black Panther Party History and Memory Project, University of Washington.

65. Interview with Aaron Dixon, Seattle Black Panther Party History and Memory Project, University of Washington; Dixon, *My People Are Rising*, 80–83.

66. Dixon, *My People Are Rising*, 99.

67. Ibid., 108, 128–129.

68. Philip Meyer, "Aftermath of Martyrdom: Negro Militancy and Martin Luther King," *Public Opinion Quarterly* 33, no. 2 (summer 1969): 170, 168.

69. Preston Woodruff, "Atlantans Express Anger," *Atlanta Constitution*, April 5, 1968.

70. Ta-Nehisi Coates, *Between the World and Me* (New York: Spiegel & Grau, 2015), 40; Charles Jackson Jr., "Atlanta University Students React with Bitterness; March Is Halted," *Atlanta Constitution*, April 5, 1968.

71. "Looting, Fires Scar Capital's Heart," *Commercial Appeal*, April 6, 1968; "Dr. Martin Luther King Jr.'s Assassination and NCSU's Reaction," January 20, 2011, Special Collections News, North Carolina State University, http://news.lib.ncsu.edu/scrc/2011/01/20/259/; Osha Gray Davidson, *The Best of Enemies: Race and Redemption in the New South* (Chapel Hill: University of North Carolina Press, 2007), 222, 224.

72. "Guard Patrols Tense Nashville and Pine Bluff," *Commercial Appeal*, April 6, 1968; "Angry Negroes Spill into Streets in Some Cities Across the Country," *Atlanta Constitution*, April 5, 1968; Jerry Thompson and Jimmy Carnahan, "Guard Seals, Patrols North Nashville Area," *Nashville Tennessean*, April 5, 1968; Jerry Thompson, "Troops Leave A & I Campus; 2 Youths Shot," *Nashville Tennessean*, April 6, 1968; Jerry Thompson, "A & I Calm as Guard Quits Area," *Nashville Tennessean*, April 7, 1968; Jerry Thompson and Frank Ritter, "ROTC Building Burns," *Nashville Tennessean*, April 8, 1968; Jerry Thompson, "Calm Grows in Nashville," *Nashville Tennessean*, April 11, 1968; "Peace Again Reigns at Tennessee State," *Chicago Defender*, April 27, 1968; Jerry Thompson and Rob Elder, "Briley Eases Bans," *Nashville Tennessean*, April 10, 1968.

73. "Disturbances By and About Negro Students," *Minerva*, Autumn–Winter 1968–1969, 320; "Tuskegee Students Ordered to Leave," *Nashville Tennessean*, April 9, 1968; Martha Biondi, *The Black Revolution on Campus* (Berkeley: University of California Press, 2012), 39–40.

74. Jimmy McIntosh, Hamilton High Essays, Folder 51, Container 8, Sanitation Strike Collection, Special Collections, McWhorter Library, University of Memphis.

75. James Wilson, Hamilton High Essays; Alice Wright, Hamilton High Essays.

CHAPTER 3: "HE KNEW THAT MILLIONS HATED KING"
1. Gary Pomerantz, *Where Peachtree Meets Sweet Auburn: The Saga of Two Families and the Making of Atlanta* (New York: Scribner, 1996), 362; David Levering Lewis, *King: A Biography*, 2nd ed. (Urbana: University of Illinois Press, 1978), 392; Benjamin Mays, *Born to Rebel: An Autobiography* (Athens:

University of Georgia Press, 1971), 360; Coretta Scott King, *My Life with Martin Luther King, Jr.* (New York: Holt, Rinehart and Winston, 1969), 334.

2. David Garrow, *The FBI and Martin Luther King, Jr.* (New York: Penguin, 1983); David Garrow, *Bearing the Cross: Martin Luther King, Jr., and the Southern Christian Leadership Conference* (New York: William Morrow, 1986), 360; Sheldon Appleton, "Martin Luther King in Life . . . and Memory," *Public Perspective*, February/March, 1995, 12.

3. David Halberstam, "The Second Coming of Martin Luther King," *Harper's*, August 1967, 48; David Halberstam, "Notes from the Bottom of the Mountain," *Harper's*, June 1968, 41; Garrow, *Bearing the Cross*, 601; "Dr. King's 1968 Speech at Grosse Pointe High School," Grosse Pointe Historical Society, www.gphistorical.org/mlk/index.htm.

4. Peter Ling, *Martin Luther King Jr.* (New York: Routledge, 2002), 288; Harvard Sitkoff, *King: Pilgrimage to the Mountaintop* (New York: Hill & Wang, 2008), 231.

5. "Memphis Blues," *Dallas Morning News*, reprinted in *Commercial Appeal*, April 2, 1968.

6. 114 Cong. Rec. S8263–8265 (March 29, 1968).

7. 114 Cong. Rec. H8380–8381 (April 1, 1968); "Kuykendall Accuses King of Sparking Memphis Clash," *Commercial Appeal*, April 2, 1968; "A Reader," Letter to the Editor, *Commercial Appeal*, April 7, 1968.

8. 114 Cong. Rec. S8946 (April 4, 1968); 114 Cong. Rec. H9035 (April 4, 1968).

9. Michael Honey, *Going Down Jericho Road: The Memphis Strike, Martin Luther King's Last Campaign* (New York: W.W. Norton, 2007), 462.

10. Maria Saporta, oral history, in Rebecca Burns, "The Remarkable Behind-the-Scenes Story of King's Funeral," *Atlanta*, April 2008, 100; Rebecca Burns, *Burial for a King* (New York: Scribner, 2011), 23.

11. Miller Taylor, "Bringing It Closer to Home," Letter to the Editor, *Sun-Bulletin* (Binghamton, NY), April 10, 1968, clipping in Box 3, Folder 7, Edwin Newman Papers, Wisconsin Historical Society.

12. Frederick C. Stern, "Eleven Hours in Chicago," *The Nation*, April 22, 1968.

13. Margaret Grealy to Carl Albert, April 5, 1968, Collection of Hon. Carl Albert, Legislative Series, Box 102, Folder 112, Carl Albert Congressional Research and Studies Center Congressional Archives, University of Oklahoma; "A Listener and Voter" to Edwin Newman, April 10, 1968, Box 4, Folder 1, Edwin Newman Papers.

14. Mike Royko, "Millions in His Firing Squad," *Chicago Daily News*, April 5, 1968.

15. Ralph McGill, "A Free Man Killed by White Slaves," *Atlanta Constitution*, April 5, 1968.

16. Ralph McGill, "Evil Played into His Hands," *Atlanta Constitution*, April 6, 1968; Burns, *Burial for a King*, 46; Douglas E. Williams to Ralph McGill, April 16, 1968, Box 18, Folder 9 (Series II: Correspondence, 1968 April 11–16), Ralph McGill Papers, Manuscript, Archives, and Rare Book Library, Emory University; Anonymous to Ralph McGill, April 8, 1968, Box 18, Folder 8 (Series II: Correspondence, 1968 April 8–10), Ralph McGill Papers; "Red Country," Letter to the Editor, *Atlanta Constitution*, April 10, 1968.

17. Carl McIntire, "'Your Land Is Full of Violence': On the Assassination of Martin Luther King," *Christian Beacon*, April 11, 1968; Responsible Businessman to Ralph McGill, April 11, 1968, Box 18, Folder 9 (Series II: Correspondence, 1968 April 11–16), Ralph McGill Papers; Olin Miller to Ralph McGill, April 7, 1968, Box 18, Folder 7 (Series II: Correspondence, 1968 April 1–7), Ralph McGill Papers; Richard Brantley, "I Am Sick to My Soul," Letter to the Editor, *Nashville Tennessean*, April 11, 1968.

18. Mrs. M. McKinney to Ralph McGill, April 10, 1968, Box 18, Folder 8 (Series II: Correspondence, 1968 April 8–10), Ralph McGill Papers.

19. E. A. McHale to Edwin Newman, April 8, 1968, Box 4, Folder 1, Edwin Newman Papers, Wisconsin Historical Society; Bronx, NY [Name illegible] to Edwin Newman, April 9, 1968, Box 4, Folder 1, Edwin Newman Papers; Ed Lehrbass to Edwin Newman, April 5, 1968, Box 4, Folder 1, Edwin Newman Papers.

20. Martin Marty, "A View of the Man and the Martyr," *New York Times Book Review*, February 16, 1969.

21. Lionel Lokos, *House Divided: The Life and Legacy of Martin Luther King* (New Rochelle, NY: Arlington House, 1968).

22. Ibid., 379, 78, 373.

23. Ibid., 459, 457–458, 462.

24. John Leo, "Students Polled on King Slaying," *New York Times*, October 6, 1968; Letter from Gordon Owen, Bobby Rogers, Billy Sutton, Steve Thompson, and Garry Dark to Ralph Abernathy, April 25, 1968, The King Center, www.thekingcenter.org/archive.

25. Age: 14, Sex: F, Years in Memphis: 12, Millington High School Essays, Container 8, Folder 52: Students' Responses to Assassination: Millington High School, Sanitation Strike Collection, Special Collections, McWhorter

Library, University of Memphis; Age: 15, Sex: F, Years in Memphis: 4, Millington High School Essays.

26. Age: 16, Sex: F, Years in Memphis: 15, Millington High School Essays; Age: 14, Sex: M, Years in Memphis: 6, Millington High School Essays.

27. Age: 14, Sex: M, Years in Memphis: 6, Millington High School Essays; Age: 17, Sex: M, Millington High School Essays; Age: 17, Sex: M, Years in Memphis: 9, Millington High School Essays; Age: 14, Sex: M, Years in Memphis: 3, Millington High School Essays.

28. Gladwin Hill, "Reagan Not Sure Johnson Has Quit," *New York Times*, April 10, 1968; "Rights and Political Leaders Voice Anguish, Shock, Grief," *Commercial Appeal*, April 5, 1968; Honey, *Going Down Jericho Road*, 485; "Civil Disobedience a Sin, Maddox Says," *Atlanta Constitution*, April 8, 1968; "Dr. King's Body at His Church," *Nashville Tennessean*, April 9, 1968; Pomerantz, *Where Peachtree Meets Sweet Auburn*, 359.

29. Age: 17, Sex: M, Years in Memphis: 17, Millington High School Essays; Age: 17, Sex: M, Years in Memphis: 9, Millington High School Essays.

30. Age: 15, Sex: F, Years in Memphis: 10, Millington High School Essays.

31. 114 Cong. Rec. S9139–9140 (April 5, 1968).

32. President Lyndon Johnson, Proclamation 3839, 114 Cong. Rec. S1621 (April 5, 1968); Joan Turner Beifuss, *At the River I Stand: Memphis, the 1968 Strike, and Martin Luther King* (Brooklyn, NY: Carlson Publishing, 1989), 435; John Shirley, "Negro Ministers Under the Confederate Flag," *Times of London*, April 6, 1968; Adam Cohen and Elizabeth Taylor, *American Pharaoh: Mayor Richard J. Daley—His Battle for Chicago and the Nation* (Boston: Little, Brown, 2000), 452; "Frank" to Edwin Newman, April 5–6, 1968, Box 4, Folder 1, Edwin Newman Papers; "'Mad Men,' A Conversation: MLK," *Wall Street Journal Online*, April 28, 2013.

33. Osha Gray Davidson, *The Best of Enemies: Race and Redemption in the New South* (Chapel Hill: University of North Carolina Press, 2007), 221–224.

34. Jerry Thompson and Rob Elder, "Briley Eases Bans," *Nashville Tennessean*, April 10, 1968.

35. "Maddox Is Upset, but Atlanta Flags Fly at Half-Staff," *New York Times*, April 10, 1968; Pomerantz, *Where Peachtree Meets Sweet Auburn*, 359; Fred Crawford, Roy Norman, and Leah Dabbs, *A Report of Certain Reactions by the Atlanta Public to the Death of the Reverend Doctor Martin Luther King Jr.* (Atlanta, GA: Center for Research in Social Change, Emory University, 1969), 83.

36. Harry Golden, "They Lowered the Flag in Virginia," *Chicago Defender*, April 20, 1968.

37. "Complains of Viet Troop Bias, Confederate Flag Before Death," *Jet*, April 4, 1968, 8–9; Ronald Spector, *After Tet: The Bloodiest Year in Vietnam* (New York: Free Press, 1993), 245, 250.

38. Zalin Grant, "The Other War: Whites Against Blacks in Vietnam," *New Republic*, January 18, 1969, 16.

39. James Westheider, *Fighting on Two Fronts: African Americans and the Vietnam War* (New York: New York University Press, 1997), 97; Wallace Terry, *Bloods: An Oral History of the Vietnam War by Black Veterans* (New York: Random House, 1984), 172; Bernard Weinraub, "Rioting Disquiets G.I.'s in Vietnam," *New York Times*, April 8, 1968; Elwood King, "Soldier's Protest to King Salute," Letter to the Editor, *Nashville Tennessean*, April 12, 1968.

40. Spector, *After Tet*, 250–251; "GIs Are Allowed to Fly Their Home State Flag," *Washington Post*, May 17, 1968.

41. David Chappell, *Waking from the Dream: The Struggle for Civil Rights in the Shadow of Martin Luther King Jr.* (New York: Random House, 2014), 93.

42. Cohen and Taylor, *American Pharaoh*, 465–466; Jonathan Tilove, *Along Martin Luther King: Travels on Black America's Main Street* (New York: Random House, 2003), 104.

43. Chappell, *Waking from the Dream*, 93; Henry Raymont, "King Family Halting Talks with Nixon for Memorial," *New York Times*, September 28, 1969; William F. Buckley Jr., "A Memorial to Martin Luther King," *Boston Globe*, October 7, 1969.

CHAPTER 4: ROSES FOR MY SOUL

1. "20,000 March in Madison," *New York Times*, April 6, 1968; "Rally Held in Austin," *New York Times*, April 6, 1968; Douglas Martin, "Chokwe Lumumba, 66, Dies; Activist Who Became Mayor," *New York Times*, February 27, 2014; Melba Joyce Boyd, "Afrocentrics, Afro-elitists, and Afro-eccentrics: The Polarization of Black Studies Since the Student Struggles of the Sixties," in Manning Marable, ed., *Dispatches from the Ebony Tower: Intellectuals Confront the African American Experience* (New York: Columbia University Press, 2000), 205.

2. "March in Tribute to Dr. King," *The Herald*, Hobart and William Smith Colleges, April 12, 1968; Stocky Clark, "A Personal Reaction," *The Herald*, April 12, 1968.

3. Interview with Alfred Price, by Brandon Holt, February 17, 2015, 35, Brandon Holt Senior Thesis Oral History Project, Princeton University Archives; Dave Huber, "Goheen Cancels Tuesday Classes," *Daily Princetonian*, April 8, 1968.

4. Huber, "Goheen Cancels Tuesday Classes"; Interview with Alfred Price, 36.

5. Huber, "Goheen Cancels Tuesday Classes"; Interview with Alfred Price, 38–39.

6. Douglas Knight, *Street of Dreams: The Nature and Legacy of the 1960s* (Durham, NC: Duke University Press, 1989), 97; Bridget Booher, "Jousting with History," *Duke Magazine*, January–February 2004.

7. Bridget Booher, "Remembering the Silent Vigil: A University Milestone," *Duke Magazine*, March–April 1998, 2; Bertie Howard, oral history, in Booher, "Remembering the Silent Vigil," 9; David Henderson, oral history, in Booher, "Remembering the Silent Vigil," 6.

8. Jack Boger, oral history, in Booher, "Remembering the Silent Vigil," 50; Theodore David Segal, *"A New Genesis": The "Silent Vigil" at Duke University, April 5th–12th, 1968*, History Honors Thesis, Duke University, April 23, 1977; Knight, *Street of Dreams*, 121; Alan Shusterman, "Too Many Whites Are Guilty," *Duke Chronicle*, April 5, 1968; Douglas Knight, oral history, in Booher, "Remembering the Silent Vigil," 4–5.

9. Knight, *Street of Dreams*, 120–121.

10. David Henderson, "Journal of the Duke Vigil," Duke Vigil Collection, Box 1, Folder 34, Rubenstein Library and University Archives, Duke University; Segal, *"A New Genesis,"* 31; David Cooper, "Duke Sit-in Spurs 'Activism,'" *Winston-Salem Journal and Sentinel*, April 14, 1968; David Henderson, oral history, in Booher, "Remembering the Silent Vigil," 6.

11. Bob Ashley, "400 Students Continue Sit-Ins," *Duke Chronicle*, April 8, 1968; Richard Smurthwaite and Clay Steinman, "Knight Endures Weekend," *Duke Chronicle*, April 8, 1968; Segal, *"A New Genesis,"* 48.

12. Segal, *"A New Genesis,"* 35–36; Henderson, "Journal of the Duke Vigil," 7; Peter Applebome, "Vigil Leaders Reflect Diversity," *Duke Chronicle*, April 8, 1968; Susan Taylor, "Everyone Was Miserable but Somehow Survived," *Duke Chronicle*, April 12, 1968.

13. Alan Ray, "The Price of a New-Found Dream," *Duke Chronicle*, April 8, 1968; Margaret Small, oral history, in Booher, "Remembering the Silent Vigil," 5.

14. Robert Creamer, "How Dr. King's Assassination and the Struggle for Collective Bargaining Changed My Life," *Huffington Post*, April 3, 2011; Segal, *"A New Genesis,"* 35; Knight, *Street of Dreams*, 123; Jack Boger, oral history, in Booher, "Remembering the Silent Vigil," 50.

15. Henderson, "Journal of the Duke Vigil," 11; Knight, *Street of Dreams*, 123.

16. Henderson, "Journal of the Duke Vigil," 17.

17. Segal, *"A New Genesis,"* v; Bertie Howard, oral history, in Booher, "Remembering the Silent Vigil," 49.

18. "Strike and Vigil," *Duke Chronicle*, April 10, 1968; "Operation Employees Demand Higher Wages," *Duke Chronicle*, April 10, 1968.

19. Henderson, "Journal of the Duke Vigil," 25; Creamer, "How Dr. King's Assassination and the Struggle"; John Strange, oral history, in Booher, "Remembering the Silent Vigil," 7.

20. Bob Ashley, "King's Death Stuns Duke," *Duke Chronicle*, April 5, 1968; Samuel DuBois Cook, oral history, in Booher, "Remembering the Silent Vigil," 8; Henderson, "Journal of the Duke Vigil," Appendix Item 6; Segal, *"A New Genesis,"* 59–60.

21. Segal, *"A New Genesis,"* 59–60.

22. Ibid., 97–98.

23. Ibid., 99.

24. Jack Burwell, "Tisdale Says 1969," *Duke Chronicle*, April 11, 1968; Segal, *"A New Genesis,"* 101.

25. Charles Heustis, oral history, in Booher, "Remembering the Silent Vigil," 8; "Mr. Tisdale," *Duke Chronicle*, April 11, 1968.

26. Richard Smurthwaite, "Four Day Silent Vigil Ends," *Duke Chronicle*, April 11, 1968.

27. Segal, *"A New Genesis,"* 102; Smurthwaite, "Four Day Silent Vigil Ends"; Henderson, "Journal of the Duke Vigil," 35.

28. Carolyn Arnold, "Council Wants Bargaining," *Duke Chronicle*, April 12, 1968; Dave Schaffer, Carolyn Arnold, and Gloria Guth, "Boycott Enters Second Week," *Duke Chronicle*, April 15, 1968; Henderson, "Journal of the Duke Vigil," 40.

29. Cliff Feingold, "Students Call Board's Proposal 'Disappointing,'" *Duke Chronicle*, April 17, 1968.

30. "Trustees Study Unit to Meet Tomorrow," *Duke Chronicle*, April 19, 1968; Ed McConville, "Diseased Workers Sue Largest Textile Maker," *Washington Post*, October 25, 1979; Marion Ellis, "The Brown Lung Battle into the Courtroom," *NC Insight*, April 1981; *National Labor Relations Board v. Hanes*

Hosiery Division, Court of Appeals for the Fourth Circuit, July 18, 1969; "A Time for Discussion," *Duke Chronicle*, April 19, 1968.

31. Henderson, "Journal of the Duke Vigil," Appendix Item 18; Henderson, "Journal of the Duke Vigil," 47–48.

32. Tom Dwiggins, "Sunday Vigil Receives Trustee's Statement," *Duke Chronicle*, April 22, 1968; Carolyn Arnold, "Workers Return to Work Today," *Duke Chronicle*, April 22, 1968; Knight, *Street of Dreams*, 101; Segal, *"A New Genesis,"* 103.

33. Smurthwaite, "Four Day Silent Vigil Ends"; "Vigilance Now," *Duke Chronicle*, April 11, 1968; "The New University," *Duke Chronicle*, April 12, 1968.

34. Cooper, "Duke Sit-in Spurs 'Activism.'"

35. Roger Kahn, *The Battle for Morningside Heights: Why Students Rebel* (New York: William Morrow, 1970), 92; Peter Millones, "Gym Controversy Began in Late 50's," *New York Times*, April 26, 1968.

36. Kahn, *Battle for Morningside Heights*, 94–95.

37. Ibid., 96.

38. Jerry Avorn, *Up Against the Ivy Wall: A History of the Columbia Crisis* (New York: Atheneum, 1970), 20; Stefan Bradley, *Harlem vs. Columbia University: Black Student Power in the Late 1960s* (Urbana: University of Illinois Press, 2009), 67; Kahn, *Battle for Morningside Heights*, 97.

39. Mark Rudd, *Underground: My Life with SDS and the Weathermen* (New York: HarperCollins, 2009), 46; Kahn, *Battle for Morningside Heights*, 105–107.

40. Rudd, *Underground*, 49–50.

41. Ibid., 50–51.

42. Kahn, *Battle for Morningside Heights*, 107.

43. Email interview with Mark Rudd, by author, June 29, 2016; Bob Feldman, "The King Memorial—Why We Disrupted," *Up Against the Ivy Wall* 3, no. 1 (April 22, 1968), Columbia University Libraries Online Exhibitions, https://exhibitions.cul.columbia.edu/exhibits/show/1968/item/5523; Avorn, *Up Against the Ivy Wall*, 28; Rudd, *Underground*, 52; Kahn, *Battle for Morningside Heights*, 107–108; Michael Stern, "Walkout Disrupts Memorial to King," *Columbia Daily Spectator*, April 10, 1968, Columbia University Libraries Online Exhibitions, https://exhibitions.cul.columbia.edu/exhibits/show/1968/item/5595.

44. Feldman, "The King Memorial—Why We Disrupted"; Email interview with Mark Rudd, by author.

45. Rudd, *Underground*, 54–56.

46. Ibid., 51.

47. Timeline of Events, 1968: Columbia in Crisis, https://exhibitions.cul
.columbia.edu/exhibits/show/1968/timeline.

48. Avorn, *Up Against the Ivy Wall*, 300–301.

49. "King Eulogy Worldwide," *Nashville Tennessean*, April 8, 1968; Michael Stern, "New York Volatile as Anger and Fear Set a Tense Mood," *New York Times*, April 6, 1968; Mary Ward, *A Mission for Justice: The History of the First African American Catholic Church in Newark, New Jersey* (Knoxville: University of Tennessee Press, 2002), 105; Rick Perlstein, *Nixonland: The Rise of a President and the Fracturing of America* (New York: Scribner, 2008), 256; "Remember When . . . Milwaukeeans Marched in Memory of Martin Luther King Jr.?," Milwaukee Public Library Digital Collections, http://content.mpl.org/cdm/singleitem/collection/RememberWhe/id/495/rec/6; Dick Looser, "2,000 March Quietly Here," *Tuscaloosa News*, April 8, 1968; Alma Baker to Edwin Newman, April 23, 1968, Box 4, Folder 1, Edwin Newman Papers, Wisconsin Historical Society.

50. "Sorrow in Alabama," *New York Times*, April 6, 1968; Jeremiah Murphy, "On Common, an Echo of April 1965," *Boston Globe*, April 9, 1968.

51. "Port Work Suspended as Tribute," *New York Times*, April 6, 1968; Michael Honey, *Going Down Jericho Road: The Memphis Strike, Martin Luther King's Last Campaign* (New York: W.W. Norton, 2007), 448; "Garment Workers Mourn Dr. King," *Amsterdam News*, April 13, 1968.

52. Rebecca Burns, Editor's Note, *Atlanta*, April 2008; Kathy Kohn, oral history, and Norm Kohn, oral history, in Rebecca Burns, "The Remarkable Behind-the-Scenes Story of King's Funeral," *Atlanta*, April 2008, 135–136; Rebecca Burns, *Burial for a King* (New York: Scribner, 2011), 110–112, 155, 160.

53. Gregory Jaynes, "I Never Have Marched Before," *Commercial Appeal*, April 9, 1968.

54. DWA, "Pretense Is Ended," Letter to the Editor, *Commercial Appeal*, April 14, 1968.

55. Jarell Watkins, "Pray Bullet Killed Indifference," Letter to the Editor, *Commercial Appeal*, April 14, 1968.

56. Interview with Jerred Blanchard, Number 66, by Carol Lynn Yellin, Anne Trotter, and Tom Beckner, May 27, 1968, Sanitation Strike Collection, Special Collections, McWhorter Library, University of Memphis, 1; William Street, "Swirling Events Make Blanchard Controversial," *Commercial Appeal*, April 11, 1968; "Peace Philosophy Is Exemplified but Speeches Betray Impatience," *Commercial Appeal*, April 9, 1968.

57. Street, "Swirling Events Make Blanchard Controversial."

58. Interview with Jerred Blanchard, Number 67, Sanitation Strike Collection, 28–29; Honey, *Going Down Jericho Road*, 393–394; Joan Turner Beifuss, *At the River I Stand: Memphis, the 1968 Strike, and Martin Luther King* (Brooklyn, NY: Carlson Publishing, 1989), 329; Interview with Jerred Blanchard, Number 68, Sanitation Strike Collection, 6.

59. Interview with Jerred Blanchard, Number 67, 31.

60. Ibid., 32–33.

61. Ibid., 35.

62. Ibid., 35–36.

63. Interview with Jerred Blanchard, Number 68, 1–2; Street, "Swirling Events Make Blanchard Controversial."

64. Interview with Jerred Blanchard, Number 68, 5; Honey, *Going Down Jericho Road*, 142.

65. Richard Lentz, "Sweet Taste of Accord Is Quickly Digested," *Commercial Appeal*, April 17, 1968; "Council Greets Agreement with Elation, Optimism," *Commercial Appeal*, April 17, 1968; "Strike-End Terms Listed," *Commercial Appeal*, April 17, 1968; "The Memphis Pact," *Tri-State Defender*, May 4, 1968.

66. Interview with Andrew Young, by Jack Bass and Walter DeVries, January 31, 1974, Interview #A-0080, Southern Oral History Program, Southern Historical Collection, University of North Carolina, Chapel Hill, http://dc .lib.unc.edu/cdm/compoundobject/collection/sohp/id/8466/rec/3.

67. Beifuss, *At the River I Stand*, 407; Interview with Dolph Smith and Jessie Smith, by Carol Lynn Yellin and David Yellin, November 21, 1971, Sanitation Strike Collection, 2, 14; Interview with Dolph Smith, by author, July 7, 2016.

68. Interview with Dolph Smith, by author; Interview with Dolph Smith and Jessie Smith, Sanitation Strike Collection, 1, 8, 11, 23–24.

69. Guy Northrop, "Morals and Monsters in Simon Collection," *Commercial Appeal*, April 14, 1968; Dolph Smith, *The Veil of the Temple Was Rent in Two*, University of Memphis Art Museum; Interview with Dolph Smith, by author.

70. Interview with Dolph Smith and Jessie Smith, 18.

71. Jonathan Binstock, *Sam Gilliam: A Retrospective* (Berkeley: University of California Press, 2005), 70, 73; *April 4, 1969*, "Oh Freedom!: Teaching African American Civil Rights Through American Art at the Smithsonian," http://africanamericanart.si.edu/items/show/30; Vinson Cunningham, "Making a Home for Black History," *New Yorker*, August 29, 2016, 39.

72. Nat Gertler, *The Peanuts Collection: Treasures from the World's Most Beloved Comic Strip* (New York: Little, Brown, 2010), 43; Michael Cavna, "Franklin Integrated 'Peanuts' 47 Years Ago Today," *Washington Post*, July 31, 2015.

73. Cavna, "Franklin Integrated 'Peanuts' 47 Years Ago Today."

74. Paul Sorene, "Why Charles M. Schulz Gave Peanuts a Black Character (1968)," *Flashbak*, November 27, 2015, http://flashbak.com/why-charles-m-schulz-gave-peanuts-a-black-character-1968–47081/.

75. Cavna, "Franklin Integrated 'Peanuts' 47 Years Ago Today."

76. Tess Cutler, "When 'Peanuts' Made History," *Tribe Magazine*, May 27, 2015; Clarence Page, "A Peanuts' Kid Without Punch Lines," *Chicago Tribune*, February 16, 2000.

CHAPTER 5: THE WORLD STANDS AGHAST

1. Taylor Branch, *At Canaan's Edge: America in the King Years, 1965–68* (New York: Simon & Schuster, 2006), 760.

2. "Martin Luther King," *Times of London*, April 6, 1968.

3. David Garrow, *Bearing the Cross: Martin Luther King, Jr., and the Southern Christian Leadership Conference* (New York: William Morrow, 1986), 595–596; Thomas Jackson, *From Civil Rights to Human Rights: Martin Luther King, Jr., and the Struggle for Economic Justice* (Philadelphia: University of Pennsylvania Press, 2007), 343; Martin Luther King Jr., *Where Do We Go from Here: Chaos or Community?* (Boston: Beacon Press, 2010 edition), 171.

4. Taylor Branch, *Parting the Waters: America in the King Years, 1954–1963* (New York: Simon & Schuster, 1988), 214.

5. Garrow, *Bearing the Cross*, 91.

6. Maria Hohn and Martin Klimke, *A Breath of Freedom: The Civil Rights Struggle, American GIs, and Germany* (New York: Palgrave Macmillan, 2010), 95–97.

7. "Dr. King in East Berlin," *International Herald Tribune*, September 13, 1964; "Crossing the Border at Checkpoint Charlie," *The Civil Rights Struggle, African-American GIs, and Germany*, http://www.aacvr-germany.org/index.php/images-7/dr-martin-luther-kings-visit-to-cold-war-berlin; "Red Berlin Admits Popular Rights Leader Without Pass," *Ebony*, November 1964. A 2014 article, published by Germany's *Deutsche Welle*, asserted that the US State Department had confiscated King's passport. In that version of the story, American leaders had no interest in encouraging King's visit to the communist territory. There is no further evidence to back up this interpretation of events. "Remembering Martin Luther King's Visit to Berlin,"

Deutsche Welle, September 11, 2014. The evidence seems to favor Taylor Branch's interpretation. Branch suggests that this was not the first time King had forgotten his passport. Branch writes, "Again having mislaid his passport, he passed through the Berlin Wall on celebrity recognition." Taylor Branch, *Pillar of Fire: America in the King Years, 1963–1965* (New York: Simon & Schuster, 1998), 483.

8. Hohn and Klimke, *Breath of Freedom*, 99; "Remembering Martin Luther King's Visit to Berlin."

9. "Remembering Martin Luther King's Visit to Berlin."

10. Hohn and Klimke, *Breath of Freedom*, 99–100.

11. Ibid., 101; Interview with Alcyone Scott, by Martin Klimke, June 8, 2009, *The Civil Rights Struggle, African-American GIs, and Germany*, http://www.aacvr-germany.org/index.php/images-7/dr-martin-luther-kings-visit-to-cold-war-berlin.

12. Interview with Alcyone Scott; Roland Stolte, "Dr. Martin Luther King Jr. in 1964 in Berlin," *The Civil Rights Struggle, African-American GIs, and Germany.*

13. "Remembering Martin Luther King's Visit to Berlin"; Chronology of Dr. King's Visit to Berlin, *The Civil Rights Struggle, African-American GIs, and Germany*, http://www.aacvr-germany.org/index.php/images-7/dr-martin-luther-kings-visit-to-cold-war-berlin; "Red Berlin Admits Popular Rights Leader Without Pass," 44; Lars-Broder Keil, "MLK in the GDR: The Rev. King's Almost Forgotten Visit to East Berlin," *OZY*, October 1, 2014.

14. Martin Luther King Jr., Draft of Article for *Amsterdam News*, September 17, 1964, The King Center, www.thekingcenter.org/archive/document/amsterdam-news-article-mlk-about-european-tour.

15. Branch, *Pillar of Fire*, 485.

16. Garrow, *Bearing the Cross*, 357; Branch, *Pillar of Fire*, 516.

17. Branch, *Pillar of Fire*, 517; Gary Pomerantz, *Where Peachtree Meets Sweet Auburn: The Saga of Two Families and the Making of Atlanta* (New York: Scribner, 1996), 335; David Levering Lewis, *King: A Biography*, 2nd ed. (Urbana: University of Illinois Press, 1978), 256.

18. Pomerantz, *Where Peachtree Meets Sweet Auburn*, 335; Ralph McGill, "Nobel Prize Reminds Us," *Atlanta Constitution*, October 16, 1964; Branch, *Pillar of Fire*, 526.

19. Lewis, *King*, 259–260, 263; Martin Luther King, "Nobel Prize Acceptance Speech," in James Washington, ed., *A Testament of Hope: The Essential Writings of Martin Luther King Jr.* (San Francisco: Harper & Row, 1986), 226.

20. Branch, *Pillar of Fire*, 546.

21. Pomerantz, *Where Peachtree Meets Sweet Auburn*, 335.

22. "Tribute to Dr. King Disputed in Atlanta," *New York Times*, December 29, 1964; Branch, *Pillar of Fire*, 568; Pomerantz, *Where Peachtree Meets Sweet Auburn*, 336–337.

23. "Tribute to Dr. King Disputed in Atlanta"; Pomerantz, *Where Peachtree Meets Sweet Auburn*, 338–339; Fred Powledge, "Atlanta Praises Dr. King at Fete," *New York Times*, January 28, 1965.

24. Lewis Baldwin, "Martin Luther King Jr., a 'Coalition of Conscience,' and Freedom in South Africa," in R. Drew Smith, ed., *Freedom's Distant Shores: American Protestants and Post-Colonial Alliances with Africa* (Waco, TX: Baylor University Press, 2006), 55–56; Martin Luther King, "South African Independence," in Martin Luther King, *"In a Single Garment of Destiny": A Global Vision of Justice*, ed. Lewis Baldwin (Boston: Beacon, 2012), 36.

25. "No Reply to Luther King Invitation," *Cape Times*, November 23, 1965, The King Center, www.thekingcenter.org/archive/document/cape-times-no-reply-luther-king-invitation; "Dr. Luther King Cause of U.S. Violence," *Cape Times*, November 25, 1965, The King Center, www.thekingcenter.org/archive/document/dr-luther-king-cause-us-violence.

26. Martin Luther King, "Let My People Go," in King, *"In a Single Garment of Destiny,"* 39–43.

27. Letter from Monica Wilson to Martin Luther King, November 12, 1965, The King Center, www.thekingcenter.org/archive/document/letter-monica-wilson-mlk; Letter from Martin Luther King to South African Embassy, February 9, 1966, The King Center, www.thekingcenter.org/archive/document/letter-mlk-south-african-embassy; Letter from South African Consulate General to Martin Luther King, March 17, 1966, The King Center, www.thekingcenter.org/archive/document/letter-n-m-nel-mlk.

28. Harvard Sitkoff, *King: Pilgrimage to the Mountaintop* (New York: Hill & Wang, 2008), 210; Martin Luther King, "Casualties of the War in Vietnam," Los Angeles, CA, February 25, 1967, www.aavw.org/special_features/speeches_speech_king02.html; Thomas Borstelmann, *The Cold War and the Color Line: American Race Relations in the Global Arena* (Cambridge, MA: Harvard University Press, 2001), 202–203.

29. Branch, *At Canaan's Edge*, 591; Martin Luther King, "A Time to Break Silence," in Washington, ed., *A Testament of Hope*, 240; King, "Casualties of the War in Vietnam."

30. King, "A Time to Break Silence," 238.

31. Ibid., 240.

32. Ibid., 240–242.

33. Marshall Frady, *Martin Luther King Jr.* (New York: Viking, 2002), 186–187; James Baldwin, "On Martin Luther King," 1978, reprinted in Jennifer Schuessler, "James Baldwin's Archive, Long Hidden, Comes (Mostly) into View," *New York Times*, April 12, 2017.

34. The Pacifica Radio/UC Berkeley Social Activism Sound Recording Project: Anti-Vietnam War Protests in the Bay Area and Beyond, www.lib.berkeley.edu/MRC/pacificaviet.html.

35. Letter from Matthias Mirschel to Martin Luther King, June 10, 1967, The King Center, www.thekingcenter.org/archive/document/letter-mr-matthias-mirschel-mlk.

36. Martin Luther King, "I See the Promised Land," in Washington, ed., *Testament of Hope*, 280.

37. "Roundup: Foreign Tributes to Dr. King," *Christian Century*, May 8, 1968, 629–630; "Africans Express Shock at Slaying of Dr. King," *New York Times*, April 6, 1968; Peter Ling, *Martin Luther King Jr.* (New York: Routledge, 2002), 304; Stephen Oates, *Let the Trumpet Sound: The Life of Martin Luther King Jr.* (New York: Harper & Row, 1982), 495.

38. "Anti-U.S. Protest in Rome," *New York Times*, April 6, 1968.

39. "Roundup: Foreign Tributes to Dr. King," 629.

40. Lyndon B. Johnson, "Remarks on Decision Not to Seek Re-Election," March 31, 1968, Miller Center Presidential Speech Archive, http://millercenter.org/president/lbjohnson/speeches/speech-3388; Branch, *At Canaan's Edge*, 749; Carlyle Morgan, "Assassination Stirs Anxieties in Europe," *Christian Science Monitor*, April 8, 1968.

41. "Shocked World Reaction to Assassination," *Times of London*, April 6, 1968; "Europe Dismayed; Fearful for U.S.," *New York Times*, April 6, 1968; "World Mourns, Fears U.S.," *Boston Globe*, April 6, 1968; "Der Schub von Memphis," *Die Welt*, April 6, 1968; "World Mourns Rights Leader," *Nashville Tennessean*, April 6, 1968; Ling, *Martin Luther King Jr.*, 305–306.

42. "L'Hommage de Paris a Martin Luther King," *Droit et Liberte*, May 1968, 9; "Une Lecon de Courage," *Droit et Liberte*, May 1968, 11.

43. "Pope Likens Dr. King to a Suffering Christ," *Boston Globe*, April 8, 1968; Gerald Miller, "Pope's Palm Mass Deplores Slaying," *Atlanta Constitution*, April 8, 1968.

44. "Africans Express Shock at Slaying of Dr. King"; "Roundup: Foreign Tributes to Dr. King," 630; "The World Honors MLK Through Stamps," *Ebony*, January 1986, 82–83; Nico Slate, *Colored Cosmopolitanism: The Shared*

Struggle for Freedom in the United States and India (Cambridge, MA: Harvard University Press, 2012), 235; Black Heritage Stamps, US Postal Service, http://uspsstamps.com/stamps/series/black-heritage.

45. Vijay Pillai, ed. *Indian Leaders on Martin Luther King Jr.* (New Delhi: Inter-State Cultural League of India, 1968), 70; "Shocked World Reaction to Assassination"; "Indian Parliament Pays King Tribute," *New York Times*, April 6, 1968.

46. Pillai, *Indian Leaders on Martin Luther King Jr.*, ix, 2, 80.

47. Ibid., 101; G. Nagarajan to Coretta Scott King and Family, April 10, 1968, The King Center, http://www.thekingcenter.org/archive/document /letter-condolence-mrs-king-and-children-nagarajan-and-family.

48. François Duvalier, *A Tribute to the Martyred Leader of Non-Violence: Reverend Dr. Martin Luther King Jr.* (Port-au-Prince, Haiti: Presses Nationales, 1968), 82, 92, 122, 98.

49. "Roundup: Foreign Tributes to Dr. King," 630; "Shocked World Reaction to Assassination"; John Daniel and Peter Vale, "South Africa: Where Were We Looking in 1968?," in Philipp Gassert and Martin Klimke, eds. *1968: Memories and Legacies of a Global Revolt* (Washington, DC: German Historical Institute, 2009), 140.

50. Brian Dooley, *Black and Green: The Fight for Civil Rights in Northern Ireland and Black America* (London: Pluto Press, 1998), 97, 96; Richard Jordan, "The 'Prophet' of Interposition: The Reverend Ian Paisley and American Segregation," *New Hibernia Review* 15, no. 2 (summer 2011): 54–55; Camilla Schofield, *Enoch Powell and the Making of Postcolonial Britain* (New York: Cambridge University Press, 2013), 219–220.

51. Allan Boesak, *Farewell to Innocence: A Socio-Ethical Study on Black Theology and Black Power* (Maryknoll, NY: Orbis Books, 1977), 15, 137; Baldwin, "Martin Luther King Jr., a 'Coalition of Conscience,' and Freedom in South Africa," 72.

52. George W. Shepherd Jr., "Who Killed Martin Luther King's Dream? An Afro-American Tragedy," *Africa Today* 15, no. 2 (April–May 1968): 2; "Roundup: Foreign Tributes to Dr. King," 629; B. S. Mofokeng, Letter to the Editor, *Johannesburg World*, April 18, 1968; D. M. Molemo, Letter to the Editor, *Johannesburg World*, April 18, 1968.

53. Bruce Oudes, "Dark Continent Weeps for King," *Commercial Appeal*, April 7, 1968; Ling, *Martin Luther King Jr.*, 304.

54. Ariel Dorfman, "A Time for Creative Suffering: Martin Luther King's Words in a Surveillance World," *TomDispatch*, August 27, 2013, www.tom

dispatch.com/blog/175741/tomgram%3A_ariel_dorfman,_martin_luther
_king_and_the_two_9_11s/.

55. Ibid.

56. Otto Kohler, "Wurzelgrund," *Der Spiegel*, April 14, 1968.

57. "West Berlin Student Revolutionary: Rudolf Dutschke," *New York Times*, April 16, 1968; David Hotham, "Rudi Dutschke, Symbol of Youth in Rebellion," *Times of London*, April 13, 1968.

58. David Caute, *The Year of the Barricades: A Journey Through 1968* (New York: Harper & Row, 1988), 97, 102.

59. Ibid., 102; Hohn and Klimke, *Breath of Freedom*, 107; Mark Kurlansky, *1968: The Year That Rocked the World* (New York: Ballantine, 2004), 152.

60. Martin Klimke, *The Other Alliance: Student Protest in West Germany and the United States in the Global Sixties* (Princeton, NJ: Princeton University Press, 2010), 116–117.

61. "How Student Leader Was Wounded," *Times of London*, April 13, 1968; "Accused Man 'Read of Dr. King Shooting,'" *Times of London*, April 13, 1968; Philip Shabecoff, "Student Rampage in West Germany Follows Shooting," *New York Times*, April 13, 1968; "West Berlin Gunman Wounds Leader of Left-Wing Students," *New York Times*, April 12, 1968.

62. Shabecoff, "Student Rampage"; "West Berlin Gunman Wounds Leader of Left-Wing Students."

63. Klimke, *Other Alliance*, 117; Hohn and Klimke, *Breath of Freedom*, 113–114. As historian Martin Klimke writes, "In a remarkable turn of interpretation, West German student activists now also began to appropriate King's legacy for their own political agenda."

64. "Powerful West German Publisher: Axel Caesar Springer," *New York Times*, April 13, 1968; David Hotham, "The Springer Press Empire, a Target of Hate," *Times of London*, April 14, 1968; Caute, *Year of the Barricades*, 104.

65. David Binder, "Kiesinger Warns Student Leaders; Unrest Continues," *New York Times*, April 14, 1968; David Binder, "Violence Rocks Cities," *New York Times*, April 13, 1968; "Students Demonstrate in Rome," *New York Times*, April 13, 1968; "How Student Leader Was Wounded."

66. Klimke, *Other Alliance*, 117–118.

67. Hotham, "Springer Press Empire"; Philip Shabecoff, "230 Arrested in Berlin," *New York Times*, April 14, 1968; Binder, "Kiesinger Warns Student Leaders"; Caute, *Year of the Barricades*, 103.

68. Philip Shabecoff, "Peaceful Rally in Berlin," *New York Times*, April 16, 1968; Caute, *Year of the Barricades*, 97, 102, 104. In West Germany as a whole,

fully 84 percent of adults still disapproved of the protests. The shift in public opinion was most apparent in West Berlin.

69. Shabecoff, "Peaceful Rally in Berlin"; David Binder, "Street Fighting Breaks Out Again in West Germany," *New York Times*, April 16, 1968.

70. Alvin Shuster, "Londoners Score Berlin Shooting," *New York Times*, April 16, 1968; "Aldermaston Rally Draws 22,000," *Times of London*, April 16, 1968; "London March on Springer Office," *Times of London*, April 16, 1968; Caute, *Year of the Barricades*, 90.

71. Shuster, "Londoners Score Berlin Shooting"; "Aldermaston Rally Draws 22,000."

72. Brian Ward, "A King in Newcastle: Martin Luther King Jr. and British Race Relations, 1967–1968," *Georgia Historical Quarterly* 79, no. 3 (Fall 1995): 604–605, 607; Brian Ward, *Martin Luther King in Newcastle upon Tyne: The African American Freedom Struggle and Race Relations in the North East of England* (Newcastle upon Tyne, UK: Tyne Bridge Publishing, 2017), 37.

73. Ward, "King in Newcastle," 612, 615; Martin Luther King, Honorary Degree Speech, University of Newcastle, November 13, 1967, www.ncl.ac.uk /congregations/assets/documents/MLKspeech.pdf.

74. Ward, *Martin Luther King in Newcastle upon Tyne*, 49.

75. Schofield, *Enoch Powell and the Making of Postcolonial Britain*, 210–211; Kennetta Hammond Perry, *London Is the Place for Me: Black Britons, Citizenship, and the Politics of Race* (New York: Oxford University Press, 2015), 191.

76. Ward, "A King in Newcastle," 618–619; Schofield, *Enoch Powell and the Making of Postcolonial Britain*, 246, 211.

77. Ward, "A King in Newcastle," 618, 626–628; Schofield, *Enoch Powell and the Making of Postcolonial Britain*, 214; Andrew Roth, *Enoch Powell: Tory Tribune* (London: Macdonald, 1970), 341.

78. Ward, "A King in Newcastle," 629–630; William Stoneman, "Britain Seeks to Solve Its Racial Rift," *Commercial Appeal*, April 10, 1968; Schofield, *Enoch Powell and the Making of Postcolonial Britain*, 212; Roth, *Enoch Powell*, 349.

79. "Many British Tributes," *Times of London*, April 6, 1968; Ward, "King in Newcastle," 628.

80. "Rioting in US Moves British," *Commercial Appeal*, April 10, 1968; David Winder, "Britain Sees Warning in U.S. Race Crisis," *Christian Science Monitor*, April 11, 1968; Schofield, *Enoch Powell and the Making of Postcolonial Britain*, 211.

81. "A Chance to Do Better," *Times of London*, April 10, 1968; Lord Walston, "Lessons from America," Letter to the Editor, *Times of London*, April 10, 1968.

82. "Intolerance," *Times of London*, April 19, 1968.

83. Schofield, *Enoch Powell and the Making of Postcolonial Britain*, 214; Ward, "King in Newcastle," 629.

84. Schofield, *Enoch Powell and the Making of Postcolonial Britain*, 208–210.

85. Enoch Powell, "Rivers of Blood," April 20, 1968, full text reprinted in *The Telegraph*, November 6, 2007; Roth, *Enoch Powell*, 346–347.

86. Powell, "Rivers of Blood."

87. Ibid.

88. Francis Cocks, "Continuing Race Bill Debate: View of Many Christians," Letter to the Editor, *Times of London*, April 26, 1968; "Mosley Speeches Recalled," *Times of London*, April 22, 1968.

89. Ward, "King in Newcastle," 630–631; John Henderson, "Voice of the People," Letter to the Editor, *Times of London*, April 23, 1968; David Le Vay, "What All Think," Letter to the Editor, *Times of London*, April 23, 1968.

90. Schofield, *Enoch Powell and the Making of Postcolonial Britain*, 209, 243–244; Tom Hopkinson, "The Thin Crust," Letter to the Editor, *Times of London*, April 26, 1968; Rita Marshall, "The Men Who Head the Marchers," *Times of London*, April 27, 1968.

91. "Coloured Family Attacked," *Times of London*, May 1, 1968; Schofield, *Enoch Powell and the Making of Postcolonial Britain*, 247–249.

92. Perry, *London Is the Place for Me*, 239; "Black Alliance Threatens to Take Militant Action," *Times of London*, April 29, 1968.

93. "MPs' Deputation," *Times of London*, April 29, 1968; "Dockers and Students in Angry Scenes," *Times of London*, May 2, 1968; Schofield, *Enoch Powell and the Making of Postcolonial Britain*, 209–223, 254–255.

94. Dan Carter, *The Politics of Rage: George Wallace, the Origins of the New Conservatism, and the Transformation of American Politics* (New York: Simon & Schuster, 1995).

CHAPTER 6: STOP THE SHOTS

1. Richard Harris, "If You Love Your Guns," *New Yorker*, April 20, 1968, 155; "Gun Controls Needed–IV," *Boston Globe*, April 25, 1968; "A First Memorial," *The Nation*, April 22, 1968, 522; Richard Stewart, "Gun Bill Caught in New Snag," *Boston Globe*, April 24, 1968.

2. David Chappell, *Waking from the Dream: The Struggle for Civil Rights in the Shadow of Martin Luther King Jr.* (New York: Random House, 2014), 3.

3. Ibid., 4–6, 11–12, 15–16, 21.

4. "Washington Is Shaken; Leaders Call for Calm," *New York Times*, April 5, 1968; Marjorie Hunter, "Dr. King's Death Is Expected to Spur Rights Bill," *New York Times*, April 6, 1968; 114 Cong. Rec. H9307 (April 9, 1968); Joseph R. L. Sterne, "Congress Pushed to Act on Rights," *Baltimore Sun*, April 6, 1968.

5. Edmund Willingham, "Open Housing Rights Bill Passes House, Goes to LBJ," *Nashville Tennessean*, April 11, 1968; Lyndon Johnson, "Remarks on Signing the Civil Rights Act," April 11, 1968, Miller Center Presidential Speech Archive, http://millercenter.org/president/lbjohnson/speeches/speech-4036.

6. Dorothy Ogle Graham, "Write Congressmen," Letter to the Editor, *Baltimore Afro-American*, April 20, 1968.

7. William Vizzard, *Shots in the Dark: The Policy, Politics, and Symbolism of Gun Control* (Lanham, MD: Rowman & Littlefield, 2000), 96, 89–91; "A First Memorial"; "Gun Controls Needed–IV"; John Chadwick, "Senate Unit Votes Gun Curbs," *Nashville Tennessean*, April 7, 1968. The Federal Firearms Act, passed in 1938, was the last major gun control law. It provided limited controls on firearms. Before that, the National Firearms Act was passed in 1934. It was designed to curtail crimes like bank robberies, and imposed licensing and registration requirements on machine guns. But the Supreme Court weakened that law in January 1968. Alan Berlow, "Gun Control That Actually Works," *New York Times*, May 31, 2016; William Galeota, "The NRA: The Gun-Men Meet in Boston," *Harvard Crimson*, April 16, 1968.

8. Robert Sherrill, *The Saturday Night Special* (New York: Charterhouse, 1973), 68; Taylor Branch, *At Canaan's Edge: America in the King Years, 1965–68* (New York: Simon & Schuster, 2006), 329.

9. Robert Sherrill, "High Noon on Capitol Hill," *New York Times Magazine*, June 23, 1968; Drew Pearson and Jack Anderson, "Gun Industry Holding Hill at Bay," *Washington Post*, April 13, 1968.

10. Sherrill, *Saturday Night Special*, 170, 222; Vizzard, *Shots in the Dark*, 93–94.

11. Sherrill, *Saturday Night Special*, 120; Adam Winkler, *Gunfight: The Battle over the Right to Bear Arms in America* (New York: W.W. Norton, 2011), 251; Richard Stewart, "N.R.A. Marshaling Opposition to Firearms Control Measure," *Boston Globe*, April 14, 1968; Harris, "If You Love Your Guns," 58, 61.

12. Vizzard, *Shots in the Dark*, 94; Harris, "If You Love Your Guns," 87–88, 122, 124; Sherrill, "High Noon on Capitol Hill"; Gabrielle Westcott, "The Fight for the Gun Control Act of 1968," Archives & Special Collections Blog, University of Connecticut, September 15, 2016.

13. Winkler, *Gunfight*, 244–247; Westcott, "Fight for the Gun Control Act of 1968"; Arica Coleman, "When the NRA Supported Gun Control," *Time*, July 29, 2016, http://time.com/4431356/nra-gun-control-history/.

14. "Ted to Speak to Convening Gun Fans," *Boston Globe*, April 5, 1968; Sherrill, "High Noon on Capitol Hill"; Galeota, "The NRA: The Gun-Men Meet in Boston"; "Gun Controls Needed–III," *Boston Globe*, April 24, 1968; Harris, "If You Love Your Guns," 57; James Doyle, "Congress Flooded by Mail Demanding Controls," *Boston Globe*, June 16, 1968.

15. Report of the National Commission on the Causes and Prevention of Violence (Washington, DC, 1969), 171; Kevin Klose, "Fairfax Chief Urges Strict Area Gun Code," *Washington Post*, May 11, 1968; Ben Franklin, "Gun Problem: The Citizens Arm as Congress Looks the Other Way," *New York Times*, April 21, 1968.

16. Thomas Dodd, Statement on the Assassination of Martin Luther King, April 5, 1968, Series III, Box 209, Folder 5618, Thomas Dodd Papers, Thomas Dodd Research Center, University of Connecticut; 114 Cong. Rec. S9197 (April 8, 1968); "A First Memorial," 523; "Gun Controls Needed–I," *Boston Globe*, April 22, 1968; "Gun Controls Needed–III"; Julius Bernstein, "How Many," Letter to the Editor, *Boston Globe*, April 12, 1968.

17. Letter from Thomas Dodd to Roman Hruska, April 17, 1968, Series III, Box 209, Folder 5619, Thomas Dodd Papers; Memo from Bob Perry to Thomas Dodd, Subject: Conference with Senator Hruska Regarding Gun Bill, April 17, 1968, Thomas Dodd Papers; Committee on the Judiciary, US Senate (April 24, 1968), 44; Stewart, "Gun Bill Caught in New Snag"; "Gun Control Bill Faces New Fight in Committee," *Washington Post*, April 24, 1968; Robert Waters, "Dodd's Gun Bill Faces New Vote," *Hartford Courant*, April 24, 1968.

18. John Finney, "Senate, Voting Crime Bill, Backs Broad Wiretapping," *New York Times*, May 24, 1968; Sterne, "Congress Pushed to Act on Rights"; Committee on the Judiciary, US Senate (April 24, 1968), 19, 31.

19. 114 Cong. Rec. S13,630 (May 16, 1968); Robert Albright, "Handgun Controls Retained," *Washington Post*, May 17, 1968; Thomas Dodd, Press Release: "Dodd Gun Bill Becomes Law, First in 30 Years," June 20, 1968,

Thomas Dodd Papers, University of Connecticut, http://doddcenter.uconn .edu/asc/images/dodd/1994–0065_210_5663.PDF.

20. Ronald Steel, *In Love with Night: The American Romance with Robert Kennedy* (New York: Simon & Schuster, 2000), 170.

21. Ray Boomhower, *Robert F. Kennedy and the 1968 Indiana Primary* (Bloomington: Indiana University Press, 2008), 63.

22. John Lewis, *Walking with the Wind: A Memoir of the Movement* (New York: Simon & Schuster, 1998), 384.

23. Ibid., 386; Boomhower, *Robert F. Kennedy and the 1968 Indiana Primary*, 2–3; Interview with Walter Sheridan, by Roberta Greene, August 5, 1969, 5, Robert F. Kennedy Oral History Collection, John F. Kennedy Library; Karl Anatol and John Bittner, "Kennedy on King: The Rhetoric of Control," *Today's Speech* 16, no. 1 (September 1968): 31.

24. Arthur Schlesinger Jr., *Robert Kennedy and His Times* (New York: Ballantine Books, 1978), 939; Boomhower, *Robert F. Kennedy and the 1968 Indiana Primary*, 63–64; Thurston Clarke, *The Last Campaign: Robert F. Kennedy and 82 Days That Inspired America* (New York: Henry Holt, 2008), 84.

25. Boomhower, *Robert F. Kennedy and the 1968 Indiana Primary*, 65; Frank Maier, "So I Ask You to Return Home and Say a Prayer," *Boston Globe*, April 5, 1968.

26. Anatol and Bittner, "Kennedy on King," 31; Boomhower, *Robert F. Kennedy and the 1968 Indiana Primary*, 135. One example of the conventional wisdom can be found in Jules Witcover's *85 Days*. Witcover writes, "It was immediately apparent that the crowd had not heard the news." Jules Witcover, *85 Days: The Last Campaign of Robert Kennedy* (New York: G.P. Putnam's Sons, 1969), 140; Robert F. Kennedy, "Remarks on the Assassination of Martin Luther King, Jr.," http://www.americanrhetoric.com/speeches /rfkonmlkdeath.html.

27. Boomhower, *Robert F. Kennedy and the 1968 Indiana Primary*, 135–136; Kennedy, "Remarks on the Assassination of Martin Luther King, Jr."; Lewis, *Walking with the Wind*, 388; Anatol and Bittner, "Kennedy on King," 32.

28. Kennedy, "Remarks on the Assassination of Martin Luther King, Jr."; Boomhower, *Robert F. Kennedy and the 1968 Indiana Primary*, 136, 69; Anatol and Bittner, "Kennedy on King," 32–33.

29. Lewis, *Walking with the Wind*, 388.

30. "RFK Denounces Slaying of Dr. King," *Washington Post*, April 6, 1968; "Bobby Calls King's Death Time of Shame," *Chicago Tribune*, April 6, 1968; Witcover, *85 Days*, 142.

31. Jack Newfield, *Robert Kennedy: A Memoir* (New York: Dutton, 1969), 248–250; Richard Dougherty, "'Violence Stains Our Land'—RFK," *Boston Globe*, April 6, 1968.

32. Daniel Patrick Moynihan, "The Democrats, Kennedy and the Murder of Dr. King," *Commentary*, May 1968.

33. Newfield, *Robert Kennedy*, 250–251.

34. John Goldman, "Kennedy Calls Death of King Turning Point," *Los Angeles Times*, April 11, 1968; Clarke, *Last Campaign*, 143.

35. David Halberstam, "Bobby's Last Campaign," *New York*, April 19, 1993, 108; David Halberstam, *The Unfinished Odyssey of Robert Kennedy* (New York: Random House, 1968), 93–94.

36. James Reston, "Washington: The Anti-Kennedy Syndrome," *New York Times*, April 24, 1968.

37. Newfield, *Robert Kennedy*, 256; Clarke, *Last Campaign*, 188.

38. Clarke, *Last Campaign*, 176.

39. Louis Harris, "Part Way with RFK: The Price He Paid," *Newsweek*, May 20, 1968, 35; Steel, *In Love with Night*, 179; Halberstam, *Unfinished Odyssey of Robert Kennedy*, 4; Witcover, *85 Days*, 180–181.

40. Finney, "Senate, Voting Crime Bill, Backs Broad Wiretapping."

41. Newfield, *Robert Kennedy*, 269.

42. John Herbers, "Kennedy Heckled in Oregon Over Gun Controls," *New York Times*, May 28, 1968; "RFK, McCarthy Hopes Rest in Oregon Today," *Newsday*, May 28, 1968; "Kennedy Booed in Oregon Gun Debate," *Los Angeles Times*, May 28, 1968; "In 1968 Robert F. Kennedy Called for Gun Control, in Roseburg," *The Oregonian*, October 4, 2015; Halberstam, *Unfinished Odyssey of Robert Kennedy*, 185–186; Clarke, *Last Campaign*, 236.

43. David Karol, *Party Position Change in American Politics: Coalition Management* (New York: Cambridge University Press, 2009), 86; "M'Carthy Cautions on Gun-Law 'Panic,'" *New York Times*, June 17, 1968; Steel, *In Love with Night*, 179; "In 1968 Robert F. Kennedy Called for Gun Control, in Roseburg."

44. Antonio Orendain, "El Malcriado," June 15, 1968, in Pierre Salinger, ed., *"An Honorable Profession": A Tribute to Robert F. Kennedy* (Garden City, NY: Doubleday, 1968), 85; James Thomas Jackson, Watts Writers' Workshop Los Angeles Underground, in Salinger, ed., *"An Honorable Profession,"* 98; Newfield, *Robert Kennedy*, 275, 289; Steel, *In Love with Night*, 187.

45. J. Anthony Lukas, "New Yorkers Awaken in Shock to a Day That Many Would Prefer to Forget," *New York Times*, June 6, 1968; Jean Stein,

American Journey: The Times of Robert Kennedy (New York: Harcourt Brace Jovanovich, 1970), 341–342.

46. "Transcript of Johnson Speech Naming U.S. Panel on Violence," *New York Times*, June 6, 1968; Max Frankel, "Johnson Appoints Panel on Violence," *New York Times*, June 6, 1968.

47. "'Cruel Hoax': Veto Called For," *New York Times*, June 7, 1968; "Johnson Statement on Strong Gun Law," *New York Times*, June 7, 1968; Max Frankel, "Johnson Asks Strong Gun Law," *New York Times*, June 7, 1968.

48. Peter Grose, "Rifle Group Head Disputes Need of Gun Controls," *New York Times*, June 8, 1968; Witcover, *85 Days*, 289.

49. Alexander Markovich, "For Total Ban on Arms," Letter to the Editor, *New York Times*, June 8, 1968; James Lincoln, "Reaction to Kennedy Assassination," Letter to the Editor, *New York Times*, June 9, 1968; Sherrill, "High Noon on Capitol Hill."

50. John Finney, "Senators Predict Strict Gun Curbs as Pressure Rises," *New York Times*, June 13, 1968; Statement by Senator Thomas J. Dodd on the Floor of the Senate, "The Sickness of Violence and the Need for Gun Control Legislation," June 11, 1968, Dodd Center, University of Connecticut; John Finney, "Rifle Group Mounts Drive Against Gun Controls," *New York Times*, June 15, 1968.

51. James Doyle, "Congress Flooded by Mail Demanding Controls," *Boston Globe*, June 16, 1968.

52. Finney, "Senators Predict Strict Gun Curbs"; Doyle, "Congress Flooded by Mail."

53. Doyle, "Congress Flooded by Mail"; Finney, "Rifle Group Mounts Drive"; Sherrill, "High Noon on Capitol Hill."

54. "Senate Fails to Protect the Public," *Los Angeles Times*, May 21, 1968; Isadore Barmash, "Retailers Cut Sale of Guns, Ammunition," *New York Times*, June 23, 1968; Sherrill, "High Noon on Capitol Hill."

55. "Transcript of Johnson's Statement on Signing Crime and Safety Bill," *New York Times*, June 20, 1968; Max Frankel, "President Signs Broad Crime Bill, with Objections," *New York Times*, June 20, 1968; "Text of Johnson Gun Message," *New York Times*, June 25, 1968; Max Frankel, "President Calls for Registering of All Firearms," *New York Times*, June 25, 1968.

56. William Borders, "Dodd Gaining Political Strength Despite Censure by the Senate," *New York Times*, June 30, 1968.

57. William Borders, "Dodd Jeered at Hartford Gun-Control Hearing," *New York Times*, July 17, 1968.

58. "Gun Control Bills Stalled in Senate," *New York Times*, July 11, 1968.

59. Marjorie Hunter, "President Signs Second Gun Bill," *New York Times*, October 23, 1968; Vizzard, *Shots in the Dark*, 97–99; Kristin Goss, *Disarmed: The Missing Movement for Gun Control in America* (Princeton, NJ: Princeton University Press, 2006), 80; Report of the National Commission on the Causes and Prevention of Violence, 176; Sherrill, *Saturday Night Special*, 280.

60. Winkler, *Gunfight*, 256–257; Vizzard, *Shots in the Dark*, 100.

CHAPTER 7: FROM OUTLAW TO SAINT

1. William Schmidt, "Looking Back at a Man Ahead of His Time," *New York Times*, January 12, 1986.

2. Robert Kellett, "Site of Slaying Becomes Shrine," *Commercial Appeal*, April 10, 1968.

3. Marcus Baram, "How Stevie Wonder Helped Create Martin Luther King Day," *Cuepoint*, January 18, 2015; "Making of the Holiday: A Chronology," The King Center, http://www.thekingcenter.org/making-king -holiday; "State Observing Holiday for Martin Luther King," *Boston Globe*, January 14, 1975; David Andelman, "Most Major Cities Will Ignore Birthday of Dr. King on Friday," *New York Times*, January 11, 1971; Robert Anglin, "Nation Pays Tribute to Dr. King," *Boston Globe*, January 16, 1976.

4. Candus Thomson, "N.H. Conservative with a Southern Accent," *Baltimore Sun*, April 29, 2001; "N.H. Blacks Answer Thomson's Attack on Young, King," *Boston Globe*, September 18, 1977.

5. Howell Raines, "Pressure Rises for Day in Georgia Hailing Dr. King," *New York Times*, January 10, 1979; Edward Walsh, "President Urges King Birthday as National Holiday," *Washington Post*, January 15, 1979; David Chappell, *Waking from the Dream: The Struggle for Civil Rights in the Shadow of Martin Luther King Jr.* (New York: Random House, 2014), 94–110; Mary Russell, "King Holiday Frustrated," *Washington Post*, December 6, 1979.

6. James Kilpatrick, "Some Unfinished Business Should Be Left That Way," *Los Angeles Times*, January 14, 1980; "Birth Date Eulogy Offered for Martin Luther King," *Los Angeles Times*, January 15, 1980.

7. Stevie Wonder, "Happy Birthday," *Hotter Than July*, Motown, 1980; Baram, "How Stevie Wonder Helped Create Martin Luther King Day"; Gil Scott-Heron, "How Gil Scott-Heron and Stevie Wonder Set Up Martin Luther King Day," *The Guardian*, January 8, 2012.

8. Carol Stocker, "A Birthday to Remember," *Boston Globe*, January 15, 1982; Lynn Simross, "Support Growing for King Holiday," *Los Angeles Times*, January 14, 1982; "Reagan Signs Extension of '65 Voting Rights Act," *Los Angeles Times*, June 29, 1982; Pedro Noguera and Robert Cohen, "Remembering

Reagan's Record on Civil Rights and the South African Freedom Struggle," *The Nation*, February 11, 2011; Hodding Carter III, "Martin Luther King Jr.: A Dream Deferred," *Wall Street Journal*, April 7, 1983; "Reagan Opposes National Holiday for Martin Luther King Birthday," *Boston Globe*, January 23, 1983.

9. Chappell, *Waking from the Dream*, 219, 115; George Lardner Jr., "Martin Luther King Jr. Day Votes," *Washington Post*, August 3, 1983.

10. "Helms Is Firm in His Opinions on Race and Drive for 'So-Called Civil Rights,'" *Wall Street Journal*, July 16, 1981; Osha Gray Davidson, *The Best of Enemies: Race and Redemption in the New South* (Chapel Hill: University of North Carolina Press, 2007), 220; Bertie Howard, oral history, in Bridget Booher, "Remembering the Silent Vigil: A University Milestone," *Duke Magazine*, March–April 1998, 49; Chappell, *Waking from the Dream*, 115–116; Paul Houston, "Helms Filibusters Against National Holiday for King," *Los Angeles Times*, October 4, 1983; Steven Roberts, "King Holiday Bill Faces a Filibuster," *New York Times*, October 4, 1983; "Helms Ends Filibuster Over King Holiday," *Los Angeles Times*, October 5, 1983; Mary McGrory, "What Did Our President Have in Mind?," *Washington Post*, October 23, 1983; Frances Romero, "A Brief History of Martin Luther King Day," *Time*, January 18, 2010; "Soundtracks: The Assassination of Martin Luther King Jr.," CNN, April 20, 2017.

11. "Senate Votes to Set a Holiday Honoring Martin Luther King," *Wall Street Journal*, October 20, 1983; "Senate Roll-call on U.S. Holiday for King," *Boston Globe*, October 20, 1983.

12. "Petition Seeks King Holiday Veto," *Boston Globe*, October 21, 1983; "Letter Gives Reagan View on King Holiday," *Boston Globe*, October 21, 1983; "Senate Votes to Set a Holiday Honoring Martin Luther King"; "Reagan Explains to Mrs. King," *Boston Globe*, October 22, 1983; McGrory, "What Did Our President Have in Mind?"

13. Gilbert Caldwell, "The Tragedy of Jesse Helms," *Washington Post*, October 23, 1983; Harry Golden, *The Nation*, April 29, 1968, 572; Gladwin Hill, "Reagan Not Sure Johnson Has Quit," *New York Times*, April 10, 1968; Noguera and Cohen, "Remembering Reagan's Record on Civil Rights."

14. Bono, The Edge, Adam Clayton, and Larry Mullen Jr., with Neal McCormick, *U2 by U2* (New York: HarperCollins, 2006), 192; Kenneth Partridge, "U2's 'The Unforgettable Fire' at 30," *Billboard*, October 1, 2014; U2, "Pride (In the Name of Love)," *The Unforgettable Fire*, Island, 1984.

15. Jeffrey Jones, "Americans Divided on Whether King's Dream Has Been Realized," *Gallup*, August 26, 2011; Sheldon Appleton, "Martin Luther King in Life . . . and Memory," *Public Perspective*, February/March, 1995, 12–13, 47.

16. Appleton, "Martin Luther King in Life," 12; Chappell, *Waking from the Dream*, 99.

17. Bernard Weinraub, "Reagan Opens Observances Leading to Dr. King's Birthday," *New York Times*, January 14, 1986; Bernard Weinraub, "Reagan Tells Pupils of Struggle Won by Dr. King," *New York Times*, January 16, 1986.

18. Roger Wilkins, "A Dream Still Denied," *Los Angeles Times*, January 19, 1986; "How to Honor Dr. King—and When," *New York Times*, January 15, 1986.

19. William Schmidt, "Nation Pauses to Remember King, Led by a Huge Tribute in Atlanta," *New York Times*, January 21, 1986.

20. Coretta Scott King, "Martin Luther King Holiday Calls for Day of World Peace," *Los Angeles Times*, January 12, 1986.

21. Noguera and Cohen, "Remembering Reagan's Record on Civil Rights"; Bernard Gwertzman, "Reagan, in Reversal, Orders Sanctions on South Africa," *New York Times*, September 10, 1985; Judi Hasson, "The Congressional Black Caucus Friday Characterized President Reagan's Comments," UPI, March 22, 1985; Andrew Glass, "House Overrides Reagan Apartheid Veto," *Politico*, September 29, 2010; "Reagan Says U.S. Favors Covert Aid to Angola Rebels," *New York Times*, November 23, 1985.

22. Howard Kurtz, "King Cited in Defense of End to Hiring Goals," *New York Times*, January 16, 1986; Lyndon Johnson, Executive Order 11246, September 28, 1965.

23. Martin Luther King Jr., *Where Do We Go from Here: Chaos or Community?* (Boston: Beacon Press, 2010 edition), 95; Martin Luther King, *Why We Can't Wait* (New York: Harper & Row, 1968 edition), 134–138; Eric Foner, Letter to the Editor, *Los Angeles Times*, August 18, 1996; Ira Katznelson, *When Affirmative Action Was White: An Untold History of Racial Inequality in Twentieth-Century America* (New York: W.W. Norton, 2005).

24. Guy Coates, "Louisiana Governor Bans Affirmative Action," *Washington Post*, January 12, 1996; Derrick Z. Jackson, "Twisting King's Dream," *Boston Globe*, October 25, 1996; B. Drummond Ayres Jr., "Affirmative Action Measure Nears a High-Profile Finish," *New York Times*, November 4, 1996; Michael Eric Dyson, "Race in America: The Tragic Abuse of King's Famous 34 Words," *Los Angeles Times*, January 16, 2000.

25. Jonathan Tilove, *Along Martin Luther King: Travels on Black America's Main Street* (New York: Random House, 2003), 11; Tanvi Misra, "The Remaking of Martin Luther King Streets," *Citylab*, November 23, 2015.

26. Tilove, *Along Martin Luther King*, 17; Michael Barnes, "The Fight Over Austin's MLK Jr. Boulevard," *Austin American-Statesman*, January 17, 2016.

27. Barnes, "The Fight Over Austin's MLK Jr. Boulevard."

28. Armando Acuna, "Stretch of 2 Streets Urged as Dr. King Ave.," *Los Angeles Times*, January 31, 1986; Ralph Frammolino, "Council OKs Market St. Change to King Way," *Los Angeles Times*, April 23, 1986.

29. Frammolino, "Council OKs Market St. Change."

30. Thomas McPhatter, "Tribute to Martin Luther King Jr.," Letter to the Editor, *Los Angeles Times*, May 11, 1986; Kinsee Morlan, "10 Freakin' Years?: The History Behind the Struggle to Build a Memorial to Martin Luther King Jr.," *San Diego City Beat*, June 28, 2006; Ralph Frammolino, "King Way Initiative Becomes Less Than Noble Issue for City," *Los Angeles Times*, October 11, 1987; Frammolino, "Council OKs Market St. Change."

31. Eric Bailey, "Merchants Protest Renaming Market Street After King," *Los Angeles Times*, May 1, 1986.

32. Jacqueline Parker, "Keep Market Street Group Demands a Vote on Name," *Los Angeles Times*, July 3, 1986; Frammolino, "King Way Initiative."

33. "Ballot on Market Street Up in Air," *Los Angeles Times*, July 8, 1986; Jacqueline Parker, "Blacks Firm in Support of Street Named for King," *Los Angeles Times*, July 11, 1986; Kathie Bozanich, "Petition Begun to Restore Market Street Name," *Los Angeles Times*, October 11, 1986.

34. Armando Acuna, "Initiative Filed to Rename King Way," *Los Angeles Times*, March 17, 1987.

35. Ibid.

36. Ralph Frammolino, "Market Street or King Way?," *Los Angeles Times*, April 21, 1987; Mike Granberry, "O'Connor to Head King Way Effort," *Los Angeles Times*, June 26, 1987; Frammolino, "King Way Initiative."

37. Frammolino, "King Way Initiative."

38. Morlan, "10 Freakin' Years?"; Jennifer Bollard, Letter to the Editor, *Los Angeles Times*, November 15, 1987; Caroline Moran, Letter to the Editor, *Los Angeles Times*, November 8, 1987; Douglas Kemp, Letter to the Editor, *Los Angeles Times*, November 15, 1987.

39. "A True Test of Motives," *Los Angeles Times*, January 10, 1988; Raymond Sanchez, "King Parade Signs Posted on Market Street," *Los Angeles Times*, February 13, 1988; Morlan, "10 Freakin' Years?"

40. Tilove, *Along Martin Luther King*, 17–18; Misra, "Remaking of Martin Luther King Streets." By 2014, there would be more than 900 King streets across the nation.

41. Thomas Knudson, "Arizona Torn by Governor-Elect's Plan to Drop King Holiday," *New York Times*, December 23, 1986; Lena Williams, "Most

of U.S. Will Honor Dr. King, but Some Still Dispute the Holiday," *New York Times*, January 18, 1987.

42. Letter from Steve Frost to Evan Mecham, January 20, 1987, State, County and Local Government Records, Arizona State Archives, http:// azmemory.azlibrary.gov/cdm/singleitem/collection/archgov/id/402/rec /1; Knudson, "Arizona Torn by Governor-Elect's Plan."

43. Lena Williams, "Holiday for Dr. King Gaining Wider Observance," *New York Times*, January 15, 1988; James Barron, "Sea to Sea, North and South, King Is Honored," *New York Times*, January 17, 1989; "Arizona Holiday for Dr. King May Face Ballot Test in 1990," *New York Times*, September 26, 1989.

44. Richard Harrington, "Public Enemy's Twisted Tribute," *Washington Post*, January 19, 1992.

45. Letter from Warren Stewart to Evan Mecham, October 26, 1987, State, County and Local Government Records, Arizona State Archives, http:// azmemory.azlibrary.gov/cdm/ref/collection/archgov/id/405; Michelle Ye Hee Lee, "Recalling Arizona's Struggle for MLK Holiday," *Arizona Republic*, January 15, 2012.

46. Richard Sandomir, "Super Bowl: A Condition of the Game," *New York Times*, January 21, 1996.

47. Héctor Tobar, "Can Latinos Swing Arizona?," *New Yorker*, August 1, 2016.

48. Evan Serpick, "Public Enemy Look Back at 20 Years of 'By the Time I Get to Arizona,'" *Spin*, November 10, 2011; Public Enemy, "By the Time I Get to Arizona," *Apocalypse '91: The Enemy Strikes Black*, Def Jam, 1991.

49. Harrington, "Public Enemy's Twisted Tribute"; Chris Willman, "Nightmarish 'Tribute' to King's Dream," *Los Angeles Times*, January 10, 1992; Seth Mydans, "For Nonviolent Legacy, a Violent Rap Message," *New York Times*, January 11, 1992; Serpick, "Public Enemy Look Back."

50. Sandomir, "Super Bowl"; "Bad Rap for Dr. King," *USA Today*, January 20, 1992.

51. Sandomir, "Super Bowl"; Harrington, "Public Enemy's Twisted Tribute."

52. Lee, "Recalling Arizona's Struggle"; Sandomir, "Super Bowl."

53. Carey Goldberg, "Contrarian New Hampshire to Honor Dr. King, at Last," *New York Times*, May 26, 1999; Michael Brindley, "N.H.'s Martin Luther King Jr. Day Didn't Happen Without a Fight," New Hampshire Public Radio, August 27, 2013; Mark Sammons and Valerie Cunningham, *Black Portsmouth: Three Centuries of African-American Heritage* (Durham:

University of New Hampshire Press, 2004), 204–205; Alina Mogollon, "N.H. Rejects King Day," *The Dartmouth*, May 3, 1993.

54. Sammons and Cunningham, *Black Portsmouth*, 205–206; Goldberg, "Contrarian New Hampshire to Honor Dr. King"; "N.H. Finally Passes MLK Holiday," UPI, May 25, 1999.

55. "Some States Boycotted MLK Day at First," UPI, January 21, 2013; Ronni Mott, "MLK Day Still a Problem in Mississippi," *Jackson Free Press*, January 21, 2013; Sarah Fowler, "State Rep Calls MLK–Robert E. Lee Shared Holiday 'Offensive,'" *Clarion-Ledger*, January 19, 2016; Elahe Izadi, "Why Arkansas Still Won't Stop Celebrating Martin Luther King Jr. and Robert E. Lee on the Same Day," *Washington Post*, January 29, 2015; "This Is Not Robert E. Lee Day," *Boston Globe*, January 15, 2016.

56. Frank Newport, "Martin Luther King Jr.: Revered More After Death Than Before," Gallup, January 16, 2006; William Manchester, *The Death of a President: November 20–November 25, 1963* (New York: Harper & Row, 1967), 624.

CONCLUSION: KING IN OUR TIME

1. "Return of the King," *The Boondocks*, Cartoon Network, 2006.

2. Ibid.

3. Ibid.

4. Ibid.

5. Barack Obama, *Dreams from My Father: A Story of Race and Inheritance* (New York: Three Rivers Press, 2004), 134; Thomas Sugrue, *Not Even Past: Barack Obama and the Burden of Race* (Princeton, NJ: Princeton University Press, 2010), 52.

6. Sam Wineburg and Chauncey Monte-Sano, "'Famous Americans': The Changing Pantheon of American Heroes," *Journal of American History* 94, no. 4 (March 2008): 1190–1192. In a further sign of the American public's unanimous embrace of King, John McCain appeared at the Lorraine Motel in 2008. McCain, the Republican presidential nominee, expressed remorse for his 1983 vote opposing a King holiday. David Remnick, *The Bridge: The Life and Rise of Barack Obama* (New York: Alfred A. Knopf, 2010), 545.

7. David Remnick, "The Joshua Generation," *New Yorker*, November 17, 2008, 70; Remnick, *The Bridge*, 24; David Remnick, "The President's Hero," *New Yorker*, February 2, 2009.

8. Jeffrey Jones, "Americans Divided on Whether King's Dream Has Been Realized," Gallup, August 26, 2011.

9. "O'Reilly: 'Martin Luther King Would Not Participate in a Black Lives Matter Protest,'" *Fox News Insider,* July 11, 2016, http://insider.foxnews.com /2016/07/11/oreilly-mlk-would-not-participate-blm-protest; Eric Bradner, "Huckabee: MLK Would Be 'Appalled' by Black Lives Matter Movement," *CNN Politics,* August 18, 2015, www.cnn.com/2015/08/18/politics/mike -huckabee-black-lives-matter-martin-luther-king/; Brian Tashman, "Sarah Palin: Black Lives Matter Is Racist," *Right Wing Watch,* July 11, 2016, www .rightwingwatch.org/content/sarah-palin-black-lives-matter-racist-and -antithesis-martin-luther-king-jrs-message.

10. Richard Land, "Black Lives Matter Doesn't Live Up to Martin Luther King's Dream," *Christian Post,* July 13, 2016.

11. Jeanne Theoharis, "MLK Would Never Shut Down a Freeway, and 6 Other Myths About the Civil Rights Movement and Black Lives Matter," *The Root,* July 15, 2016; Martin Luther King, "Letter from Birmingham City Jail," in James Washington, ed., *A Testament of Hope: The Essential Writings of Martin Luther King Jr.* (San Francisco: Harper & Row, 1986), 295; King, Dear Friend Letter, April 1968, SCLC Papers, Part 1, Reel 2.

12. Shaun King, "Clemson Coach Dabo Swinney's Speech on Injustice in America Is the Dumbest Thing I've Ever Heard," *New York Daily News,* September 14, 2016; Dabo Swinney on National Anthem, www.youtube.com /watch?v=Z7sBNkUkRdA.

BIBLIOGRAPHY

A Note on Sources

Of the many excellent books on King's life, I have relied most on the following: Taylor Branch, *Parting the Waters: America in the King Years, 1954–1963*; Taylor Branch, *Pillar of Fire: America in the King Years, 1963–1965*; Taylor Branch, *At Canaan's Edge: America in the King Years, 1965–68*; David Garrow, *Bearing the Cross: Martin Luther King, Jr., and the Southern Christian Leadership Conference*; David Levering Lewis, *King: A Biography*; Stephen Oates, *Let the Trumpet Sound: The Life of Martin Luther King Jr.*; Thomas Jackson, *From Civil Rights to Human Rights: Martin Luther King, Jr., and the Struggle for Economic Justice*; Peter Ling, *Martin Luther King Jr.*; Adam Fairclough, *To Redeem the Soul of America: The Southern Christian Leadership Conference and Martin Luther King Jr.*; and Harvard Sitkoff, *King: Pilgrimage to the Mountaintop*. Many of these books conclude at the Lorraine Motel, with King's confidants arrayed on the balcony, pointing in the direction of the assassin.

There are countless works on America in the 1960s, some of which cover 1968 alone. See Mark Kurlansky, *1968: The Year That Rocked the World*; David Caute, *The Year of the Barricades: A Journey Through 1968*; Charles Kaiser, *1968 in America: Music, Politics, Chaos, Counterculture, and the Shaping of a Generation*; Irwin Unger, *Turning Point: 1968*; and Jules Witcover, *The Year the Dream Died: Revisiting 1968 in America*. Many of these authors highlight white activists in the New Left and the antiwar movement. Others explore the drama of the 1968 presidential campaign, spinning tales about Robert Kennedy, Richard Nixon, or George Wallace. Many of these books tend to mention King's death only in passing.

The King assassination has indeed received attention. Many such books focus on James Earl Ray, the manhunt to catch him, and the question of whether Ray acted alone. These include Hampton Sides, *Hellhound on His Trail: The Stalking of Martin Luther King Jr. and the International Hunt for His*

Assassin; Gerald Posner, *Killing the Dream: James Earl Ray and the Assassination of Martin Luther King*; and Gerold Frank, *An American Death: The True Story of the Assassination of Dr. Martin Luther King, Jr., and the Greatest Manhunt of Our Time.*

The Memphis sanitation strike and King's funeral are both the subjects of wonderful studies. Michael Honey and Joan Turner Beifuss have each written gripping accounts of the Memphis strike. See Michael Honey, *Going Down Jericho Road: The Memphis Strike, Martin Luther King's Last Campaign*, and Joan Turner Beifuss, *At the River I Stand: Memphis, the 1968 Strike, and Martin Luther King*. Rebecca Burns has focused on Atlanta during King's funeral in her book *Burial for a King: Martin Luther King Jr.'s Funeral and the Week That Transformed Atlanta and Rocked the Nation*. One of the few books to examine the larger import of King's death is Michael Eric Dyson's *April 4, 1968*. Dyson explores "how King embraced death's inevitability to shape his social agenda" (Dyson, *April 4, 1968: Martin Luther King Jr.'s Death and How It Changed America* [New York: Basic Civitas Books, 2008], x–xi). Dyson assesses racial inequality at the beginning of the twenty-first century and ruminates on the extent, and limits, of change wrought by the civil rights movement. There are also two major accounts of the riots that gripped American cities after King's assassination. Shortly after the riots, the staff of the *Washington Post* compiled a volume of reporting entitled *Ten Blocks from the White House*. In 2009, Clay Risen published *A Nation on Fire*. Risen's book is the definitive text on the riots, and on this period in American history. Both of these works show that African Americans rebelled because of the underlying conditions in their cities. King's death was the catalyst for the riots more than the cause. See Ben W. Gilbert and the Staff of the *Washington Post, Ten Blocks from the White House: Anatomy of the Washington Riots of 1968*; Clay Risen, *A Nation on Fire: America in the Wake of the King Assassination*; Michael Eric Dyson, *April 4, 1968: Martin Luther King Jr.'s Death and How it Changed America*. David Chappell's *Waking from the Dream* is a recent addition to the literature on King's legacy. Chappell focuses on the Fair Housing Act of 1968, the legislative battle over the King holiday, and the rise of Jesse Jackson. See David Chappell, *Waking from the Dream: The Struggle for Civil Rights in the Shadow of Martin Luther King Jr.*

ARCHIVAL COLLECTIONS

John F. Kennedy Library
  Robert F. Kennedy Oral History Collection
Lyndon B. Johnson Library
  White House Central Files

Manuscript and Rare Book Library, Emory University
Ralph McGill Papers
Newsweek Collection
SCLC Papers
Moorland-Spingarn Research Center, Howard University
Ralph Bunche Oral History Collection
Rubenstein Library and University Archives, Duke University
Duke Vigil Collection
Scholars Room, Paley Center for Media
Special Collections, University of Memphis
Sanitation Strike Collection
Thomas Dodd Research Center, University of Connecticut
Thomas Dodd Papers
Wisconsin Historical Society
Edwin Newman Papers

SELECTED NEWSPAPERS

Amsterdam News
Atlanta Constitution
Boston Globe
Chicago Defender
Commercial Appeal
Daily Spectator
Die Welt
Duke Chronicle

The Guardian
Johannesburg World
Los Angeles Times
Nashville Tennessean
New York Times
Times of London
Washington Post

BOOKS

Abernathy, Ralph. *And the Walls Came Tumbling Down.* New York: Harper & Row, 1989.

Albert, Peter, and Ronald Hoffman, eds. *We Shall Overcome: Martin Luther King, Jr. and the Black Freedom Struggle.* New York: Da Capo Press, 1993.

Allen, Ivan, Jr., with Paul Hemphill. *Mayor: Notes on the Sixties.* New York: Simon & Schuster, 1971.

Appy, Christian. *Patriots: The Vietnam War Remembered from All Sides.* New York: Penguin, 2003.

Avorn, Jerry. *Up Against the Ivy Wall: A History of the Columbia Crisis.* New York: Atheneum, 1970.

Baldwin, Lewis. *To Make the Wounded Whole: The Cultural Legacy of Martin Luther King Jr.* Minneapolis, MN: Fortress Press, 1992.

————. *Toward the Beloved Community: Martin Luther King, Jr., and South Africa*. Cleveland, OH: Pilgrim Press, 1995.

Beifuss, Joan Turner. *At the River I Stand: Memphis, the 1968 Strike, and Martin Luther King*. Brooklyn, NY: Carlson Publishing, 1989.

Bernstein, Irving. *Guns or Butter: The Presidency of Lyndon Johnson*. New York: Oxford University Press, 1996.

Binstock, Jonathan. *Sam Gilliam: A Retrospective*. Berkeley: University of California Press, 2005.

Biondi, Martha. *The Black Revolution on Campus*. Berkeley: University of California Press, 2012.

Bloom, Joshua, and Waldo Martin. *Black Against Empire: The History and Politics of the Black Panther Party*. Berkeley: University of California Press, 2013.

Boesak, Allan. *Farewell to Innocence: A Socio-Ethical Study on Black Theology and Black Power*. Maryknoll, NY: Orbis Books, 1977.

Bono, The Edge, Adam Clayton, and Larry Mullen Jr., with Neal McCormick. *U2 by U2*. New York: HarperCollins, 2006.

Boomhower, Ray. *Robert F. Kennedy and the 1968 Indiana Primary*. Bloomington: Indiana University Press, 2008.

Borstelmann, Thomas. *The Cold War and the Color Line: American Race Relations in the Global Arena*. Cambridge, MA: Harvard University Press, 2001.

Bradley, Stefan. *Harlem vs. Columbia University: Black Student Power in the Late 1960s*. Urbana: University of Illinois Press, 2009.

Brady, Diane. *Fraternity*. New York: Spiegel & Grau, 2012.

Branch, Taylor. *At Canaan's Edge: America in the King Years, 1965–68*. New York: Simon & Schuster, 2006.

————. *Parting the Waters: America in the King Years, 1954–1963*. New York: Simon & Schuster, 1988.

————. *Pillar of Fire: America in the King Years, 1963–1965*. New York: Simon & Schuster, 1998.

Burns, Rebecca. *Burial for a King: Martin Luther King Jr.'s Funeral and the Week That Transformed Atlanta and Rocked the Nation*. New York: Scribner, 2011.

Califano, Joseph. *The Triumph and Tragedy of Lyndon Johnson: The White House Years*. College Station: Texas A&M University Press, 2000.

Cannato, Vincent. *The Ungovernable City: John Lindsay and His Struggle to Save New York*. New York: Basic Books, 2001.

Carter, Dan. *The Politics of Rage: George Wallace, the Origins of the New Conservatism, and the Transformation of American Politics*. New York: Simon & Schuster, 1995.

Caute, David. *The Year of the Barricades: A Journey Through 1968.* New York: Harper & Row, 1988.

Chafe, William. *Civilities and Civil Rights: Greensboro, North Carolina, and the Black Struggle for Freedom.* New York: Oxford University Press, 1980.

Chappell, David. *Waking from the Dream: The Struggle for Civil Rights in the Shadow of Martin Luther King Jr.* New York: Random House, 2014.

Clarke, Thurston. *The Last Campaign: Robert F. Kennedy and 82 Days That Inspired America.* New York: Henry Holt, 2008.

Cleaver, Eldridge. *Post-Prison Writings and Speeches.* New York: Random House, 1969.

Cohen, Adam, and Elizabeth Taylor. *American Pharaoh: Mayor Richard J. Daley—His Battle for Chicago and the Nation.* Boston: Little, Brown, 2000.

Crawford, Fred, Roy Norman, and Leah Dabbs. *A Report of Certain Reactions by the Atlanta Public to the Death of the Reverend Doctor Martin Luther King Jr.* Atlanta: Center for Research in Social Change, Emory University, 1969.

Dallek, Robert. *Flawed Giant: Lyndon Johnson and His Times, 1961–1973.* New York: Oxford University Press, 1998.

Davidson, Osha Gray. *The Best of Enemies: Race and Redemption in the New South.* Chapel Hill: University of North Carolina Press, 2007.

Dixon, Aaron. *My People Are Rising: Memoir of a Black Panther Party Captain.* Chicago: Haymarket Books, 2012.

Dooley, Brian. *Black and Green: The Fight for Civil Rights in Northern Ireland and Black America.* London, UK: Pluto Press, 1998.

Dorfman, Ariel. *Heading South, Looking North: A Bilingual Journey.* New York: Farrar, Straus and Giroux, 1998.

Dudziak, Mary. *Exporting American Dreams: Thurgood Marshall's African Journey.* New York: Oxford University Press, 2008.

Duvalier, François. *A Tribute to the Martyred Leader of Non-Violence: Reverend Dr. Martin Luther King Jr.* Port-au-Prince, Haiti: Presses Nationales, 1968.

Dyson, Michael Eric. *April 4, 1968: Martin Luther King Jr.'s Death and How It Changed America.* New York: Basic Civitas Books, 2008.

Elfenbein, Jessica, Thomas Hollowak, and Elizabeth Nix, eds. *Baltimore '68: Riots and Rebirth in an American City.* Philadelphia: Temple University Press, 2011.

Estes, Steve. *I Am a Man! Race, Manhood, and the Civil Rights Movement.* Chapel Hill: University of North Carolina Press, 2005.

Fairclough, Adam. *Martin Luther King Jr.* Athens: University of Georgia Press, 1990.

————. *To Redeem the Soul of America: The Southern Christian Leadership Conference and Martin Luther King Jr.* Athens: University of Georgia Press, 1987.

Fitzpatrick, Ellen. *Letters to Jackie: Condolences from a Grieving Nation.* New York: Ecco, 2010.

Frady, Marshall. *Martin Luther King Jr.* New York: Viking, 2002.

Frank, Gerold. *An American Death: The True Story of the Assassination of Dr. Martin Luther King, Jr., and the Greatest Manhunt of Our Time.* New York: Doubleday, 1972.

Garrow, David. *Bearing the Cross: Martin Luther King, Jr., and the Southern Christian Leadership Conference.* New York: William Morrow, 1986.

————. *The FBI and Martin Luther King Jr.* New York: Penguin, 1983.

Gassert, Philipp, and Martin Klimke, eds. *1968: Memories and Legacies of a Global Revolt.* Washington, DC: Bulletin of the German Historical Institute, 2009.

Gertler, Nat. *The Peanuts Collection: Treasures from the World's Most Beloved Comic Strip.* New York: Little, Brown, 2010.

Gilbert, Ben W., and the Staff of the *Washington Post. Ten Blocks from the White House: Anatomy of the Washington Riots of 1968.* New York: Praeger, 1968.

Goss, Kristin. *Disarmed: The Missing Movement for Gun Control in America.* Princeton, NJ: Princeton University Press, 2006.

Halberstam, David. *The Children.* New York: Random House, 1998.

————. *The Unfinished Odyssey of Robert Kennedy.* New York: Random House, 1968.

Hampton, Henry, and Steve Fayer, eds. *Voices of Freedom: An Oral History of the Civil Rights Movement from the 1950s Through the 1980s.* New York: Bantam Books, 1990.

Harding, Vincent. *Martin Luther King: The Inconvenient Hero.* Maryknoll, NY: Orbis Books, 1996.

Hill, Lance. *The Deacons for Defense: Armed Resistance and the Civil Rights Movement.* Chapel Hill: University of North Carolina Press, 2006.

Hilliard, David, and Lewis Cole. *This Side of Glory: The Autobiography of David Hilliard and the Story of the Black Panther Party.* Boston: Little, Brown, 1993.

Hohn, Maria, and Martin Klimke. *A Breath of Freedom: The Civil Rights Struggle, African American GIs, and Germany.* New York: Palgrave Macmillan, 2010.

Honey, Michael. *Black Workers Remember: An Oral History of Segregation, Unionism, and the Freedom Struggle*. Berkeley: University of California Press, 1999.

———. *Going Down Jericho Road: The Memphis Strike, Martin Luther King's Last Campaign*. New York: W.W. Norton, 2007.

Jackson, Thomas. *From Civil Rights to Human Rights: Martin Luther King, Jr., and the Struggle for Economic Justice*. Philadelphia: University of Pennsylvania Press, 2007.

Jeffries, Hasan Kwame. *Bloody Lowndes: Civil Rights and Black Power in Alabama's Black Belt*. New York: New York University Press, 2009.

Johnson, Lyndon. *The Vantage Point: Perspectives of the Presidency, 1963–1969*. New York: Holt, Rinehart and Winston, 1971.

Joseph, Peniel. *Stokely: A Life*. New York: Basic Civitas Books, 2014.

Kahn, Roger. *The Battle for Morningside Heights: Why Students Rebel*. New York: William Morrow, 1970.

Kaiser, Charles. *1968 in America: Music, Politics, Chaos, Counterculture, and the Shaping of a Generation*. New York: Weidenfeld & Nicolson, 1988.

Karol, David. *Party Position Change in American Politics: Coalition Management*. New York: Cambridge University Press, 2009.

Katznelson, Ira. *When Affirmative Action Was White: An Untold History of Racial Inequality in Twentieth-Century America*. New York: W.W. Norton, 2005.

King, Coretta Scott. *My Life, My Love, My Legacy*. New York: Henry Holt, 2017.

———. *My Life with Martin Luther King Jr.* New York: Holt, 1969.

King, Martin Luther, Jr. *"All Labor Has Dignity."* Edited by Michael Honey. Boston: Beacon Press, 2011.

———. *"In a Single Garment of Destiny": A Global Vision of Justice*. Edited by Lewis Baldwin. Boston: Beacon Press, 2012.

———. *The Trumpet of Conscience*. New York: Harper & Row, 1968.

———. *Where Do We Go from Here: Chaos or Community?* Boston: Beacon Press, reprinted in 2010.

———. *Why We Can't Wait*. New York: Harper & Row, 1964.

Klimke, Martin. *The Other Alliance: Student Protest in West Germany and the United States in the Global Sixties*. Princeton, NJ: Princeton University Press, 2010.

Knight, Douglas. *Street of Dreams: The Nature and Legacy of the 1960s*. Durham, NC: Duke University Press, 1989.

Kurlansky, Mark. *1968: The Year That Rocked the World.* New York: Ballantine, 2004.

Lentz, Richard. *Symbols, the News Magazines, and Martin Luther King.* Baton Rouge: Louisiana State University Press, 1990.

Lewis, David Levering. *King: A Biography.* 2nd ed. Urbana: University of Illinois Press, 1978.

Lewis, John. *Walking with the Wind: A Memoir of the Movement.* New York: Simon & Schuster, 1998.

Lindsay, John. *The City.* New York: W.W. Norton, 1969.

Ling, Peter. *Martin Luther King Jr.* New York: Routledge, 2002.

Lokos, Lionel. *House Divided: The Life and Legacy of Martin Luther King.* New Rochelle, NY: Arlington House, 1968.

Lukas, J. Anthony. *Common Ground: A Turbulent Decade in the Lives of Three American Families.* New York: Alfred A. Knopf, 1985.

Manchester, William. *The Death of a President: November 20–November 25, 1963.* New York: Harper & Row, 1967.

Marable, Manning, ed. *Dispatches from the Ebony Tower: Intellectuals Confront the African American Experience.* New York: Columbia University Press, 2000.

Mays, Benjamin. *Born to Rebel: An Autobiography.* Athens: University of Georgia Press, 1971.

McKnight, Gerald. *The Last Crusade: Martin Luther King, Jr., the FBI, and the Poor People's Campaign.* Boulder, CO: Westview Press, 1998.

Miami Herald. Miami Negroes: A Study in Depth. Miami, FL: *Miami Herald,* 1968.

Moore, Leonard N. *Black Rage in New Orleans: Police Brutality and African American Activism from World War II to Hurricane Katrina.* Baton Rouge: Louisiana State University Press, 2010.

Murch, Donna. *Living for the City: Migration, Education, and the Rise of the Black Panther Party in Oakland, California.* Chapel Hill: University of North Carolina Press, 2010.

Newfield, Jack. *Robert Kennedy: A Memoir.* New York: Dutton, 1969.

Oates, Stephen. *Let the Trumpet Sound: The Life of Martin Luther King Jr.* New York: Harper & Row, 1982.

Obama, Barack. *Dreams from My Father: A Story of Race and Inheritance.* New York: Three Rivers Press, 2004.

Painter, Nell Irvin. *Creating Black Americans: African-American History and Its Meanings, 1619 to the Present.* New York: Oxford University Press, 2006.

Payne, Charles. *I've Got the Light of Freedom: The Mississippi Organizing Tra-dition*. Berkeley: University of California Press, 1995.

Pearson, Hugh. *The Shadow of the Panther: Huey Newton and the Price of Black Power in America*. Reading, MA: Addison-Wesley, 1994.

Perlstein, Rick. *Nixonland: The Rise of a President and the Fracturing of Amer-ica*. New York: Scribner, 2008.

Perry, Kennetta Hammond. *London Is the Place for Me: Black Britons, Cit-izenship, and the Politics of Race*. New York: Oxford University Press, 2015.

Pillai, Vijay, ed. *Indian Leaders on Martin Luther King Jr.* New Delhi: Inter-State Cultural League of India, 1968.

Pomerantz, Gary. *Where Peachtree Meets Sweet Auburn: The Saga of Two Families and the Making of Atlanta*. New York: Scribner, 1996.

Posner, Gerald. *Killing the Dream: James Earl Ray and the Assassination of Martin Luther King Jr.* New York: Random House, 1998.

Powell, Colin, with Joseph Persico. *My American Journey*. New York: Ran-dom House, 1995.

Ralph, James. *Northern Protest: Martin Luther King Jr., Chicago, and the Civil Rights Movement*. Cambridge, MA: Harvard University Press, 1993.

Remnick, David. *The Bridge: The Life and Rise of Barack Obama*. New York: Alfred A. Knopf, 2010.

Risen, Clay. *A Nation on Fire: America in the Wake of the King Assassination*. Hoboken, NJ: Wiley, 2009.

Rogers, Peter. *With Malice Toward None: The Night Martin Luther King Jr. Was Killed: A Memoir*. Awesome Wonder Press, 2013.

Rosenberg, Tina. *Children of Cain: Violence and the Violent in Latin America*. New York: Penguin, 1991.

Roth, Andrew. *Enoch Powell: Tory Tribune*. London, UK: Macdonald & Co., 1970.

Rudd, Mark. *Underground: My Life with SDS and the Weathermen*. New York: HarperCollins, 2009.

Salinger, Pierre, ed. *"An Honorable Profession": A Tribute to Robert F. Kennedy*. Garden City, NY: Doubleday, 1968.

Sammons, Mark, and Valerie Cunningham. *Black Portsmouth: Three Centu-ries of African-American Heritage*. Durham: University of New Hampshire Press, 2004.

Schlesinger, Arthur, Jr. *Robert Kennedy and His Times*. New York: Ballantine Books, 1978.

Schofield, Camilla. *Enoch Powell and the Making of Postcolonial Britain*. New York: Cambridge University Press, 2013.

Sherrill, Robert. *The Saturday Night Special*. New York: Charterhouse, 1973.

Shih, Bryan, and Yohuru Williams, eds. *The Black Panthers: Portraits from an Unfinished Revolution*. New York: Nation Books, 2016.

Sides, Hampton. *Hellhound on His Trail: The Stalking of Martin Luther King Jr. and the International Hunt for His Assassin*. New York: Doubleday, 2010.

Sitkoff, Harvard. *King: Pilgrimage to the Mountaintop*. New York: Hill & Wang, 2008.

Slate, Nico. *Colored Cosmopolitanism: The Shared Struggle for Freedom in the United States and India*. Cambridge, MA: Harvard University Press, 2012.

Smiley, Tavis. *Death of a King: The Real Story of Dr. Martin Luther King Jr.'s Final Year*. New York: Little, Brown, 2014.

Smith, R. Drew, ed. *Freedom's Distant Shores: American Protestants and Post-Colonial Alliances with Africa*. Waco, TX: Baylor University Press, 2006.

Spector, Ronald. *After Tet: The Bloodiest Year in Vietnam*. New York: The Free Press, 1993.

Steel, Ronald. *In Love with Night: The American Romance with Robert Kennedy*. New York: Simon & Schuster, 2000.

Steele, Shelby. *The Content of Our Character: A New Vision of Race in America*. New York: St. Martin's Press, 1990.

Stein, Jean. *American Journey: The Times of Robert Kennedy*. New York: Harcourt Brace Jovanovich, 1970.

Sugrue, Thomas. *Not Even Past: Barack Obama and the Burden of Race*. Princeton, NJ: Princeton University Press, 2010.

Suri, Jeremi. *The Global Revolutions of 1968*. New York: W.W. Norton, 2007.

Terry, Wallace. *Bloods: An Oral History of the Vietnam War by Black Veterans*. New York: Random House, 1984.

Tilove, Jonathan. *Along Martin Luther King: Travels on Black America's Main Street*. New York: Random House, 2003.

Tuck, Stephen. *The Night Malcolm X Spoke at the Oxford Union: A Transatlantic Story of Antiracist Protest*. Berkeley: University of California Press, 2014.

Tuck, Stephen, and Robin Kelley, eds. *The Other Special Relationship: Race, Rights, and Riots in Britain and the United States*. New York: Palgrave Macmillan, 2015.

Tye, Larry. *Bobby Kennedy: The Making of a Liberal Icon*. New York: Random House, 2016.

Tyson, Timothy. *Radio Free Dixie: Robert F. Williams and the Roots of Black Power*. Chapel Hill: University of North Carolina Press, 1999.

Unger, Irwin. *Turning Point: 1968*. New York: Scribner, 1988.

Vincent, Rickey. *Party Music: The Inside Story of the Black Panthers' Band and How Black Power Transformed Soul Music*. Chicago, IL: Lawrence Hill Books, 2013.

Vizzard, William. *Shots in the Dark: The Policy, Politics, and Symbolism of Gun Control*. Lanham, MD: Rowman & Littlefield, 2000.

Ward, Brian. *Martin Luther King in Newcastle upon Tyne: The African American Freedom Struggle and Race Relations in the North East of England*. Newcastle upon Tyne, UK: Tyne Bridge Publishing, 2017.

Ward, Brian, and Tony Badger, eds. *The Making of Martin Luther King and the Civil Rights Movement*. New York: New York University Press, 1996.

Ward, Mary. *A Mission for Justice: The History of the First African American Catholic Church in Newark, New Jersey*. Knoxville: University of Tennessee Press, 2002.

Washington, James, ed. *A Testament of Hope: The Essential Writings of Martin Luther King Jr.* San Francisco: Harper & Row, 1986.

Westheider, James. *Fighting on Two Fronts: African Americans and the Vietnam War*. New York: New York University Press, 1997.

Wilkins, Roger. *A Man's Life: An Autobiography*. New York: Simon & Schuster, 1982.

Winkler, Adam. *Gunfight: The Battle over the Right to Bear Arms in America*. New York: W.W. Norton, 2011.

Witcover, Jules. *85 Days: The Last Campaign of Robert Kennedy*. New York: G.P. Putnam's Sons, 1969.

———. *The Year the Dream Died: Revisiting 1968 in America*. New York: Warner Books, 1997.

Young, Andrew. *An Easy Burden: The Civil Rights Movement and the Transformation of America*. New York: HarperCollins, 1996.

INDEX

Page numbers in italics refer to illustrative material.

Nina Morrison

Jason Sokol is the Arthur K. Whitcomb Associate Professor of History at the University of New Hampshire. The author of two critically acclaimed books on the history of the civil rights movement, Sokol lives in Newburyport, Massachusetts.